PLACING SORROW

UNIVERSITY OF NORTH CAROLINA
STUDIES IN COMPARATIVE LITERATURE

Number 60

WERNER P. FRIEDERICH, *Founder*
EUGENE H. FALK, *Editor*

PLACING SORROW

A Study of
the Pastoral Elegy Convention
from Theocritus to Milton

ELLEN ZETZEL LAMBERT

Chapel Hill
THE UNIVERSITY OF NORTH CAROLINA PRESS
1976

Copyright © 1976 by
The University of North Carolina
Studies in Comparative Literature
All rights reserved
Printed in the United States of America
ISBN 0-8078-7060-9
Library of Congress Catalog Card Number 76-23154

Library of Congress Cataloging in Publication Data

Lambert, Ellen Zetzel, 1940–
    Placing sorrow.

    (University of North Carolina studies in comparative
literature; no. 60)
    Includes bibliographical references and index.
    1. Elegiac poetry—History and criticism.
2. Pastoral poetry—History and criticism. I. Title.
II. Series.
PN1389.L3   809.1'3   76-23154
ISBN 0-8078-7060-9

In memoriam:

MURIEL BASHLOW ZETZEL

ELIZABETH ROSENBERG ZETZEL

CONTENTS

ACKNOWLEDGMENTS

I am grateful to the following publishers for permission to quote passages from the works cited: the Cambridge University Press, from *Theocritus* (1952) and *The Greek Bucolic Poets* (1953), both edited and translated by A. F. S. Gow; to Farrar, Straus and Giroux Inc., from "Wash Far Away," by John Berryman, originally published in *American Review* 22 (1975), copyright Kate Berryman; to Houghton Mifflin Company, from *The Complete Poetical Works of John Milton* (1965), edited by Douglas Bush; to the University of Texas Press, from *The Pastoral Elegy: an Anthology* (1939), edited by Thomas P. Harrison, Jr., with translations by Harry Joshua Leon; and to Wayne State University Press, from Jacopo Sannazaro's *Arcadia and Piscatorial Eclogues* (1966), translated with an introduction by Ralph Nash. Translations not otherwise documented are my own.

Two professors at Bryn Mawr College stimulated my interest in pastoral poems and pastoral sorrows: Robert Burlin, under whose directorship I explored medieval literary gardens, and Isabel Gamble MacCaffrey, who first taught me to read "Lycidas." Thomas M. Greene of Yale University directed the thesis out of which the present work grew and has furthered, in more ways than I can here acknowledge, both my understanding of literary conventions and (at all stages) this study. Toni Burbank, Irma Brandeis, Harry Levin, and Reeve Parker read my manuscript and made many valuable suggestions. My brother, James Zetzel, helped me in my struggles with the neo-Latin texts and cast a classicist's cool eye over my opening chapters. Needless to say, I am responsible for any errors which remain. My typist, Anne Granger, has provided more than technical support. Blanche Lambert and Adele Clark helped generously with the proofreading. To all of these I am enormously grateful—but most of all, to my husband Mark, who knows (I hope) how much he has given.

E. Z. L.

INTRODUCTION

*The Form and its Boundaries;
Ends and Beginnings*

In death we are all one, but in our responses to death how various! Sir Thomas Browne marvels at that paradox as he catalogues in loving detail the funeral customs of peoples long since vanished. Browne's interest is never simply that of the antiquarian. What intrigues him is the way each diverse set of customs expresses a particular society's way of coming to terms with the inevitable end. A ritual, he knows, is never elaborated in mere happenstance; and in our rites of death, as elsewhere, each separate "ceremony of bravery" (in Browne's fine phrase)[1] is "founded upon some bottom of reason."[2] Here I shall be considering just one of the ceremonies of bravery through which man confronts his fated end, and a literary ceremony rather than a social one: the poetic convention we call the pastoral elegy. But the central question I shall be asking of this form is the one Browne asks: how does this ceremony embody a distinctive response to death? For a literary convention is, like a convention of behavior, always something more than a series of allusions or inherited forms: it is a way of seeing things.

Initially we may be more impressed by the diversity than the unity of the pastoral elegist's vision of death. Here we are dealing, after all, not with the customs of a single, uniform culture, but with the diverse responses of individual men in various ages, men whose cultures dictate a variety of answers to the perennial questions raised by humanity's shared fate. And we should not be surprised to discover that pastoral elegists do indeed have different things to say about death—and sometimes have no answers, as such, to offer us. The very first pastoral elegy we know, the first ✗ *Idyll* of the Hellenistic poet Theocritus, is not properly speaking a lament at all. Here a herdsman sings a song about the death of a ✗ certain <u>neatherd</u>, Daphnis: when Daphnis dies, the waters close over him. That is all; we are not told anything further about this Daphnis' fate, nor do we mourn his death. What poetic traditions, ✗ folk songs or rituals may lie behind this third century B.C. poem is now obscure to us, though we can, and shall, hazard some guesses. What lies ahead is a long, and a varied, poetic tradition. In Vergil's ✗ fifth *Eclogue*, several centuries and several elaborations later, we find a Daphnis already dead at the song's opening. One herdsman laments his death; a second then raises him to the stars. Now a deified Daphnis looks down on us from the threshold of a Roman Olympus. And later still (fourteen hundred years later) in the pastoral elegies of Renaissance humanists, Daphnis is revived once more to die a Christian death and be translated to a Christian heaven.

The subjects of these pastoral elegies are, moreover, as various as the afterworlds in which their heroes repose. The Theocritean Daphnis is a neatherd simply, albeit a mythical one. But Vergil's Daphnis is the guardian of the whole Roman countryside—is, perhaps, Julius Caesar himself. And the hero of a Renaissance pastoral elegy may be, *inter alia*, the poet's patron, or his poetic father, or the father of his country.

Pastoral elegies do differ from one another. They differ more, one would imagine, and differ more significantly, than two men's rehearsals of the same behavioral convention will differ. And this literary convention is, at least in certain obvious respects, more varied than most literary conventions. Pastoral elegists, writing over an extended period of time, describe varied kinds of losses and propose varied remedies to the problems of death and mourning. A pastoral elegy in which the hero leaves this world for a better one elsewhere affects us differently from one in which the hero simply leaves; and both of these affect us somewhat differently from a lament in which we are told that the hero now watches over us from on high. Similarly, a lament for a shepherd will not sound just like a lament for a king or one for an intimate friend; and neither of these last two will sound quite like one composed for a poetic mentor, who is at once both friend and father to the elegist.

In the preceding paragraphs I have told the story of the pastoral elegy's evolution in such a way as to highlight the convention's diversities. But there is a second way of telling this story, one which will bring out unities more fundamental, it seems to me, than those diversities. And it is this second story which chiefly concerns me in these pages. When we use the word "convention" (and I do think that is the right word to use here), we imply that there is something more involved in the development of a particular literary tradition than what we might call imitation or reminiscence. We imply that the various poems in that tradition share a certain outlook as well as certain formal similarities. "Convention," as Harry Levin has reminded us, means a "coming together."[3] Without a common center of feeling, conventionality confers no true participation, only a facade of sameness. Thus Pope, and even Shelley, while retaining a number of the pastoral elegy's traditional formulae, address us from outside that common center of feeling; Milton, questioning many of these same formulae, addresses us from inside it. It is this common center of feeling, or way of seeing things, uniting works by such various poets as Theocritus, Vergil, Spenser and Milton, that I propose to analyze here.

The pastoral elegy, I would suggest, proposes no one *solution* to the questions raised by death but rather a *setting* in which those questions may be posed, or better, "placed." It offers us a landscape. A lament for a king will not sound just like a lament for a fellow poet; but both king and poet can be brought into the pastoral world; both can be mourned here. This landscape itself varies from one poet and one subject to the next. But, and this is the important point, it remains a concrete, palpable world, a world in which the elegist can place diffuse, intangible feelings of grief and thereby win his release from suffering.

"*Here* are oaks and galingale; *here* sweetly hum the bees about the hives. *Here* are two springs of cold water . . . "[4] says one Theocritean herdsman to another. Later, Vergil's Gallus invites his wayward Lycoris to join him in another pastoral retreat in much the same terms: "*hic* gelidi fontes," he says, "*hic* mollia prata, Lycori, / *hic* nemus; *hic* ipso tecum consumere aeuo"[5] ("here are cool springs; here are soft meadows, Lycoris; here woods; here with you only time itself would slowly waste me away"). And later still Ben Jonson's sad shepherd speaks with the same accent, the accent of pastoral: "*Here*! she wont to goe! / and *here*! and *here*! / Just where those Daisies, Pinks, and Violets grow."[6] Milton's Comus is (for good reason) less specific about the precise nature of the pleasures he invites the Lady to share with him when he welcomes her to his bower, but his gesture and inflections deliberately recall those earlier ones: "*Here* dwell no frowns, nor anger; from these gates / Sorrow flies far. See, *here* be all the pleasures. . . . "[7] Exactly what we are asked to share in these different landscapes—this changes from one pastoral poem and poet to the next; but that it is something tangible, something, as the herdsman says, "here"—this remains the same.

The very first words of the first pastoral elegy we know point to the setting and its consolations: "Sweet is the whispered music of that pinetree by the spring, goatherd," says the shepherd Thyrsis to his friend, "and sweet too your piping."[8] And from this Theocritean song on down into Milton's "Lycidas," the music of the pinetree amplifies and supports that of the herdsman's pipe, and it places his human sorrows as it does so.

This poetic world to which the pastoral elegist "escapes," this imaginary world, is not—as it is sometimes said to be—*less* substantial than the world he actually inhabits. On the contrary, it is in important ways made to seem *more* substantial (*more* concrete, *more* comprehensible) than the "real" world. Landscape, as Adam Parry has said, always has a metaphorical value in poetry; and the pastoral landscape, like other literary landscapes, points toward values outside itself.[9] But "pastoral" describes, first of all, a setting; it is only secondarily a country of the mind or an attitude toward life in general.[10] It is the setting, the rural scene as it is composed by the poet and experienced by the herdsman, which consoles us.

Further, this concrete, palpable world is "real" in a second and deeper sense—real because it can contain pain and suffering. The point has been contested. Critics often suggest that the pastoral world is defined precisely by its exclusion of sorrowful themes. They suppose that suffering simply does not exist here; or if it does intrude, it is viewed as an interloper whose very presence undermines the whole delicate pastoral edifice of bliss.[11] But, in fact, the pastoral ideal, from Theocritus on, has never been that of a *hortus conclusus*. Neither suffering nor death has ever been excluded from this paradise. And one can make at least a plausible case for the view that the pastoral dirge is the original pastoral song. We do not know enough about the origins of pastoral poetry to prove such a case. What we do know is that from Theocritus on, pastoral poetry is full of wrangling and complaints, love laments and funeral songs. Death is indeed no stranger in Arcadia.[12] We might, I think, go so far as to maintain that the presence of death enhances the pastoral version of felicity. For it is not the herdsmen who are happy in pastoral poetry; theirs is not the state of Adam and Eve in Eden. It is rather we who are happy hearing (as most often we do) of their sorrows—happy because those sorrows seem so much simpler than our own. The pastoral landscape pleases us not, like the vanished groves of Eden, because it *excludes* pain, but because of the way it includes it. Pastoral offers us a vision of life stripped not of pain but of complexity.[13]

Moreover, once we recognize that it is a setting, not a solution, which the pastoral world offers the funeral poet, we are in a better position to appreciate the continuity between pagan and Christian laments. Endings of poems do matter; but they are not all that matters. They are not all that consoles. Rosemond Tuve's fine observation that "the affirmations of *Lycidas* begin with its first line"[14] will hold for the convention as a whole. And everything in these laments, from the opening lines of the frame to the herdsmen's final exchange, bears upon the healing process, works to console us. Indeed a pastoral elegy need not culminate (as Theocritus' does not) in any explicit words of consolation in order to be experienced as consoling, to place our sorrow. And if later pastoral elegists generally do want more explicit assurances than Theocritus gives us, those final answers are not necessarily the only answers they discover—or necessarily the most important ones. As critics we have, perhaps, paid too much attention to purely doctrinal revisions in considering the way Christian poets revive this and other classical forms. We have asked where a poet is going, but less often how he gets there. My attention to the setting in which the elegist places his grief and the process whereby he moves toward his recovery will not, I hope, obscure the differences between pagan pastoral elegies and Christian ones. But it will draw the reader's attention to the continuity of both form and feeling between the two.

In shifting the focus of our attention from the solution of the poet's dilemma to its setting, we can also better appreciate the varieties of that setting. All pastoral landscapes are "sweet," as the Theocritean herdsman says, but they are sweet in different ways. All are consoling, but they console us in different ways. When we come to analyze how a particular landscape consoles us, we will be looking less at its component objects—the streams, the trees, the grove, etc., which are relatively unchanging—than at its atmosphere. We will be considering, that is, how a particular scene is composed and how it affects us. A poem is, of course, a structure of words, not pictures. But in speaking of these pastoral landscapes and how they work to console us, it will be useful to borrow from the terminology of the visual arts. We will want, for instance, to discriminate between a warm landscape and a cool one, between an animated scene and a static one. We will want, too, to consider spatial effects and relationships: to distinguish an open, unbounded scene from a closed one, a crowded from a bare setting. Such considerations have a good deal to do with how a particular poetic landscape affects us, with how it consoles us. In the following chapters, then, I shall be analyzing these "pictorial" effects among others, asking not simply *what* we see in a given setting, but *how* we are invited to see and feel it.

We will be exploring this pastoral landscape in all its rich diversity in the following chapters of this study. Here let us begin to consider in somewhat more detail what distinguishes this particular ceremony of bravery from others: what kinds of response to loss it encourages and what, conversely, it discourages. It would be interesting to chart Browne's funeral customs on a literary rather than a social map—to analyze, that is, the various attitudes toward death expressed through different literary forms. Here I can only sketch in a few of the frontiers one would want to place on such a map by way of outlining the territory under discussion in these pages.

The pastoral landscape offers the elegist, above all, the opportunity to place his human sorrows within the universal, but also manifestly concrete, world of living and dying things in nature. The pastoral sunlight simplifies as it clarifies. It reveals the elegist's human suffering and loss to be like, or at least not all that unlike, death in nature. The two realms are not one; but we can speak of one in terms of the other. And if nature's grasses return in the following season, or her sunlight on the following day, so we too will, if not recover the one we have lost, at least recover ourselves. "Clear sky one day, rain the next,"[15] says one Theocritean herdsman to another to console his friend for the loss of a mistress. Men's feelings, the herdsman suggests, are like the weather: they fluctuate. What is certain is that life renews itself. To place a lament in the pastoral world is, then, to imply some form of regeneration.

We win our release from suffering here chiefly by yielding to it. Nature's child, the herdsman is also nature's victim, the victim of nature in him. "Clear sky one day, rain the next," speaks for the herdsman's vulnerability to inner as well as outer storms. He cannot alter his feelings any more than he can change the weather or the course of fate herself. But if he cannot control that fluctuation, he can yield himself to the eternal ebb and flow.

In bringing death into the pastoral world, the elegist divests it of some of its grandeur. There is no room here for a sacrificial death, for a death which owes its allegiance to something beyond the individual's existence. Pericles (as Thucydides reports it) consoled the Athenians for the loss of their city's finest youths in battle by recalling to them the ideal of civilization for which these men gave their lives. Such deaths are to be envied, not mourned. This is always the heroic consolation: what the hero died for was something worth dying for. But the pastoral hero knows no allegiance but to life itself, the life lived *here* among these streams and fields. This existence is not to be defended but simply enjoyed. Death can never be preferred to life in the pastoral world. It may be made intelligible; it can, indeed it must, be endured. But it is never to be desired. One yields here, but only to the inevitable.

Pastoral consoles us by enfolding us in nature's sympathies. And its capacity to absorb our sufferings in this way makes it inhospitable to a tragic view of death. Tragedy isolates man, strips him of those sympathies which pastoral would gather about him. Lear on the heath tears at his clothing in order to get at "the thing itself; unaccommodated man." In pastoral poetry we do not see man thus in his nakedness. Nature surrounds the herdsman, clothes him in her sympathies, reminds him that his suffering belongs to the life and death of all living things. If he must die, he will not die alone. And his fate seems less terrible because it is, in various ways, shared.

But if the pastoral world enfolds man in nature's sympathies, it divests him of other sorts of involvement. It strips him, for instance, of his social identity. In pastoral elegies we do not find that density of texture, that awareness of the social fabric of life, which lends weight and conviction to these lines from Ben Jonson's elegy on the death of his friend, Vincent Corbet:

> *Much from him I profess I wone,*
> *And more, and more, I should have done,*
> *But that I understood him scant;*
> *Now I conceive him by my want.* [16]

Here it is the acknowledgment of multiple layers of personality, some of which will always remain impenetrable to another person, that makes Jonson's poem so moving. The pastoral elegist sacrifices nuance when he simplifies. And he sacrifices with it that sense of intimacy which is conferred by the very effort to penetrate the barriers between one human being and another. The pastoral elegist relinquishes the complexities of the individual human situation that he may better portray this loss in its deeper relation to other losses, both human and nonhuman ones. When we weep for Lycidas we weep for all young men dead ere their prime.

One final distinction: the reminder that the one we mourn, though he no longer lives *here* with us, still lives in some better world elsewhere, may be consoling; but it is not in itself a pastoral consolation. We shall see in Renaissance pastoral elegies the flowering of a second landscape, a world of unfading blossoms and fields forever green. Its distinctive topography and atmosphere inform us that this landscape exists to give substance to assurances other than those which the pastoral world can provide: the assurances of the eternal life. The pastoral world, I have already suggested, includes death within the cycle of nature's annual renewal. From that other world death has been banished; there we see an eternal springtime, one beyond mutability. The Renaissance pastoral elegist may be able to navigate his poetic course between these two landscapes. Indeed Vergil teaches him how to raise his shepherd-hero to the stars—and then to bring us down to earth again. But these remain two settings, two ways of seeing things. And to the extent that the pastoral elegist (pagan or Christian) detaches himself from his earthly setting, to the extent that he shifts his perspective from *here* to *there*, he must forfeit the consolations of the pastoral landscape.[17]

Let us turn now for a moment to the matter of the name. The term "pastoral elegy" belongs to our own age, not to that of the poems themselves. Indeed, as a description of classical and Renaissance funeral laments it is anachronistic. The classical "elegiac" describes a meter, not a mood—and not even the meter of pastoral poetry, which is the hexameter. In the Renaissance period an "elegy" is a poem which might once have been written in that elegiac meter; a poem which addresses itself to the emotions. Renaissance elegies include love poems as well as funeral laments. It is only in the Romantic period that the term takes on its modern meaning, only then are "elegiac" sentiments those associated exclusively with death. I might then find some accurate label for the classical and Renaissance poems discussed here, "pastoral dirge" perhaps or "pastoral epicedium." I have chosen, however, to retain our modern term "pastoral elegy": it will do as well as any, and it is the term we know.

We who write about the convention in retrospect feel the need for a single, unifying name. The poets who wrote in that convention did not. Our term was apparently first introduced by Spenser, when he called his "Astrophel" (1595) a "Pastorall Elegie upon the Death of . . . Sir Phillip Sidney." But there is nothing final in this designation; the name does not "stick." A Renaissance pastoral elegy is called a "monody," a "pastoral," an "eclogue," a "lament," and all possible combinations of the above terms. It may be designated by the name of the shepherd-singer, as "Lycidas" or "Damon." Or it may be identified simply by its place in a pastoral sequence, as the fifth *Eclogue*.[18] The various names are not arbitrary: each tells us something important about the poem in question. But it is surely significant that neither Renaissance poets nor Renaissance theorists felt a need to give the convention as a whole its own particular name.[19]

It is not that the form itself lacks definition. On the contrary; the Renaissance pastoral elegy convention has a good many internal rules, more in fact than any other pastoral form[20] and more than most literary conventions. But they are unwritten rules. It is perhaps a sign of the vitality as well as the fluidity of the Renaissance convention that it goes by many names and sometimes no name. Like the word "convention" itself (which only acquires its modern sense when the idea of conventionality in both art and life has become suspect),[21] so this particular convention too only acquires a name when the form itself has rigidified, when the pastoral elegist's way of placing sorrow is felt to be an unnatural way. Milton knew, when he began "Lycidas" with the words "yet once more," what earlier poets and poetic visions he was summoning. He knew theirs was a vision in which, *mutatis mutandi*, he shared. He did not have to give it a name.[22]

A way of seeing things and the individual visions of particular men—I have tried in these pages to strike a balance between the two, between the anatomy of a convention and the analysis of poems in that convention. I have selected for detailed commentary some fourteen poems, the ones which seem to me most worthy of discussion in their own right and which best illuminate the evolution of the form. What follows is, then, offered as an analysis of a convention, not a comprehensive historical survey of its development.[23] Brief summaries and footnotes will, I hope, serve at least to acquaint the reader with some of the byways not explored here. I have, however, tried to discuss enough and sufficiently varied examples of the form to indicate its range as well as its continuing preoccupations. My concern throughout, as I have said, is with the encounter between the poet and the landscape and the way this landscape is modified to accommodate different kinds of loss. Thus funeral laments in which the landscape functions merely as an allegorical cover do not concern me here. What we choose to call such poems is not important; for my purposes they are not pastoral elegies. The poems I am analyzing here all depend for their central effects on what follows from an elegist's bringing his sorrow to a particular natural setting. It is this encounter we shall be following as we move from Alexandrian Cos to the Roman countryside, from the banks of the Tiber to the Loire, until in 1637 Milton brings the convention to its climax and, as he brings his Lycidas home to an English shore, makes the pastoral elegist's special way of seeing things seem everyone's way, humanity's way of seeing them. Milton universalizes in "Lycidas"; he does not, finally, repudiate. His elegist's assault upon the convention's traditional way of placing sorrow is only exceeded by (as indeed it is predicated upon) the poet's larger faith in this ceremony of bravery.

What are the sources of the literary convention whose boundaries, or recurrent concerns, I have sketched in the preceding paragraphs? What earlier ceremonies (whether literary or nonliterary ones) might have helped to shape the form we will be studying here? How—and when—did the pastoral elegy's various internal motifs "come together" as a convention? Here, let us admit at the outset we enter an intriguing but treacherous realm of almost pure speculation. The teasing, elusive hero of Theocritus' first *Idyll*, who hints only obliquely at the cause of his suffering and taunts Aphrodite as he goes to his death, still keeps the secrets of his own origins closely guarded from us today. What myths, what other dying neatherds, what literary traditions or experiences may lie behind this first pastoral elegy we do not know. Nor do we know what would be most useful for us to know: the extent to which the origins of the pastoral elegy are involved with or distinct from those of the pastoral genre as a whole. Did Theocritus think of the "pastoral song" which his Thyrsis sings in the first *Idyll* as essentially the same kind of song that herdsmen sing in his other idylls? Did he think of these pastoral songs as conforming to a type at all? We cannot answer these questions with any assurance, for the pre-Theocritean history of the pastoral genre remains obscure. And that is itself something of a mystery, since by the third century B.C., when Theocritus wrote his pastoral (or "bucolic") idylls, the other major categories of Greek literature (epic, drama, etc.) had been long established and their various sub-species and internal conventions analyzed. Are we, then, to suppose that pastoral was a relative latecomer to this repertory of forms? It rather looks that way. Possibly there were earlier pastoralists (and earlier pastoral elegists) whose poems have since been lost to us. One thing that is unlikely is that the pastoral elegy sprang full blown from the pen of Theocritus. Doubtless there were literary precedents of some sort. The inventiveness of the Alexandrian poets tends to be of the sort that operates through novel combinations of pre-existent materials. Yet, whatever may lie behind the Theocritean presentation of Daphnis' death, that image which is in turn the ancestor of all subsequent ones, it is at least tempting to suppose that the convention crystallizes, takes on its definitive shape, in this first Theocritean idyll.

Tempting, for one thing, because it seems so likely that the Alexandrian age should have been the age to produce pastoral and the pastoral elegy. The Alexandrians at the Ptolemaic court for whom Theocritus wrote his poems looked on theirs (much as we look on ours today) as an over-civilized age. To such a people, a poet's call to return to some simpler, more "natural" way of life strikes an answering chord. Clearly the Theocritean call to Sicily or (closer at hand) to Cos is not the call of a wild songbird but of one too long in cities pent. William Empson's definition of pastoral, as poetry written about "the people" but neither by nor for them, applies well (so far as we can judge of the poet from his poems) to Theocritus.[24] The poet's preference for slight, highly finished forms; the very innocence of his herdsmen, whose actions often raise that indulgent smile we reserve for the comic misadventures of the clown who tries to play a hero's part; and the fine balance Theocritus himself maintains, as he contemplates his subjects, between affectionate sympathy and amused detachment—these are not the hallmarks of a primitive art or a primitive artist. On the contrary, Theocritus presents his brief *Idylls* as the happy alternative to the ponderous and pretentious volumes turned out by those of his fellow poets who still labor on in the outworn epic tradition. Clearly Theocritus' "primitivism" must be read against the background of the Alexandrian world's disillusionment with the heroic and republican assertions of an earlier age.[25]

The pastoral elegy, too, as we see it in Theocritus (and leaving aside for the moment the question of its ultimate ancestry), is most satisfactorily explained as a response to these same outworn conventions. Certainly the Theocritean presentation of a dying herdsman becomes more intelligible, more expressive, if viewed against the background of earlier literary representations of dying heroes than if viewed as the vestigial survival of some earlier, more primitive funeral lament. We will return shortly to the various primitivistic theories of the origins of our convention. For the moment let us examine very briefly the literary context. Epic poems continue to be written by Alexandrian poets and their heroes continue to die heroic deaths—but we are not greatly moved by them. The stark splendor of Achilles' lament for Patroklos is not to be recaptured in the faded formulae of the old epic convention; and the eloquent understatement with which Aeneas tells us of his grief at his father's death is still ahead of us. Adam Parry has suggested that pastoral functions as a cover in an age of irony: at a time when men find it difficult to experience strong feelings directly, the pastoralist creates a fictive world through which to reunite us with the world of feeling.[26] Here we can still be moved by a man's loves or by his sorrows. But in transferring them from the epic arena to the pastoral grove, the feelings themselves are qualified. Instead of the warrior exalted in his death, the pastoral poet gives us the herdsman who yields to the common fate of nature's creatures. Instead of heroic awe, he gives us poignancy. At the same time, the herdsman's gestures seem sweeter to us, his drama more moving, if we bring to this death memories of earlier, nobler deaths. That was splendid, the pastoral elegist suggests, but this is fine too. The pastoral vision of death, like the pastoral vision of life, gains significance through its implied contrast with other ways of seeing things.

Today we are, for a variety of reasons, inclined to look with scepticism on the image of Theocritus favored by nineteenth- and early twentieth-century critics: the poet of the people, the home-sick Sicilian transcribing (perhaps polishing) the folk songs of his native countrymen.[27] Our increasing awareness, sharpened by several recent studies of Theocritus,[28] of the sophistication of this poet's verses and our better understanding of the nature of folk composition force us to abandon the image of Theocritus as a primitive or quasi-primitive poet. However, to dismiss as naive the notion that Theocritean pastoral springs directly out of the herds-man's own soil need not be to dismiss altogether the possibility of primitivistic or folk influences upon Theocritus. Indeed it is diffi-cult *not* to speculate along these lines when one contemplates the pastoral elegy, with its image of a dying youth "whom universal nature did lament." As I have already suggested, the sources of Theocritean pastoral are likely to be several; and there is no reason why, if Theocritus himself is surely not a poet of the folk, there may not be among his sources popular materials of various kinds. The most sophisticated poets everywhere have felt free to draw upon popular traditions; there is no reason to suppose that this poet is an exception. We do not, in any case, know enough about the pre-Theocritean history of pastoral simply to dismiss this pos-sibility out of hand. Some of these popular sources are worth exploring—worth, that is, setting alongside the image of death we see in the first *Idyll*. We cannot, of course, prove anything by such explorations. All we can do—and all I propose to do in this brief discussion—is to estimate how close or how remote certain ac-tivities, both literary and non-literary, may be to what I think Theocritus is doing in his poem.

What about "primitive" attitudes toward death? Does the pas-toral elegist's conception of death, whatever its immediate sources, have anything in common with the views of men less civilized than himself? This is a particularly difficult question to answer. For probably the single most important discovery of modern anthropology is that there is no one "primitive" way of looking at life or at death. The primitive has as many ways of responding to death as we have. Moreover, at least one of these ways is *prima facie* alien to that of the pastoral elegist. The death rites of many primitive tribes serve to effect a desired separation between the world of the living and that of the dead. What distresses such peoples is not the discontinuity wrought by death but just the opposite: the possibility of the continuing and baneful influence of the dead man's spirit upon the world of the living. The basic thrust of the pastoral elegy is to affirm continuity; life, albeit in new forms, goes on. The difference between these two responses is a fundamental one. And if one were to define (somewhat arbitrarily) the first kind of response as "primitive," then we might say that mourning, which presumes there is a grief to be assuaged, a gap to be breached, is an essentially civilized act.

There are, however, other ways of looking at death—some of which may be particularly congenial to men who live on more intimate terms with nature than most of us do today. The pastoral elegist, we have said, considers human death by placing it in nature's world, within her annual cycle of decay and regeneration.

Now to the civilized urbanite this setting is an artificial one. But what of the rustic? Is it not probable that death first presents itself to his imagination in just this aspect? That may be. But the next questions are more difficult for us to answer. Might the Theocritean pastoral elegy be the descendant of some earlier, primitive lament in which actual herdsmen sought to come to terms with the awesome fact of human mortality by placing it in the world they knew? And might such herdsmen have asked nature to weep or to reverse her course for their sake and expected nature to comply with their demands? Are these same demands in later pastoral elegies the figurative residue of what was once taken quite literally? We cannot answer these questions. But most recent anthropological research supports the view that primitive men are no more likely to confuse the human and the nonhuman realms than we are. If Lévi-Strauss is to be believed, many primitive myths and rituals serve to elaborate basic distinctions between the two realms. And we can all appreciate the fact that the man who lives in close contact with nature is more likely to be aware of such distinctions. He feels, as we do not, his own helplessness when nature releases her thunder or when she refuses her rains. Surely he does what he can to propitiate the gods. But he is not inclined to suppose that nature looks on him with any special sympathy—that she would, of her own accord, and purely out of affection, bend her order to his. It is not a primitive impulse which dictates a shepherd to say, "let all be changed because Daphnis is dying."

But if not characteristically primitive, this is a wish which is entertained at certain times by all men—perhaps especially in moments of unusual stress. In funeral laments from all cultures and from all stages of civilization we see a desire on the part of the mourner (expressed either as wish or as fact) to involve the whole world in his own particular sorrows. Nature is made culpable, is made to suffer, is made to sympathize. Thomas Rosenmeyer cites the lament of a Chinook Indian woman for her dead infant in which the mother's grief is deflected into anger at some ripe berries hanging above her head.[29] In one of the most ancient sections of the Old Testament, David, mourning the deaths of Saul and Jonathan, demands that a blight infect the place where they were slain: "Ye mountains of Gilboa, let there be no dew, neither let there be rain upon you . . ." (II Sam. 1:19). And in a first century B.C. lament by the Chinese poet Mei Sheng, "sad winds sing in the white aspens" and "their long murmuring" kills the mourner's heart with grief.[30] In these several instances of what Ruskin calls the "pathetic fallacy," that is, the transferral of human feelings onto the nonhuman world,[31] the important thing, it seems to me, is not *whether* nature feels with us but *what* she or what we ask her to feel. For we ask different things from nature in our moments of extreme need: we ask her to ease the burden of our anger; we ask her for revenge; we ask her to share our melancholy. And in each case the speaker asks nature to do something he knows she would not ordinarily do. His demand that nature (in some manner or other) go out of her way for him testifies, then, not to an underlying confusion about the sort of response appropriate to nature and that appropriate to man, but to the particular way in which grief heightens or dislocates his sense of reality. The "pathetic fallacy," whether invoked by a primitive or the most sophisticated of poets, is never, I suspect, invoked except as a conscious distortion—is never, that is, a fallacy.

Now in the pastoral elegy, when we invite nature to turn her order upside-down or to weep with us, what we are asking for is not a display of anger, or a promise of revenge, or even (primarily) a display of grief. We are asking for a demonstration of love. I think we would do better to explore the possible ancestry of this particular wish, this particular way of dislocating reality under the pressure of an extraordinary situation, than to look for the origins of such dislocations in primitive world-views. That nature feels a special affection for man does not, I have already suggested, appear to be a belief particularly characteristic of societies more primitive or rustic than our own. There is some evidence, moreover, to support the view that Theocritus' more immediate source for his image of nature's sympathy in the first *Idyll* comes, not from folk culture, but from the world of art.

Our evidence comes from a passage in another of the bucolic idylls, the seventh. A herdsman tells of the celebration he will make if his friend comes safely home from a sea voyage. He describes the ritual feasting, the drinking and the story-telling which will mark the occasion. The song for the beloved's safe return (or "propemptikon") is itself a conventional form, and the context suggests that the songs to be sung at the festival will also deal with familiar conventional subjects. One of these songs, like that song in the first *Idyll* which is our special concern, deals with the death of Daphnis:

> and close at hand Tityrus shall sing how once Daphnis the neatherd loved Xenea, and how the hill was sorrowful about him and the oaktrees which grow upon the river Himeras' banks sang his dirge, when he was wasting like any snow under high Haemus or Athos or Rhodope or remotest Caucasus.
>
> (72–77)[32]

This is all we hear of Daphnis or his death in the seventh *Idyll*. The speaker continues with a summary of another song to be sung on the same occasion.

We cannot be sure that the Daphnis whose death the Sicilian hills and trees lament in the seventh *Idyll* is the same Daphnis whose death is the subject of Theocritus' much fuller treatment in the first. The eighth *Idyll* features an evidently quite different Daphnis. And the Xenea of the seventh is not mentioned in the first *Idyll*. But the situations are alike enough to invite our comparison: in the first *Idyll* we also see a Daphnis "pining away" (or literally, "melting") for love; there too nature joins in the lament; and there too we see the hero's death impinging, first on his immediate environment, then, by successive stages, on more distant realms. But when we compare these two dying Daphnises, we are aware of important differences as well as similarities. In the seventh *Idyll*, where Daphnis' death is only alluded to in what appears to be a conventional context, the association between the hero and nature is a far more intimate one than it is in the first *Idyll*, where we see the neatherd's death enacted before us. In the seventh *Idyll* the hill is sorrowful and the oak-trees sing the dirge; in the first, the animals mourn for the death of the neatherd (their master), but hills and trees do not. And, conversely, in the seventh *Idyll* Daphnis himself "melts" into nature, like snow beneath the mountains, at his death; but when Daphnis is "melting" again in the first *Idyll*, the usage of the term is restricted to the erotic sphere.

We should be cautious about making any large generalizations about the sources of the first *Idyll* on the basis of a comparison with this brief passage in the seventh *Idyll*. But it looks as though Theocritus inherited from the literary repertory of available forms a conventional topic, "the woes of Daphnis," dealing with a particular part of the familiar Daphnis myth, namely, the neatherd's death. And it looks further (if we can trust the evidence I have deduced from this passage in the seventh *Idyll*) as though there were also a traditional way of presenting this topic—a highly idealized, romantic way in which the human and the nonhuman worlds are very nearly merged. If Theocritus did inherit such a conception of the "woes of Daphnis," to which he alludes in the seventh *Idyll*, then we must be struck by the degree to which he departs from that traditional presentation when he tells the story himself in the first *Idyll*. For here, as we shall see in our closer study of this poem, though nature sympathizes with Daphnis' death, there is no question of "oneness" between the two worlds. In the first pastoral elegy we know that the distinction between man and nature is already firmly established. It is more appealing (to me at least) to look on Theocritus, not as the heir to a primitive tradition in which man and nature are "as one," but rather as the true father of the convention because, in revising the conventional literary presentation of Daphnis' death, he separates Daphnis from his world. Without the sympathy between man and nature, the pastoral elegist could not *place* his sorrow. But without the distinction between the two realms, the very source of his sorrow would be obscured.

Thus far we have considered the possibility that the pastoral elegist's association between man and nature might be derived from some earlier funeral lament in which the meaning of human life and death is clarified by placing those events in a nonhuman setting. But there is another and an opposite theory—one which takes nature, not man, as its starting point and considers the herdsman to be originally but a metaphor for events taking place in the nonhuman realm. According to this theory (which is still probably the most widely accepted view of the origins of the convention), the pastoral elegy is the descendant of ancient vegetation rites, such as continued to flourish, and indeed enjoyed a considerable revival, in the Alexandrian age. This theory has its own origins in the pioneering anthropological research of Sir James George Frazer at the turn of the century. Frazer described the annual rituals held in Mesopotamia in honor of such dying and reviving gods as Adonis and Tammuz—rituals which, as he thought, served to commemorate "the yearly decay and revival of life, especially of vegetative life."[33] And Frazer went on to cite verses in which the youthful god is compared to plants that wither before their time. Tammuz, for instance, is "a tamarisk that in the garden has drunk no water / Whose crown in the field has brought forth no blossom."[34]

The pastoral elegist also tells of a lovely youth cut off in the springtime of his life and surrounded by a natural world that often denies her own fertility to express her sympathy with him. Was this "dying" natural world once the original subject of the lament? Might we have in such verses as those Frazer describes the source of the pastoral elegy convention? Frazer himself did not make the connection. But literary critics since then have done so. Indeed such a derivation is often simply assumed. T. P. Harrison, for instance, in his anthology of pastoral elegies (1939), states that "the Daphnis legend is a late Greek development of the symbol under which earlier peoples mourned the withering vegetation of summer. . . . 'This dirge over the fading beauty of the year soon assumed the form of the lament over the death of a young shepherd-poet.'"[35] And this from Frank Kermode in 1952: "Theocritus in his first *Idyll* celebrates the death of the shepherd-hero Daphnis, which in folklore had represented the annual death of Nature."[36] Of course one of the chief reasons we, as critics, are interested in derivations (which may or may not be a good reason) is because they seem to tell us something about what *is* as well as what *was*. Harrison and Kermode do not suggest that, because the first *Idyll* of Theocritus derives from a lament for a vegetation god, the poem is such a lament, but Northrop Frye does: "the poem [*Lycidas*] will not be about King but about his archetype, Adonis, the dying and rising god, called Lycidas in Milton's poem."[37]

It is just because this sort of identification is so tempting and so easily made that we must be particularly careful here. It is not impossible that the first *Idyll* is derived from these vegetation rites. But the fact has not by any means been proven. What does seem unlikely, in view of the eclecticism and sophistication of Alexandrian art, is that it could be quite this simple. It seems highly unlikely that the pastoral elegy, as we see it in Theocritus, is the direct descendant of this single extra-literary source. We do know that Theocritus was familiar with these vegetation rites. And he may have drawn upon them in the first *Idyll*. But it need not be an all or nothing affair, and it may well have been a highly self-conscious one.

Again I think another Theocritean idyll (this time not one of his bucolic poems) helps us to gauge the sort of influence which this extra-literary phenomenon may have had on the first *Idyll*. For Theocritus not only knew about these vegetation rites, but he also wrote about them; and in the fifteenth *Idyll* we get some idea of how he felt about them. The poem, a dialogue between two Alexandrian women, describes their visit to the palace where the annual festival in honor of Adonis is being held. The exoticism of the ritual serves here as an antidote to the banality of every-day reality. The world of ritual, at least in the fifteenth *Idyll*, is the world of romance, an escape world. And in the end the grand pageant of the god's annual death and rebirth simply brings home to these spectators the fact that in their own lives nothing changes, from day to day, from year to year. The poem ends with one of the women returning home to a hungry husband with an acid tongue; she hopes, but does not really expect, that things may be different for her when Adonis comes again in the following year. In the fifteenth *Idyll*, then, Theocritus uses the image of nature's annual round to point up the differences between ritual and reality, nature's round and our own. To be sure, the fifteenth *Idyll* is urban and satiric. It is possible that in the pastoral milieu of the first *Idyll* Theocritus may have chosen to impose ritualistic patterns on human experience in a more straightforward fashion. But the example of the fifteenth *Idyll* should at the least remind us how sensitive this poet is to the dissonances between nature's course and the way in which human events take shape.

The image of a dying god who symbolizes nature's annual death was certainly current in the Alexandrian world of the third century B.C., when men (and more often women) were busily reviving these ancient fertility cults. I would guess that it does contribute something to the presentation of the neatherd's death in the first *Idyll*. But if Theocritus may invite us to compare his Daphnis with Adonis, he by no means identifies the two. For the critical identification of the Theocritean Daphnis with the dying and reviving god of vegetation we are, I think, less indebted to Theocritus himself than to a later historical accident—namely, the gathering together, perhaps as early as the Augustan age, of the Theocritean idylls with the poems of the later Greek "bucolic" poets. Included among these later poems is Bion's "Lament for Adonis," a poem with little or no indebtedness to the first Theocritean *Idyll* but one which obviously has a great deal to do with vegetation or fertility rituals.[38] Because the "Lament for Adonis" descends into the Renaissance along with the first *Idyll*, it does then have an influence on the development of the Renaissance pastoral elegy. But that, of course, is a later story.

Furthermore, in the most familiar of the Daphnis myths current in the third century B.C. there is nothing to suggest that Daphnis himself was ever the object of a fertility cult like Adonis or Tammuz. On the contrary, the myth tells a rather different story. Here is one version of the legend which comes to us indirectly from the Sicilian historian Timaeus (c. 346–250 B.C.):

> Some say that Daphnis the neatherd was Mercury's friend, others his son; and that he had this name from an accident: for he was born of a nymph and as soon as born exposed under a laurel tree. . . . While Daphnis kept cows in Sicily, being very beautiful, a nymph fell in love with him, whom he enjoyed, being in his blooming years. . . . They agreed that he should not enjoy any other, but if he transgressed, she threatened him, that it was decreed by fate he should lose his sight. . . . Afterwards the King's daughter falling in love with him, he being drunk violated the agreement and lay with her. This was the first occasion of Bucolic verses, the subject whereof was to bewail the misfortune of Daphnis, and the loss of his eyes. Stesichorus the Himerean first used this kind of verse.
>
> (10.18)[39]

The first century B.C. Sicilian historian Diodorus supplements this account with the further elaboration that Daphnis, "being endowed with an unusual gift of song," was himself the inventor of bucolic poetry (4.84).[40] And Servius (*Ad Ecl.*, 5.20) records another version of this Daphnis myth in which at Daphnis' death Hermes takes him up to heaven and causes a spring to well up in the spot where he died.

The testimony of these ancient historians cannot persuade a modern scholar to seek the origins of pastoral poetry in songs sung by and in honor of a mythological neatherd: clearly the historians are extrapolating here (from familiar literary motifs) an imagined extra-literary source. But if we cannot make the connection, it is at least interesting that Theocritus' contemporaries (or some of them) do make it. For the Daphnis myth to which they trace the origins of pastoral is, from our point of view, a suggestive one. In the myth, as in the pastoral elegy but not the vegetation ritual, we celebrate an intimacy rather than an absolute identification between the hero and his setting. An offspring of Hermes and a nymph, named for the laurel tree beneath which he is exposed, the Daphnis of the myth is protected both by nature and a god. Yet this Daphnis must live in a human realm, and neither gods nor nymphs nor laurels can save him when, intoxicated by drink and eros, he violates his oath; Daphnis must pay the human penalty—blinding or (in another version) death. Now we cannot even be sure that this Daphnis myth to which the ancient historians trace the origins of the pastoral genre is the same Daphnis myth which Theocritus is using in his first *Idyll*. As we shall see, the allusiveness of his presentation makes possible the conjecture that his poem is about some entirely different dying Daphnis. I think this *is* Theocritus' story, and that those ancient commentators are right who suppose this myth to be the immediate source for his first *Idyll*. For the myth not only fits the "facts" as we see them (somewhat obscurely to be sure) in the Theocritean poem; it fits in a deeper sense. I am not suggesting that the myth and the poem are doing the same thing; for the myth, as we see it here in its bare outlines, can scarcely be said to "do" anything at all. What I am suggesting is that this is the sort of material out of which Theocritus might have shaped his poem; it allows for, perhaps even encourages, the attitude toward death we see fully developed in the poem—an attitude of poignant yet controlled sympathy on the part of nature and the poet for the dying herdsman.[41]

To sum up this brief and admittedly inconclusive discussion: perhaps the key term is self-consciousness. There is a new self-consciousness, first of all, about art, about their own literary traditions, on the part of the Alexandrian poets. Whatever else Theocritus is doing in his first *Idyll*, he is almost certainly looking back over his shoulder at earlier (and generally more heroic) literary representations of death. He may also be looking at earlier pastoral representations. The allusiveness of the first *Idyll* and of its hero suggests other poems, perhaps other dying herdsmen. There is at least a hint that Theocritus may have inherited a literary tradition which portrayed the bond between that dying herdsman and his world as a very close one, and that in giving us a hero who is himself conscious of his own separateness from nature, he revises that tradition. Nor need we rule out the possibility of more "primitivistic" or popular influences upon Theocritus as long as we recognize that these influences may be absorbed (and criticized as they are absorbed) in the same spirit of self-consciousness as literary ones. Indeed there is a possibility that Theocritus modified these popular sources along the same lines as the literary sources. If the popular image of the dying god, Adonis, serves as one model for the Theocritean Daphnis, then again Theocritus reduces the degree of identification between the hero and his world. And finally, if any of these speculations contain some measure of truth, then Theocritus is indeed the true father of our genre: for it is the recognition that human life cannot, after all, be subsumed within nature's annual course which, along with that affirmation of nature's sympathy for man, defines the pastoral elegist's vision of death.

PLACING SORROW

ABBREVIATIONS

1. PERIODICALS:

AJP	*American Journal of Philology*
AR	*American Review*
HLB	*Harvard Library Bulletin*
HSCL	*Harvard Studies in Comparative Literature*
JHS	*Journal of Hellenic Studies*
KR	*Kenyon Review*
MLN	*Modern Language Notes*
PMLA	*Publications of the Modern Language Association*
SEL	*Studies in English Literature, 1500–1900*
SP	*Studies in Philology*
TAPA	*Transactions of the American Philological Association*
UTQ	*University of Toronto Quarterly*
YCS	*Yale Classical Studies*

2. BOOKS:

Darbishire	*The Poetical Works of John Milton*, ed. Helen Darbishire, 2 vols., Oxford, 1955, 2.
Harrison-Leon	*The Pastoral Elegy: An Anthology*, with introduction, commentary and notes by Thomas Perrin Harrison, Jr. and English translations by Harry Joshua Leon, Austin, 1939.
Patrides	*Milton's "Lycidas": The Tradition and the Poem*, ed. C. A. Patrides, New York, 1961.

1

THEOCRITUS

Placing Sorrow in a Sweet World

We cannot know the original place of the poem we call the "first *Idyll*" within the Theocritean corpus. This poem is, however, given first place in each of the three manuscript families which have come down to us; and it is tempting to think that it came first for the poet himself. In no other bucolic idyll does Theocritus contain his central dramatic episode within so artfully contrived a setting.[1] In no other idyll is there so much to contain. Though Daphnis has much in common with herdsmen in other Theocritean idylls, though they all belong to the same world, we see more deeply into that world in this poem than in any other idyll. Theocritus contains Daphnis' death within the sweetness of pastoral, indeed makes it share in that sweetness; but he also makes us feel here the tension between the dying hero and the world he lives in, between the passionate energies of life and the fate which decrees death.

Theocritus places Thyrsis' song, the "woes of Daphnis," within an elaborate frame, in fact a series of frames. These not only contain the interior drama; they establish the context in which sorrow and death are defined in this world. Let us look at the outermost of these frames (or the first half of it): the initial dialogue between two herdsmen, a shepherd Thyrsis and an unnamed goatherd. What the relation of these speakers may be to Daphnis himself we are not told. For Daphnis' sorrows do not penetrate this outer world. The action of the initial dialogue is minimal. Its function is to create the landscape in which Thyrsis' song will be set. Indeed, the very first words of the herdsmen place human melodies in nature's melodious world:

Thyrsis: Sweet is the whispered music of that pinetree by the springs, goatherd, and sweet too your piping. You will take second prize to Pan. If he chooses the horned goat, you will have the she-goat, and if he has the she-goat for his prize, the kid falls to you. And the flesh of a kid is sweet before one milks her.

Goatherd: Sweeter, shepherd, falls your song than that stream which tumbles splashing from the rocks. If the Muses take the ewe for their gift, you shall have as prize the stall-fed lamb, and if it be their pleasure to have the lamb, you shall carry off the ewe after them.

Thyrsis: In the Nymph's name, goatherd, will you sit down and pipe, here by this sloping knoll and the tamarisks? and meanwhile I will tend your goats.

Goatherd: No, shepherd, no; at noontime we may not pipe, for fear of Pan. For then, surely, he is resting wearied from the chase. And he is quick-tempered and bitter wrath sits ever on his nostril. But you, Thyrsis, are wont to sing the woes of Daphnis and have come to mastery in pastoral song. Come here then, and let us sit beneath the elm, facing Priapus and the springs, by that shepherds' seat and the oaks. . . .

$(1-23)^2$

This is, first of all, a world to be enjoyed. "Sweet" ("hedu") is the first word of the poem and sweetness becomes the leitmotif of the little scene. The herdsman's song is sweet; so is the sound of the waterfall and of the wind in the pine tree. Later Thyrsis will introduce "the woes of Daphnis" by commending the sweetness of his own voice. It is, above all, within a sweet world that the pastoral elegist places sorrow, and a world in which one sweet thing is not all that different from another. There is, to be sure, a hierarchy of sweets: the natural music of pine tree and brook yields to the human music of pipe and song, while these in turn yield to the music of the gods. But one sort of sweetness can be compared to another. For both art and nature offer us gratifications of an immediate, palpable kind. Underlying these several parallel assertions is the basic assumption that life itself is sweet and we are here to enjoy that sweetness. This is not to say that the herdsman's

desires will always be gratified; the Cyclops in the elventh *Idyll* is
not granted his nymph, nor will Daphnis be granted his. But the
value of a life dedicated to the enjoyment of sensuous pleasures is
not questioned here. It is the basic assumption of the herdsmen's
world, and the meaning of death in his world is conditioned by
that assumption.

Implicit in the ideal of sweetness is the value placed on sensa-
tion. Sweetness (as opposed, for instance, to beauty) requires that
someone be there to savor or taste it. In fact it is a catalogue of
sensations, not objects, that the herdsmen offer us. The whisper-
ing of the pine, the warbling of the brook, the sound of pipe and
voice are sweet. But if they speak of sensations, the herdsmen
"objectify" their feelings, endow them with the clarity of outline,
the palpability and essential impersonality of objects. Thyrsis tells
us that the sounds of the pine tree and pipe are sweet, not that he
finds them so. Presumably anyone else would find them sweet
too. Sensations are presented here as tangible facts from which
those who experience and record them maintain a certain detach-
ment.[3] The catalogue style of presentation with its separate, par-
allel units serves to isolate and distinguish one sensation from
another; each is sweet, but there is no sense of one sensation or
response merging with another.[4]

We feel as if we were in a world whose objects we could reach
out and grasp, and this is because the speakers themselves appear
to do just that. Thyrsis and the goatherd make their setting come
alive for us less by describing objects than by pointing to them. The
pine tree is not distinguished *sui generis*; the important thing about
it is that it is *that* pine tree, the one by the springs. The goatherd
points to a spot "here by this sloping knoll," and Thyrsis to an-
other one, "here . . . beneath the elm . . . by that shepherds' seat
and the oaks." By *placing* objects in this way rather than describing
them, Theocritus gives us a sense of participating in the scene from
within, of registering its objects and sensations as the herdsmen
register them, rather than of contemplating it from without. He
gives us that sense of "hereness" which is more important to the
pastoral elegist than the elements of the landscape in themselves.

This is, further, as these "stage directions" imply, a well-ordered little world. We could make a fairly coherent diagram of this scene. Here everything has its place. And in the human sphere as well, nothing is left unaccounted for. If Pan chooses the buck, then the goatherd will have the doe; but if the god should prefer the doe, then the kid remains for him. And, should the goatherd wish to pipe, Thyrsis will tend his goats.

Yet, if we could make a coherent diagram of this scene, we could not so easily place the scene as a whole on a map. There are no clues which point to a particular locale; we might be anywhere in the Greek world. Internally both space and time are carefully established; externally both are left open. This delightful grove simply exists, here and now—perhaps also there and then. And thus we experience at once a sense of internal security and of unfetteredness. We feel that this delightful grove must be located in some precious place far away from the world we live in. But by not locating his bucolic paradise on the map Theocritus frees it from comparisons with actuality. We do not have to ask ourselves where this place is or whether it is even a real one. We do not, so to speak, have to build a wall around it. There need be, then, no sacrifice of freedom. The Theocritean version of Eden is not contingent.

All the features of this initial scene we have mentioned—the sweetness, the immediacy, the clarity of outline, the sense at once of security and unboundedness—are summed up and concentrated in the noonday sun which illuminates it. The goatherd, we observe, puts some stress upon the fact that the noon hour is at hand, de-clining to play on his pipe at this time. As he describes it, noon is a period of suspended animation. Pan is only resting; wrath sits on his nostril and soon the chase will begin again. The herdsman's proffered seat beneath the elm testifies not to *ennui* but to the intensity of the sun's heat. We are forced into repose here by an in-tensification, not a diminution, of life's energies. Beyond the shelter of the elm tree the sunlight transfixes each object in its bright, shadowless gaze. The noon stillness is charged with the passionate activities of the day, which it for the moment holds in abeyance. Similarly, Daphnis' death will be surrounded by images of life, of vitality, of sweetness. And Daphnis will convert even his dying into an affirmation of life. The Theocritean herdsmen sing of death at high noon, and their funeral song participates in the values of the daylight world: clarification, simplification, intensification.

The opening dialogue establishes the physical and emotional climate in which the "woes of Daphnis" will be placed. The next scene, a second, interior frame, takes us a step closer to the themes of the lament. The goatherd offers Thyrsis a special cup if he will sing "the woes of Daphnis." And as the goatherd describes the intricate carving on that cup, he uncovers a world in miniature with a dramatic life of its own. Such picture-poems, or "ekphrases," were a favorite device of Alexandrian poets. But here the "digression" leads us toward, rather than away from, the subject at hand. For in each of the scenes on the cup a potentially threatening or painful situation is transformed into a pleasing aesthetic pattern. Here is the goatherd's description:

> And I will give you a deep cup, washed over with sweet wax, two-handled, and newly fashioned, still fragrant from the knife. Along the lips above trails ivy, ivy dotted with its golden clusters, and along it winds the tendril glorying in its yellow fruit. And within is wrought a woman, such a thing as the gods might fashion, bedecked with a cloak and circlet. And by her two men with long fair locks contend from either side in alternate speech. Yet these things touch not her heart, but now she looks on one and smiles, and now to the other she shifts her thought, while they, long hollow-eyed from love, labour to no purpose. By these is carved an old fisherman, and a rugged rock whereon the old man eagerly gathers up a great net from a cast as one that labours mightily. You would say that he was fishing with all the strength of his limbs, so do the sinews stand out all about his neck, grey-haired though he is; yet his strength is as a youth's. And a little way from the sea-worn old man there is a vineyard with a fair load of reddening clusters, guarded by a little boy who sits upon its dry-stone wall. About him hang two foxes, and one goes to and fro among the vine-rows plundering the ripe grapes, while the other brings all her wit to bear upon his wallet, and vows she will not let the lad be until [she has raided his breakfast-bread]. But the boy is plaiting a pretty cricket-cage of bonded rush and asphodel, and has more joy in his plaiting than care for wallet or for vines. And every way about the cup is spread the pliant acanthus. A wondrous thing it is to goatherds' eyes, a marvel that will strike thy heart with amaze; for it I paid the ferryman of Calydna a goat and a great cheese of white milk. . . .
>
> (27–58)

The first episode sounds the theme of rejected love and pride which will have a central place in the woes of Daphnis. These three figures on the cup are, like the Theocritean herdsmen, victims of their emotions, fated to act out their little drama over and over again. But just as these figures serve quite literally a decorative end on the cup itself, so the goatherd's description of them re-creates the pattern traced by the three participants and not the painfulness of an actual situation. Ardor has been converted here into a charming design. In the second scene a similar sort of conversion takes place. Age ought to be taking its toll on the old man, as suffering ought to take its toll on the young lovers. But instead the energy (as it were, of the scene itself) keeps him going. The pattern re-creates itself; the ravages of time are held in abeyance. And in the third scene we know that the child will always be secure on his stone wall despite the plundering foxes. Here it is not simply that, as in the "cold pastoral" of Keats' urn, art has suspended the progress of time; the child is secure because in his world the delicate cricket cage will always count for more than niggardly caution—or indeed than the grapes themselves. He is simply indifferent to the foxes, and we delight in his indifference.

In the interior world of the lament, Daphnis' world, the tyranny of love, the loss of one's vitality and the taunts of one's adversaries will pose more serious threats than they do here. The figures on the cup are aesthetic objects still. Daphnis will make a larger claim on our emotions. We enter into his drama, hear him speak. And the song of Thyrsis aims to dispel a larger threat than the ones we see here—that of death itself. But there, too, art works to convert pain into sweetness.[5]

The larger difficulty of that artistic endeavor is hinted at in the final lines of the goatherd's speech:

> Gladly I would please you with it [the cup], my friend, if you will sing that lovely song. I do not mock you; no, come, man, for surely you cannot carry your singing to Hades that brings forgetfulness of all things.
>
> (60–63)

Daphnis too must make his song heard even in Hades. More is involved here than a playful challenge; for, in the end, everything depends on how far our songs can carry.

Now Thyrsis tells us, as he begins his song, who he is, and he commends his own voice to us:

Begin, dear Muses, begin the pastoral song.

Thyrsis of Etna am I, and sweet is the voice of Thyrsis.

(64–65)

Thyrsis commends the sweetness of his own voice in the same detached, objective way he earlier commended the sweetness of music made by the waterfall. His song will be a sweet song, and its sweetness is something palpable, measurable, objective. The lament participates in the sweetness of pastoral, for it is, we are told, a *pastoral* song. We will be reminded of this participation at regular intervals throughout the song, moreover, for this line, "begin, dear Muses, begin the pastoral song," is the refrain which recurs (with some variation) between each of the song's eighteen stanzas. Periodically, then, this refrain interrupts the narrative flow; and as it does so it brings us back to the affirmations of pastoral and the impersonality of art. To announce at the outset the song's beginning is, moreover, to imply a middle and an end. Toward the middle of the song, the refrain modulates to "begin again the pastoral song"; and then, finally, it changes to "cease, Muses, come cease the pastoral song." The refrain calls our attention to the formal structure of the composition as a whole. It tells us where we are at various points along the way and speaks for a world in which it is possible to know where one is. Thyrsis announces at the outset that both he and his song are composed.

And only now does he identify himself, as "Thyrsis *of Etna*." In the initial dialogue, we saw, the speakers do not appear to be associated with any particular locale. One geographical point of reference is established there, however. The goatherd tells Thyrsis that he purchased his cup from the ferryman of Calydna. Now Calydna is most likely Calymnos, an Aegean island not far from Cos. And Cos (a favorite country resort of Alexandrians, a nursing ground for Ptolemaic princes, and home of a poetic school with which Theocritus may have been associated) is, quite explicitly, the setting for some of the other bucolic idylls, most notably the seventh.[6] The framing dialogue in this first *Idyll* may, then, also be set on Cos. But Theocritus does not, significantly, tie his herdsmen down to any specific locale, be it Cos or any other place. He leaves the setting open, indeterminate, evoking Coan associations just strongly enough to suggest that the little grove by the stream is the place from which one can (as the Alexandrian poet can from the vantage point of his Coan retreat) look back toward a mythical (or mythicized) past.

Thyrsis begins with nature's love for Daphnis. Before we see the neatherd himself, we see the natural world which gathers itself about him—or rather, gathers and yet does not gather:

> Where were you, Nymphs, where were you, when Daphnis was wasting? In the fair vales of Peneius or of Pindus? for surely you kept not the mighty stream of Anapus, nor the peak of Etna, nor the sacred rill of Acis.
>
> *Begin, dear Muses, begin the pastoral song.*
>
> (66–70)

The nymphs love Daphnis; yet they cannot save him. Or, Theocritus gracefully equivocates. Surely if the nymphs *had* been in Sicily, they would have saved him; they must therefore have been detained elsewhere. Theocritus permits us to indulge in the fantasy that their sympathy might somehow have saved Daphnis from his death, even as that wish is acknowledged to be a fantasy. For the Daphnis we see in the next verse is already dead, and nature can only mourn his loss:

> For him the jackals howled, for him the wolves; for him dead even the lion of the forest made lament.
>
> *Begin, dear Muses, begin the pastoral song.*
>
> (71–73)

The natural world in which Theocritus places Daphnis' death is one which balances sympathy against detachment. One impulse, that of love, bears us inward, toward Sicilian Anapus, Etna, Acis and the scene of convocation about the "wasting" Daphnis; a contrary impulse, dictated by reality, bids us rather turn outward, toward Thessalian Peneius and Pindus, as we acknowledge that the nymphs were not here, did not save Daphnis. A statement about the strength of nature's sympathy for man is combined with an awareness of the limitations of that sympathy.

The neatherd's death creates sympathetic reverberations throughout the whole Greek world (wolves were native to Theocritus' Sicily, jackals may have been, lions certainly were not). The diffusion of the lament into distant, exotic realms, on the one hand, magnifies the lament; it forces us to take Daphnis more seriously than the heroes of other Theocritean idylls. On the other hand, the passage is deliberately hyperbolic. Even African lions are mourning . . . and mourning whom? a Sicilian neatherd. This Daphnis must be very important indeed; perhaps more important than any herdsman can ever be—or any man, even if he is the darling of the nymphs. This suggestion of an overreaction is no more than an innuendo, an undercurrent in the great tide of love that sweeps through nature at Daphnis' death. But it is there. And it is just strong enough so that our dominant, sympathetic response to the passage—how much the Nymphs, the pastoral creatures, and we too care for Daphnis—is tempered by our awareness of how little is finally altered by that caring. It is this combination of the tenderest sympathy with a half-amused detachment that defines Theocritus' way of placing sorrow.

Nature's love for Daphnis is qualified in another way because it is nature's sympathy, not man's. The animals who mourn the neatherd who loved them mourn as animals: the jackals "howl"; they do not weep. As I have already said, there are no weeping rivers or trees in Theocritus' lament.[7] In fact, Daphnis himself will be distinguished from these creatures of nature by his refusal to release his own grief in this unrestrained fashion. Here man is self-contained, not nature.

The nymphs cannot save Daphnis; he is, we see, already dead. But as we read on, the convocation becomes a convocation about a still-living hero. Fate is accomplished but we are allowed to experience it as still somehow potentially reversible. The lions mourn a dead Daphnis. But the kine at Daphnis' feet in the next stanza,

Kine in plenty about his feet, and bulls, many a heifer and many a calf lamented . . .

(74–75)

suggest an upright rather than a prone figure. And in the following lines we realize, perhaps with some surprise, that Daphnis is still alive, still "wasting." Gods and men now gather about him, not, it now appears, to mourn Daphnis but to comfort him:

> First came Hermes from the hill, and said, 'Who torments you, Daphnis? of whom, friend, are you so enamoured?'
>
> *Begin, dear Muses, begin the pastoral song.*
>
> The neatherds came, the shepherds came, and goatherds, and all asked what ailed him. . . .
>
> (77–81)

We know, then, at the outset, that death is final and that the hero must in the end yield to his fate. But we are allowed to back-track in time, to see the still-living Daphnis taking that fate upon himself and, as we shall see, acting it out in his own way.

The pastoral poet places sorrow in nature's world. But that world, just because it is an impersonal world, can be cruelly de-humanizing as well as consoling. The animals have come to comfort Daphnis, as does Hermes. Priapus, who follows next, begins in a sympathetic tone, but by the end of his speech it is the mocking god of animalistic sexuality whose voice we hear:

> Priapus came, and said, 'Poor Daphnis, why are you wasting? while for you the maiden wanders by every fount and glade —
>
> *Begin, dear Muses, begin the pastoral song—*
>
> searching. Ah, truly, cursed in love and helpless are you. Neatherd you were called, but now you are like the goatherd, for he, when he sees the nannies at their sport, weeps that he was not born a goat.
>
> *Begin, dear Muses, begin the pastoral song.*
>
> And you, when you see how the maidens are laughing, weep because you are not dancing with them.' To these no answer made the neatherd, but bore his bitter love, bore it even to his appointed end.
>
> (81–93)

Priapus "places" Daphnis' love by reducing it to a *merely* natural-istic event. The precise nature of the predicament to which he alludes is somewhat obscure, but the point of the teasing is clear enough. To Priapus Daphnis is just another victim of his passions, to be set alongside the foolish goatherd who wishes he could couple with his own goats. Why not, suggests the sex god, take advantage of what is at hand? Here is a maiden "searching" for you; here are maidens dancing; yet you don't join them. Why then waste away?

Why indeed? The question is at the heart of the critical controversy surrounding the song of Thyrsis, and upon its answer depends our understanding of the meaning of Daphnis' death. According to one view, Daphnis refuses the love of the "searching" maiden and declines also to dance with her because, though he loves the maid, he is a "second Hippolytus" bound by a vow of chastity who would rather die than submit to his passions.[8] If we follow this reading, then we assume that Theocritus is not following the Daphnis myth we know (the one cited in the previous chapter)[9] but some quite different story, whether of his own invention or another's. Daphnis then dies at the hands of the vengeful love goddess, Aphrodite, for refusing to love, a martyr to the ideal of chastity. His death marks the culmination of his withdrawal from life.[10]

The events to which Priapus alludes can, however, be accommodated to our myth (the story the scholiasts know) and, so interpreted, yield in my opinion a richer and a more "Theocritean" reading of the poem. According to this view, Priapus alludes to both maidens of that myth in his taunts (the nymph and the princess), one of whom desires Daphnis and the other of whom he now desires. The passion for which Daphnis is wasting might, then, be either a recalcitrant affection for the princess who seduced him, while his betrothed nymph still "searches" in vain;[11] or Daphnis might be wasting with a renewed passion for his nymph, in which case it is the princess who "searches."[12] In either case, the point is that "love" has led Daphnis to break his vow and now the "love" he desires (for whichever maiden) is denied him and he pines away in grief. Daphnis' excesses and not his deficiencies in love, according to this view, are the cause of his death.

Certainly nothing in any other Theocritean idyll suggests that a herdsman might act in a way contrary to his impulses, that he might choose not to yield to his passions. Nothing suggests that there is even room in his imagination for a distinction between what one feels and what one chooses to do about one's feelings.[13] The opening dialogue of this idyll, as well as those lovers figured on the goatherd's cup, prepare us to see feelings here too presented as sensations which, be they sweet or bitter, simply impress themselves upon us: received, recorded, above all, given. We are not prepared for a drama of renunciation. None of these things do, of course, in themselves preclude such a drama. What does, I think, preclude it is the language (albeit teasing and allusive) of Priapus' speech. If Daphnis were a willing martyr to chastity he would certainly be frustrated, but it is hard to see why he would be described as one "helpless in love." If Daphnis had chosen his fate, had chosen renunciation, the one thing he would not be is helpless. He is helpless only if he cannot help but yield to his feelings—and consequently to his death. This, it seems to me, is indeed his situation. Daphnis' drama is a drama of acquiescence to the inevitable, not of withdrawal and renunciation. It is the same drama acted out by other Theocritean herdsmen in other bucolic idylls but acted out more passionately here: for never does the herdsman's world seem as sweet as it does in this idyll and in no other idyll does the acquiescence to a given passion entail an acquiescence to death itself.[14] We are forced to leave the pastoral world behind us at the moment it seems most dear to us. Daphnis' death touches us so because, seeing the strength of his attachment to this world, we see what it is for him to have to leave it. But he does have to. To turn this submission to fate into a voluntary withdrawal is to lose much of its pathos.

Daphnis can die for love but he cannot choose not to love. Priapus' ethic is different. He suggests another kind of yielding. Why not, he asks, since the maiden you love now spurns you, take the one at hand? Forget about what you cannot have, the procreative god urges Daphnis. Daphnis' heroism, an altogether human heroism, consists in his rejection of this impersonal, animalistic sexuality, not in his rejection of all sexuality.

Priapus places Daphnis' love within his sphere of animalistic sexuality; and Aphrodite, who comes next, places it within her own province of eroticism. She sees Daphnis as a victim in Love's eternal contest:

> Aye and Cypris came too, with a sweet smile, craftily smiling but with heavy wrath held back, and said, 'Surely, Daphnis, you vowed that you would give Love a fall, but have you not been thrown yourself by cruel Love?'
>
> (95–98)

In one sense both Priapus and Aphrodite are quite right about Daphnis: he *is* the victim of his passions; he cannot escape the consequences. Their words reinforce other voices in the poem which stress the tyranny of Eros, the inexorability of fate. It is a recurrent voice in the Theocritean bucolic idylls. But these cruel taunts are not all-important, for Daphnis himself rejects them. Though love's victim, he refuses to play the game:

> To these no answer made the neatherd, but bore his bitter love, bore it even to his appointed end.
>
> (92–93)

The end may indeed be fated, but Daphnis insists upon having it on his own terms. By his silence he affirms that his love is something more than animalistic passion and more than a game—that it is something well worth dying for. As he keeps his silence, bearing his bitter love (bearing it, perhaps, deep inside himself), he affirms that his love and his fate are his own. This attitude of self-containment may be one reason why Theocritus presents Daphnis' story so allusively (indeed cryptically) in his poem: by keeping the facts of that story also to himself, though of course it is all over now and nothing can be altered, Daphnis becomes the master of his own fate.

Daphnis triumphs over his fate by converting that fate into an act of free will. When he finally answers Aphrodite, his words unite defiance with acquiescence:

> And to her at length Daphnis made answer: 'Cypris, grievous to bear, wrathful Cypris, Cypris detested by mortals, do you think, then, that all my suns are set already? Even in Hades shall Daphnis be a bitter grief to Love.'
>
> (100–03)

The insistence that he still has many suns left sounds like a denial of death. But in the very next line Daphnis admits that henceforth it is only in the sunless realm that he will be "a bitter grief to Love." He can admit that he is indeed vanquished because, at the same time, he is showing us just how alive, how human, he is. He too, we see now, can play the mocking game; with a series of allusions to episodes in which it was she, not (as now) he, who was love's victim (105–113), Daphnis teases Aphrodite in turn. Then, having placed himself on par with the destructive love goddess, Daphnis puts aside the bantering tone and with a new serenity he says farewell to his world.

Daphnis sings his own funeral song. Thus, in the most emphatic way possible, he takes fate upon himself. He insists that he, finally, be the one to place his sorrows—placing them not, as Priapus and Aphrodite had done, from without but from within. In his rejection of their taunts and his insistence on "bearing his bitter love even to its appointed end," Daphnis frees himself from the tyranny of nature's round. Unlike the goats, or the goatherd who tends them, or Aphrodite's lovers locked in their endless struggle, Daphnis is not condemned to re-enact again and again the same drama.

But now, as he accepts his fated end and freely goes to his death, Daphnis re-establishes the bonds of sympathy and love between himself and nature. The moment of death for the pastoral hero is a moment of self-definition, of placing himself in his world:

> I am that Daphnis that herded here his cows, and watered here his bulls and calves.
>
> (120–21)

Again, we see that what the pastoralist values in his landscape is not so much its particular charms but the fact that it is his world, the one he lives in: it is "here."

Now Daphnis leaves this world and its sweetness behind him. His words linger over the names of cherished places, the creatures, the gods, the haunts he has loved:

> Farewell, you wolves and jackals and bears in your mountain caves. No more to your woods, to your groves and thickets no more, fares

the neatherd Daphnis. Farewell, Arethusa, and you rivers that down Thybris pour your fair waters.

(115–18)

If at the song's opening it was Thyrsis who asked after the absent nymphs, now it is Daphnis himself who commands the ceremony of convocation. He invites Pan to come from his native Arcadia in Greece to this Sicilian isle, not, now, in a vain effort to forestall his death, but to commemorate it, to receive from him the herdsman's pipe, instrument of his song:

> O Pan, Pan, whether you are on the high hills of Lycaeus, or range mighty Maenalus, come to the Sicilian isle and leave the mountain peak of Helice and that high tomb of Lycaon's son wherein even the Blessed Ones delight.
>
> *Cease, Muses, come cease the pastoral song.*
>
> Come, my lord, and take this pipe, fragrant of honey from its compacted wax, with binding about its handsome lip, for now to Hades am I haled by Love.

(123–30)

In yielding to death Daphnis is a commanding figure, for he can compel, by the sweetness of his song, the pastoral god to his side.

And he can, perhaps, compel nature too, if not to prevent his fate, then at least to share it with him:

> Now violets bear, you brambles, and, you thorns, bear violets, and let the fair narcissus bloom on the juniper. Let all be changed, and let the pine bear pears since Daphnis is dying. Let the stag worry the hounds, and from the mountains let the owls cry to nightingales.

(132–36)

Daphnis' plea testifies to each man's sense that the outrageousness of his own death ought to involve the whole world in chaos. If nature loves us, surely she ought to die with us or to turn her own order upside-down.[15] And Daphnis almost makes us believe that it might happen.

Almost, but not quite. Daphnis' demand enforces the pathos of his situation even as it proclaims his verbal mastery over his fate. Compare for a moment the description of Lear on the heath,

> *Contending with the fretful elements;*
> *[He] bids the wind blow the earth into the sea,*

> [He] bids the wind blow the earth into the sea,
> Or swell the curled waters 'bove the main,
> That things might change or cease.
>
> (3. 1. 4–7)

Lear's demand that nature turn upside-down for him has an authority Daphnis' lacks. For Lear is, imaginatively speaking, larger than the fretful elements. We believe that he could compel nature to match his own inner storms. Daphnis making the same demand is a touching rather than a terrifying figure. We know how little will be changed by his pleas. The dissonance between what the neatherd's death means to him and what it means to us is expressed in the playful nature of the inversions Daphnis invites. These are more charming than cataclysmic. Indeed they seem to share in the sweetness and whimsicality of the pastoral hero himself.

This brings us to another important quality of the Theocritean passage. Lear demands "that things might change or cease." The second demand is but an extension of the first. For changes in the fabric of the universal order Lear once knew can only be destructive changes. To alter that order is to destroy it. But when Daphnis asks that "all be changed," life does not cease. On the contrary, the reversals Daphnis invites promise renewed fertility. Order reasserts itself in new, fanciful ways. Now brambles and thorns will bring forth violets; the narcissus blooms on the juniper bush and even the pine will bear fruit. The reversal of the traditional progress of the hunt ("let the stag worry the hounds") suggests, not a continuation of the slaughter, but a transformation of destructiveness into play. (We recall the transformations of pain into pleasing patterns on the goatherd's cup.) In Daphnis' command to turn the world upside-down, then, we feel two things: the pathos of the plea, which reminds us the neatherd's words will not change anything; and the persistence of the life-energy which, despite fate, converts even death into an affirmation of freedom and vitality.[16]

As Daphnis goes to his death we feel once more the sense of an act which is at once fated and, at the same time, freely undertaken:

> So much he said, and ended; and Aphrodite would have raised him
> up again, but all the thread the Fates assigned was run, and Daphnis

went to the stream. The waters closed over him whom the Muses loved, nor did the Nymphs mislike him.

(138–41)

However much Aphrodite now may wish it were otherwise, fate will not be denied. But again Theocritus reverses the sequence of events: we are told that Aphrodite would have raised him up again (Daphnis appears to be already beneath the waters); *then* we see him walking to the stream. And again the sense is of the hero taking that destined end freely upon himself, thus making it his own.

As for the stream itself, there is some uncertainty as to which stream Theocritus has in mind here. We would expect it to be Acheron, the river which, in Greek mythology, separates the world of the living from that of the dead. But ordinarily one crosses over Acheron to the other side, whereas the image here appears to be of a submersion in the waters. Perhaps Theocritus is again being deliberately vague in order to have it both ways: the image suggests at once the finality of death, a passing beyond the borders of this world, and a reabsorption back into the stream of life. For this second meaning Theocritus may have recalled the version of the Daphnis myth in which Hermes causes a spring to well up in the spot where Daphnis dies.

But, equally significant, any such assurance is only hinted at here. There is no explicit consolation for death in Theocritus' poem. Though Daphnis boasts of his continued existence in Hades, that existence (as he describes it) is but a continuation of life here. In Thyrsis' song it is the sweetness of life in this world that counts. The song ends as it began, with sympathy—recalling the love of the Muses, the Nymphs, and even of Aphrodite herself, for Daphnis. Protest is laid to rest. Even the waters of death seem particularly gentle with the pastoral hero.

The return to the world of the frame is abrupt. Thyrsis does not ask us to grieve for Daphnis. His song has been a performance, a gift, and he asks for its reward:

And give me the goat and the bowl, so I may milk her and make libation to the Muses. Farewell, many times farewell, Muses. I will sing a sweeter song for you next time.

(143–45)

The song is placed once more among the other objects of the pastoral world and can indeed be exchanged for one (or several) of these. Its sweetness (recalled now again) is something measurable, objective. This song has been sweet but another one might be sweeter.

Thus Thyrsis distances us from the pathos of Daphnis' death. But the music of that song continues to reverberate quietly through this closing exchange. We hear an echo of Daphnis' repeated "farewell"'s in the "farewell"'s which Thyrsis now extends to the Muses. And the exchange of the song for the goat and the bowl recalls Daphnis' bequeathal of his pipe (the instrument of his own song) to Pan at his death. Here, as there, the exchange of precious objects enforces continuity. Thyrsis, like Daphnis, participates in the pastoral rhythm, the give and take of life itself.

It is the sense of on-going life that Theocritus leaves us with in the goatherd's final speech:

> May your fair mouth be filled with honey, Thyrsis, and with the honeycomb; and may you eat the sweet figs of Aegilus, for your singing outdoes the cicada. See, here is the cup; mark, friend, how sweet it smells; you will think it has been dipped at the well of the Hours. Come here, Cissaetha; and you milk her. And she-goats, don't be so frisky or the he-goat will rouse himself.
>
> (146–52)

We end with this image of resurgent vitality in a world whose energies (whether combative or sexual) are but with difficulty contained. Nature, if she is not held in check, will "rouse herself." It is this outer world, sweet, buoyant, objectifying, which encloses and supports the inner world of Daphnis' suffering and death. Thyrsis' song is placed alongside the sweets of nature (the song of the cicada) and those of art (the carved cup).

Daphnis has turned even death into an affirmation of pastoral sweetness and vitality. But if the same life-energies flow through Daphnis' world and the outer world of the frame, there are also differences between the two. The he-goat who cannot contain himself recalls Priapus' taunt that Daphnis is like the goatherd who would like to couple with his own she-goats. Daphnis, we have seen, belongs to nature's world; he is the victim of his passions.

But, because he is self-contained, because he can die and not just live for love, because he can keep silent as well as speak his sorrows, he is something more than one of nature's creatures. Only man can make a free act out of what is fated.

There are two ways in which all later pastoral elegies differ from this one. First: all later poems treat a dead hero rather than a dying one; the lament is sung by a friend, not by the victim himself. Secondly: all later poems in the tradition look back, directly or indirectly, to this one. Combined—and indeed their effects are not wholly separable—these two changes confer a more retrospective, more meditative character on later pastoral elegies. But we must also be impressed by the degree of continuity between this Theocritean idyll and what follows it, particularly by the degree to which motifs implicit here become explicit in later poems.

The shift from a dying hero to a dead one transfers us from the realm of dramatic narrative to that of elegy proper. In the later poems there is less room for protest, more for grief. The love-intrigue and the mysteries surrounding Daphnis' death are sloughed off. Once one is dead, the causes count for little. And with the intrigue goes the bantering which surrounds Daphnis' death and gives an edge to the pathos in Theocritus. In later laments the hero does not have to wrest his dignity for himself; a dead hero is automatically an honored one. Generally in the later pastoral elegies ("Lycidas" is the great exception here) the sentiment flows more easily, often too much so. We miss the tension between speech and silence, between protest and acquiescence which characterizes Daphnis' encounter with his fate.

But the post-Theocritean pastoral elegist concerns himself with a new drama: that of the mourner's resolution of his grief. His arduous, and sometimes wayward, progress toward that resolution takes the place of Daphnis' struggle with his fate. Though the elegist now mourns the death of another, as he echoes phrases first uttered by Daphnis, he reveals the continuing preoccupation of the tradition with the concerns of those still living. What matters most in the pastoral elegy is how we deal with death, not the fate of the dead themselves. That matters too; but it matters less in an absolute, metaphysical sense than in a human one, i.e., as it affects us here. When the elegist places his sufferings in an earthly landscape, he suggests that it is through his relation to earthly things that he will work toward his resolution.

Daphnis comes to accept his fated end, we saw, by taking it freely upon himself. In later pastoral elegies we see a new kind of integration between the elegist's own feelings and the destined end that awaits him. For later pastoral elegists come to the convention knowing, in another way, where they are headed. They know because they are following other poets who have gone before them. These elegists bring to an ever-increasing body of conventionalized expression the particular burden of their own private feelings. And, like Daphnis, they must make that destined end, that end which others have accomplished before them, their own, as they must make Daphnis' landscape their landscape.

To participate in a literary convention is a kind of sharing. To the various ways of placing sorrow we find in the first *Idyll* we must add now the placing of the individual poet's feelings in a convention. (It is, of course, possible that this element plays a part in the Theocritean poem as well, one we cannot assess.) I suspect that the reduced proportions of the frame and the omission, generally, of the second, interior frame altogether can be attributed to the fact that its placing function is largely taken over by the element of conventionality itself. When we hear the echoes of earlier pastoral elegies we know what sort of world we are in and what sort of response is solicited. These literary echoes become themselves part of the sweet music of pastoral—and no small part.

All the later poems in the convention are, in some sense, commentaries on this one and hence different from it. Theocritus' first *Idyll* is not *about* death in the sense that later laments are. Theocritus offers us neither explanation nor consolation for Daphnis' death. Nor does he generalize from this death to other deaths. Here there are no morals, no messages. Theocritus simply presents us with "the woes of Daphnis," much as his herdsmen point to the beauties of their little grove. "Meanings" can be extracted from these presentations; that, of course, is what I have been trying to do in these pages. But it is, at best, a clumsy process, for Theocritus' poem offers us an utterly smooth surface. It makes no reference to anything outside itself. Later pastoral elegies do, however, refer to things outside themselves: they refer to other poems. And, as later elegists look back on the sweet, elusive figure of Daphnis, they look for meanings in his death; as they recall the earlier poem, they cannot choose but to comment on it, to interpret it. Gradually, meanings submerged or implied in Theocritus come to the surface. The tension we perceive in the first *Idyll* between the course of nature's life and the course of Daphnis' human life becomes an explicit contrast, and one which involves, moreover, not only one man and one landscape, but all men and all our landscapes: *that* realm renews itself; *ours* does not. As the particular "truths" of Theocritus' poem are formulated, they tend to be generalized.

Later elegists will be—indeed will have to be—more explicit, too, about whom they mourn and why. Theocritus does not tell us why we should mourn for Daphnis. We see the animals howl; we see men and gods converge about the dying herdsman; most importantly, we see Daphnis himself. He himself commands our sympathy as he goes to his death. But with the shift from a dying to a dead hero, we have to be told why we should mourn—and then, why we should cease to mourn. When eulogy is admitted, consolation follows close behind it.

Yet, to a remarkable extent, the later pastoral elegist shares in the vision of death that informs this first Theocritean *Idyll*. He too places sorrow in a special world, in some sweet, sunlit landscape which helps him to clarify his grief and so, finally, to put it aside. And, whatever its particular features (which, as we shall see, vary considerably), this landscape remains, above all else, *his* landscape—the place where he stands, a world he knows.

·◆✦⊱▏◈▕⊰✦◆·⊱▏◈▕⊰✦◆·⊱▏◈▕⊰◆·

Two Greek laments of the second century B.C. have, from antiquity on, been classified with the Theocritean bucolic poems and were regularly included in Renaissance collections of pastoral.[17] One, the "Lament for Adonis," which may or may not be by Bion, is not really a pastoral elegy at all. The other, the "Lament for Bion," attributed in the Renaissance to Moschus but evidently by an Italian pupil of Bion, imitates the first *Idyll* at several points but is, I should say, on the periphery of our convention. The "Lament for Adonis" exerts some influence upon the Renaissance form and the "Lament for Bion" a greater one; but it is significant that Vergil, who would have been familiar with both these laments, makes very little use of them and turns instead directly to Theocritus.[18] Doubtless he saw that what is missing from them is the most important thing: the pastoral setting itself. My treatment of these two intermediate poems, then, will be but a summary one.

The "Lament for Adonis" offers us a good example of what a dirge is like when it is for a representative of the natural rather than the human world. Rather than attempt to appropriate this poem for our tradition, I want to suggest here why it is not a pastoral elegy. And this is, essentially, because here there is not—and cannot be—a distinction between the dying hero and the natural world that mourns for him: for Adonis is no less than (and no more than) the incarnation of nature's own annual death and rebirth. Thus there can be no tension between our distinctive, human fate and that eternal round. Blood drips from the god's thigh; nature's flowers flush red with grief. From Adonis' wound springs up a rose; from Aphrodite's tears, a windflower. Our sorrows and nature's sorrows are the same; as she is reborn so are we. Here there is no gathering of the suffering individual into himself, no proud check upon the flow of tears. The general sense of slackness is reflected in the extravagance of the imagery—a striking contrast to that isolation of particular effects we saw in Theocritus:

> Cruel, cruel the wound Adonis bears upon his thigh, but deeper the wound Cytherea bears within her heart. About the lad howl the hounds he loved: the Mountain Nymphs make wail for him, and Aphrodite, her tresses loosed, has gone roaming in the thickets, sorrowful, unkempt, and bare of foot. The brambles tear her as she goes, and draw her sacred blood. . . .
> 'Alack for the Cyprian,' cry all the hills, and the oak-trees, 'Alas for Adonis.' The rivers wail for Aphrodite's sorrows; the springs weep for Adonis on the hills. The flowers turn brown for grief. . . .
> (16–22, 31–35)[19]

The monotonous quality of these ejaculations is an accurate reflection of the fact that death can have no finality here. Neither the god nor his grieving mistress can break free from the consoling but ultimately tyrannizing round of nature. Adonis dies only to be reborn, to die again, to be mourned again. The poetic structure echoes these cyclical repetitions. We end with a forecast of the ritual repeating itself:

> Cease thy laments today, Cytherea; stay thy dirges. Again must thou lament, again must thou weep another year.
>
> (97–98)

Whatever its own merits or defects, the "Lament for Adonis" provides us with a convenient measure of the insufficiency of the purely "archetypal" approach to the pastoral elegy proper: Lycidas (to revise Northrop Frye) is not Adonis.

The atmosphere of the "Lament for Bion" is, in some respects, very much like that of the "Lament for Adonis," though the two laments are at opposite ends of the spectrum. Adonis is wholly identified with the natural world. Bion has very little relation to that world. And in both poems we see a very generalized image of nature herself. Thus in the opening lines of the "Lament for Bion" we find:

> Wail sorrowfully, ye glades and waters of the Dorians; weep rivers, for our beloved Bion. Now make lament, all green things; now moan, all groves, and, flowers, expire with unkempt clusters. Now, roses and anemones, don mourning crimson; speak out thy letters, hyacinth, and add more cries of sorrow to thy petals. The fair singer is dead.
>
> (1–7)[20]

In both these poems what is missing is the sense of a human presence in, and interacting with, a landscape. In the "Lament for Adonis," the human world seems wholly absorbed by the non-human one. Here the two worlds tend to pull apart from one another. We have, on the one hand, those generalized images of nature grieving and, on the other hand, men who inhabit a quite different world. Here for the first time we mourn not a herdsman but a contemporary, one who is only a herdsman by proxy—that is, as the author of poems *about* herdsmen. The poet wants us to think of his subject as the heir to the Theocritean Daphnis. But he also knows, and wants us to know, that this "Daphnis" is a second

Homer and that "every famous city and every town" mourns his death. When Vergil places Caesar's death in the pastoral world he shows us why this world, above all others, should mourn the custodian of a whole civilization. But the author of the "Lament for Bion" seems less sure why he should come to pastoral with his sorrows. And indeed he does not. He gives us generalized descriptions of nature weeping, but he does not create a particular setting in which either the elegist or the one whose death he mourns is placed.

It is appropriate that the "Lament for Bion" should be the first pastoral elegy to formulate the contrast between human life and life in nature explicitly. Here for the first time we see the elegist set the annual cycle of vegetative life against the finality of his own life in this world:

> Alas, when in the garden wither the mallows, the green celery, and the luxuriant curled anise, they live again thereafter and spring up another year, but we men, we that are tall and strong, we that are wise, when once we die, unhearing sleep in the hollow earth, a long sleep without end or wakening.
>
> (99–104)

This contrast is, we said, already implied in the first *Idyll*. But there, we feel, Daphnis is a part of nature even as he is distinguished from it. He differs from the animated world around him, not by his possession of qualities utterly foreign to that world, but by the way he deals with energies he shares with nature's creatures. Daphnis can keep his feelings to himself if he cannot alter them. The difference between the neatherd and his world is not articulated; it is something we sense as we read the poem. But the author of the "Lament for Bion" alters the force of the original contrast as he brings it to the surface. For now we differ from nature precisely by that speculative faculty which permits us to stand back from her world and comment in a generalized way on the differences between the two realms. We are distinguished from nature by our wisdom.

The contrast between nature's course and the course of human life becomes a commonplace in Renaissance pastoral elegies. The elegist who brings his grief to the pastoral world sees similarities between that world and his own, but he also sees differences. The differences may be cause for sorrow or for rejoicing. Like Theocritus and this later Greek poet, each elegist perceives the contrast in his own terms. It may be his affections, or his intellect, or his self-consciousness, or his spirituality that sets him apart. In one form or another, the contrast is an integral part of the pastoral elegist's way of looking at death. But it is only a part of what he sees. If he is to draw upon the consolations of this same regenerative nature, he must also see his place *in* nature's order. Theocritus balances the two complementary insights against one another. In the "Lament for Bion" it is mainly the separateness we see.

The poem ends inconclusively, with a turn away from pastoral. The elegist imagines himself a second Orpheus who might descend to Hades and retrieve his friend thence as Orpheus sought once to retrieve Eurydice. But is he a second Orpheus? Would his song avail? The poet leaves us in doubt as he pictures himself standing before Plutus. There is no return either for the elegist or his friend to the pastoral hills. For the pastoral world is not, finally, very real here, is not, as it was in the first *Idyll* and will be again in Vergil's fifth *Eclogue*, a place to come home to.

2

VERGIL

"Otium" and Exile

Theocritean pastoral is characterized by its openness, its freedom from constraints. Vergilian pastoral is characterized—and enhanced—by the warring world which threatens its borders. Its pleasures are most invitingly spread out before us by one who can no longer enjoy them. And, like most exiles, Vergil's Meliboeus in the first *Eclogue* longs for the pleasures he must forfeit less for their own sake than for that of the precious continuity they embody. That is what he has really lost. Thus the envied Tityrus is no youthful lover but an old man ("fortunate senex"), one who has lived in the same spot for a long time. Vergil appeals to our love of familiar places and rituals: the *known* river; bees that hum *as they have always done*; sheep that need eat *no unaccustomed* food; pigeons whose cooing *will never cease* (1. 46–58). The Vergilian pastoralist asks, not, how sweet? but, how long? The threat of destruction casts its shadow, not only over Vergil's lament for Daphnis, but over his whole eclogue series. For now death is not only an event *in* the pastoral world; it is also something that happens, or may at any time happen, *to* that world. Daphnis' death in the fifth *Eclogue* brings with it the death of a whole way of life.

That way of life which Vergil celebrates in the *Eclogues* is best summed up by the key term "otium." For Vergil "otium" means something more than leisure as opposed to work or duty ("negotium").[1] "Otium" is peace as opposed to warfare, fertility as opposed to destruction. The contemporary historical world, the world of political uncertainty and civil war which followed the assassination of Julius Caesar in 44 B.C., presses in on us here and will not be denied. The eviction of Italian landowners from their homes to make way for demobilized troops (whether or not Vergil's own farm was, as legend has it, saved from such confiscation by Octavius himself) is the central experience behind all these pastoral poems. The exiled farmer is the immediate subject of two of the eclogues; but the opposition between exile and "otium," warfare and peace, wandering and stability, governs the series as a whole.

In Vergilian pastoral we long, not for the freedom of the grove, but for a land made dear through cultivation and love. In moving from Theocritus to Vergil we move from a genuinely pastoral—that is, a nomadic, shepherding—way of life to an agricultural one. (We see the Vergilian singers both as herdsmen and as farmers, but it is in the latter role that they seem most themselves.) An easy, unfettered existence is associated now, not with the herdsman's liberation from the constraints of urban life, but with the random destructiveness of the soldier. We do not ask what lies beyond the Theocritean herdsman's grove, or where he goes when the singing match is over. That such questions do not arise is a measure of his freedom. But the Vergilian singer goes home.[2] The cyclical pattern of the farmer's life, from dawn to sunset, activity to repose, shapes the poetic rhythms of the *Eclogues*. In Theocritus we experience life in discrete units, from moment to moment. In Vergil we feel the passage of time. The song that begins at noon often concludes with the shadows of evening.[3] If the frisky kid with her sweet flesh is a nice emblem of the Theocritean pastoral world, a world in which vitality counters the threat of enervation, attenuation of feeling, then the well-fed ewe, heavy with milk or with young (a recurrent figure in the *Eclogues*),[4] expresses the values of a world in which the stability and fertility of the homeland are menaced by the more active threat of destruction.

"Otium," as we see it in the *Eclogues*, is a dependent state. The Theocritean creatures have a life of their own; the frisky she-goats, we remember, will rouse the buck unless the goatherd calms them. But the kids in the first *Eclogue* (14–15) are helpless without their master. The Vergilian pastoral ideal seems so precarious in part because we are not allowed to forget how much depends upon the human presence. Just beyond Tityrus' farm the uncultivated marshland with its bare rocks and reeds encroaches. In the *Georgics* Vergil will present the farmer in an active guise, insuring peace and continuity with his own careful labor. But in the passive world of the *Eclogues* the ideal must be sustained in more imaginative terms, through the vision of the herdsman-farmer who is also, of course, a poet. And, as the land depends on him, so he depends on the sustaining presence of a protector from without, a "deus." Should this protector fail him, the farmer (like Meliboeus in the first *Eclogue* or Moeris in the ninth) becomes a mere herdsman-wanderer again—that is to say, for Vergil: an exile. Thus in the fifth *Eclogue*, when this protector dies, the whole pastoral world dies with him; and we are all (until the god's rebirth) exiles.

It is perhaps because Vergil makes us so aware of the vulnerability of his pastoral world that some have supposed it to be an insubstantial one as well.[5] But it is our own Romantic heritage which associates a precarious existence with an unreal one. That association is not Vergilian; indeed it is not characteristic of pastoral poetry generally.[6] Vergil transplants his own Mantuan landscape (intermittently) to the remote province of Arcadia to suggest that "otium" is a state that we have, physically and spiritually, lost touch with. If his pastoral landscape is saturated with nostalgia for what we may have left behind us, it is not therefore unreal. On the contrary, the Vergilian ideal is to be reunited with what is most real: the basic human affections, the attachment to the land. Tityrus' peace is nothing without the beech tree beneath which he reclines.

His existence is, nonetheless, a privileged if not an imaginary one. In the *Eclogues* we hear of soldiers seizing the farmers' lands, we know that Meliboeus will soon be on his exile's way, and we are told that at Daphnis' death the crops will fail. But if in the *Aeneid* we see the destruction of a beloved homeland, follow the exiles across the seas, learn what it is to go without food, in the *Eclogues* we see all these things from the perspective of pastoral. The dangers are perfectly real—but we do not have to pursue them too far.

They serve rather to enhance than to qualify the pleasures of pastoral. In spite of the troubles all around him, Tityrus remains secure beneath his beech tree. Imaginatively speaking, his existence counts for more than what threatens it. The emphasis in the first *Eclogue* falls not on Meliboeus' forthcoming journey (though we know what lies ahead for him); the emphasis falls rather on this last evening Meliboeus will enjoy as his friend's guest, with green leaves for his bed and ripe apples for his dinner. And in the fifth *Eclogue* the emphasis falls, not on death itself, but on the way this most potent threat is, if not dismissed, contained. In the fifth *Eclogue* we celebrate a peace that can outlast the ravages of war.

That Vergil's *Eclogues* are arranged in a deliberate and meaningful sequence has long been recognized.[7] I should say that the basic concentric design of this series supports the Vergilian image of pastoral as an enclosed and a besieged world. The poet opens the suite with a qualified invitation to his pastoral world (1.79–83) and closes it with an equally qualified withdrawal from it (10.70–77). The pastoral world is set against other experiences, other worlds. As we move inward from the two extremities the eclogues become increasingly affirmative, increasingly secure in their celebration of the pastoral peace. At the center of this sphere is the fifth *Eclogue*. And here, pre-eminently it is not simple pleasure which counts, but the triumph of "otium" over the forces of death and destruction. Death is admitted into the very heart of Vergil's pastoral sanctuary (indeed it is dealt with most explicitly in this eclogue); but it is admitted so that it may be vanquished. Exile and death are here contained within, even as they are set against, the pastoral peace.

In its smallest effects, as in its largest design, the fifth *Eclogue* is organized by the principle of harmony through opposition or alternation.[8] In Thyrsis' song we saw life *in* death; in the paired songs of Mopsus and Menalcas life and death, "otium" and exile, are set against one another. Now lamentation is answered by rejoicing and Daphnis' death is answered by his deification. The dialectical pattern is established in the opening frame, which prepares us for the larger juxtapositions of the two songs which follow it. Indeed we learn a good deal by looking closely at some of the minor alterations Vergil makes as he revises the parallel exchange in the first *Idyll* of Theocritus. For once again the frame does more than offset the song (or songs) within. It tells us how death will be placed in that inner world. Indeed it is the small changes that are perhaps the most revealing in this respect. The slight alterations of setting and atmosphere prepare us, indeed force us, to consider the whole subject in a new light. Here, then, is the Vergilian version of the opening dialogue between the two herdsmen:

Menalcas   Mopsus

Me. *Cur non, Mopse, boni quoniam conuenimus ambo,*
      tu calamos inflare leuis, ego dicere uersus,
      hic corylis mixtas inter consedimus ulmos?

Mo. *Tu maior; tibi me est aequum parere, Menalca,*
      siue sub incertas Zephyris motantibus umbras
      siue antro potius succedimus. aspice, ut antrum
      siluestris raris sparsit labrusca racemis.

Me. *Montibus in nostris solus tibi certat Amyntas.*

Mo. *Quid, si idem certet Phoebum superare canendo?*

Me. *Incipe, Mopse, prior, si quos aut Phyllidis ignis*
      aut Alconis habes laudes aut iurgia Codri.
      incipe: pascentis seruabit Tityrus haedos.

Mo. *Immo haec, in uiridi nuper quae cortice fagi*
      carmina descripsi et modulans alterna notaui,
      experiar: tu deinde iubeto ut certet Amyntas.

Me. *Lenta salix quantum pallenti cedit oliuae,*
      puniceis humilis quantum saliunca rosetis,
      iudicio nostro tantum tibi cedit Amyntas.
      sed tu desine plura, puer: successimus antro.[9]

[*Me*. Mopsus, since we've met and both are skilled—you at blowing on the thin reed pipe, I at singing verses—why don't we sit here where hazel trees are mingled among the elms.

Mo. You are older; it is for me to yield to you, Menalcas, whether it be here, beneath the shifting shade which stirs in the wind, or at the cave. Look how the wild woodland vine has sprinkled it with clusters here and there.

Me. In our mountains only Amyntas rivals you.

Mo. But isn't he the one who would strive to outsing Apollo?

Me. You start, Mopsus, if you have any songs of fiery love for Phyllis, or praise of Alcon or quarrels against Codrus. Begin; Tityrus will look after our grazing kids.

Mo. I would rather try out this song which I wrote down on the green bark of a beech tree and set to music, marking the alternations of voice and pipe. Then you can ask Amyntas to compete with me!

Me. As the pliant willow yields to the pale olive, as the humble nard to the crimson rose, so much, I think, Amyntas yields to you. But no more talk, boy; we have reached the cave.]

If we have the first *Idyll* of Theocritus in mind—and that is how Vergil wishes us to read his poem—all of this seems at first quite familiar. Again rustics gracefully converse in a landscape as charming as they are. Again allusion is made to the separate talents of each speaker and to playful rivalries with other members of the pastoral company. Again several different sites are suggested for the ensuing songs. And again the leisure essential to the herdsmen's recreation is established: the flock will be cared for. Like its Theocritean prototype, the Vergilian scene establishes a world of sweet things in which the sorrows of death can be placed. It prepares us to consider the lament as an aesthetic performance, not an outpouring of personal feeling.

Yet each of these "Theocritean" motifs has been subtly altered, and along the same lines: a sequence of individual objects and sensations is converted into a series of *encounters*, or contrasts, between one thing and another. First of all, the scene itself is staged as an encounter. The Theocritean speakers are simply there (or "here"); but the Vergilian speakers meet each other ("conuenimus"). Moreover, the differences between the two speakers now entail a definite relationship. Instead of a shepherd and a goatherd we have here a younger speaker and an elder one to whom the former defers. Similarly, where Theocritus enumerates various pleasures, of which the goatherd's piping and the shepherd's singing are two, Vergil's line, "tu calamos inflare leues, ego dicere uersus," relishes the contrast between two different talents. It is not a contrast of opposites: piping and singing, like the herdsmen themselves, belong to the same world. But Vergil invites us to savor the different kinds of pleasure which his speakers bring to their encounter.

Another revision which points in the same direction is Vergil's conversion of the Theocritean subordination of the goatherd's piping to that of the god Pan into the more active rivalry between Mopsus and Amyntas. This passing reference to a competition between members of the same class hints at Vergil's strategy in the poem as a whole: his conversion of the solo performance of the Theocritean singer, Thyrsis, into the two-part exchange between Mopsus and Menalcas. Vergil borrows the amoebean contest (in which one singer's donnée must be "answered", or capped, by his successor's) from Theocritus, but Theocritus does not employ that form in his lament for Daphnis. It is Vergil who brings the dialectical structure of the amoebean exchange to the pastoral elegy and thereby creates a new form in which sorrow is "answered" by rejoicing, death by rebirth.[10]

The landscape too in this initial scene has become a study in relationships. Hazels are intermingled among the elms, not placed somewhere nearby, as the elm is near the oaks in the first *Idyll* (21–23). Scattered clusters of ivy here half-hide and half-expose the mouth of the cave. Where Theocritus surrounds his shady seat with bright sunlight, Vergil delights in the interplay between light and darkness. Shadows come and go in the uncertain breeze beneath the elms. Again, it is not a matter of neat antitheses but of more subtle contrasts, as between such near kin (or look-alikes) as the willow and the olive, the wild nard and the rose.

The way in which the site is selected has changed too—and along the same lines. In the first *Idyll* Thyrsis invites the goatherd to sit "here, by this sloping knoll." But then, a few lines later, the goatherd says, "Come here, then, and let us sit beneath the elm." Vergil converts this indeterminate situation with its amplitude of possibility into one which requires a choice: here or there. The singers' selection of the cave rather than the open grove as the site for the match is not arbitrary: it expresses Vergil's own preference for a sequestered pastoral.

All these contrasts, between the various objects in the landscape and between the singers themselves, prepare us to see Daphnis' death, too, as a study in contrasts or juxtapositions. As the Vergilian "otium" is defined by its relation to other less congenial states without, so too death and destruction are measured here by what we have lost. At the same time we contemplate these alternations from the perspective of "otium," not exile. As piping and singing, hazel trees and elms, the willow and the olive, sequestered cave and open grove, the elder singer and the younger all belong to the same world, the pastoral one, so too do the two songs which follow. In the fifth *Eclogue* we see death through the eyes of the bereaved farmer, not those of the exile. And, as we hear in the frame the sweet harmony of one note played off against another, contrasting one, we are prepared for that larger harmony of the poem itself in which the sorrowful song of Mopsus is "answered" by the joyous song of Menalcas.

Mopsus begins his song where the Theocritean Thyrsis ended his: Daphnis is already dead; the nymphs (and perhaps Aphrodite) are embracing him:

> *Exstinctum Nymphae crudeli funere Daphnin*
> *flebant (uos coryli testes et flumina Nymphis),*
> *cum complexa sui corpus miserabile nati*
> *atque deos atque astra uocat crudelia mater.*
> (20–23)

[For Daphnis cut off by a cruel death the Nymphs wept. You hazels and rivers bear witness to the Nymphs; while his mother holds to herself the body of her unfortunate son and calls on the gods and the cruel stars.]

The rest of Mopsus' song explores the meaning of Daphnis' death.

The Daphnis whose death Mopsus laments is no longer, like his Theocritean original, a simple herdsman. For this Daphnis' death (we soon see) threatens the life of the whole pastoral world. Theocritean nature mourns Daphnis, but it can live without him. Vergilian nature, a cultivated world, cannot. Who is this Daphnis? Tradition identifies him with the custodian of the whole Roman world: Julius Caesar.[11] But what has Caesar, the warrior, the very symbol of the power of the state, to do with the farmer's fruitful fields? For Vergil, a good deal. If Theocritean pastoral is self-sustaining, Vergilian pastoral needs a "deus" from Rome, needs a Caesar. In the ninth *Eclogue* that need is made explicit: there a herdsman points to the star of a deified Caesar that gladdens all the corn with grain and ripens the grapes (46–50). Good arguments can be made both for and against identifying the apotheosized Daphnis of the fifth *Eclogue* with the Julius Caesar of the ninth. But perhaps the most important thing is simply the fact that we are not invited in this fifth *Eclogue*, as we are in the ninth, to identify the "deus" with any particular Roman ruler. For by leaving it open, by calling his "deus" simply Daphnis here, Vergil emphasizes our permanent need—not for the particular man, Caesar—but for the ideal custodian, whom Caesar may, in a glancing reference, represent. In the fifth *Eclogue*, the symbol, the ideal, is more important than the man.

It is as a custodian, or "custos," that we mourn Daphnis here. He was the leader of his people; unlike his Theocritean counterpart, a civilizer (as the reference to the Bacchic rites informs us):

> *Daphnis et Armenias curru subiungere tigris*
> *instituit, Daphnis thiasos inducere Bacchi*
> *et foliis lentas intexere mollibus hastas.*
>
> (29–31)

[Daphnis taught us to fasten the Armenian tigers to the car, and Daphnis taught us to lead the revellers of Bacchus in the dance and to entwine the light wands with soft leaves.]

In the Theocritean pastoral world we value vitality for its own sake; here we value what we can do with it. This Daphnis taught the herdsmen how to harness nature's energies for their own human ends.

Who is he? Not so much the particular man as the principle of inner order, or *decorum*, which sustains the pastoral vision. He is that which gives life to the whole. Significantly, Mopsus describes this Daphnis through similitude:

> *uitis ut arboribus decori est, ut uitibus uuae,*
> *ut gregibus tauri, segetes ut pinguibus aruis,*
> *tu decus omne tuis.*
>
> (32–34)

[As the vine glorifies the tree, and the grapes the vine, as the bull the flock, and the corn the fertile fields: so you are all the glory of your people.]

As the vine, though the weaker member, brings to her "marriage" with the elm the precious gift of fertility,[12] so in the subsequent pairs the subject confers on its object not mere "decoration" but vital sustenance.

Without the "custos," pastoral cannot sustain itself. Here death is presented as a reversion to a *merely* natural state—that is, for Vergil, a state of wildness. Now instead of the barley planted by the farmer, barren wild oats come up:

> *grandia saepe quibus mandauimus hordea sulcis,*
> *infelix lolium et steriles nascuntur auenae;*
> *pro molli uiola, pro purpureo narcisso*
> *carduus et spinis surgit paliurus acutis.*
>
> (36–39)[13]

[Often in the furrows where we planted fat grains of barley, infertile darnel and barren oats come up instead. Where once the soft violet, the purple-eyed narcissus, now rise thistles and thorns with their sharp spikes.]

With the death of the one who nurtured us, all nurture in this world ceases: the herdsmen cease to lead their beasts to water; even animals refuse their food:

> *non ulli pastos illis egere diebus*
> *frigida, Daphni, boues ad flumina; nulla neque amnem*
> *libauit quadripes, nec graminis attigit herbam.*
>
> (24–26)

[No one drove the oxen from their pastures to the cool streams in those days; not one beast drank water or touched a blade of grass.]

And the protective gods of the countryside, Pales and Apollo, withdraw as well. When the Theocritean Daphnis died, we felt nature's sympathy. Here we feel her helplessness. Grief is presented in more passive terms now: the woods give back the echo of the dirge (28); the hazel trees and brooks bear witness to the suffering of the Nymphs (21).

In Mopsus' song, as in the opening frame, Vergil describes a scene or event through contrast. We learn the meaning of Daphnis' death not (as in Theocritus) by seeing it enacted before us, but by setting our present state against our former one. Daphnis' death transports us from the world of "otium" to that of exile; but the exile's world, here as elsewhere in Vergil, takes its coloring from the one left behind. Barren oats recall the barley once planted in those same furrows; thistles and thorns bring back memories of violets and narcissi. The evocation of a time of happiness in a time of sorrow heightens the poignancy of Mopsus' lament—and softens it. His words recreate for us the banished pleasures: the cool streams, the furrows of fat grain, the gay flowers. If Daphnis has died, if the farm and the farmers can no longer sustain themselves . . . what then? Mopsus does not ask. He looks backwards, not forwards. He expresses neither bitterness nor anxiety for the future—only regret for what has been lost. And thus he still speaks to us from the perspective of pastoral. Though the farm animals refuse their food and the fields bring forth barren oats, we have not left that world or its vision of life behind us. It is here the herdsman places his sorrow; here Mopsus, in the last lines of his song, bids the shepherds build a tomb for Daphnis; here his deeds will be recorded:

> spargite humum foliis, inducite fontibus umbras,
> pastores (mandat fieri sibi talia Daphnis),
> et tumulum facite, et tumulo superaddite carmen:
> 'Daphnis ego in siluis, hinc usque ad sidera notus,
> formosi pecoris custos, formosior ipse.'
>
> (40–44)

[Strew leaves on the ground, draw shade over the fountains, shepherds: Daphnis demands these rites. Build a tomb and on it inscribe this song: "Daphnis am I in the woodlands, known from here to the stars, guardian of the fair flock—but fairer I."]

The epitaph that the Vergilian Daphnis commands to be engraved upon his tomb invites comparison with his Theocritean predecessor's farewell to his world: "I am that Daphnis who herded here his cows and watered here his bulls and calves" (120–121). In both passages the herdsman affirms his place in this world, affirms it even as he acknowledges death's power to take him from that world. The thrust of the Theocritean epitaph, however, is Daphnis' act of self-assertion. He makes even his death a proof of his own vitality. Vergil, however, affirms, not *that* the hero is, but *what* he is. His epitaph serves to define the ideal. For Theocritus' straightforward declarative Vergil substitutes a mediated comparison. Again, we learn the value of things in this pastoral world by seeing them in relation to other things: the open grove and the cave; sterile oats and plump grains of barley; the flock and the herdsman who tends it. Vergil's comparison points, too, to the changed nature of the ideal: the flock is fair but the man who tends it is fairer still, and he is fair because he tends them. The Vergilian pastoral ideal is expressed in the action of caring for things. In "custos" Vergil pronounces his Daphnis the custodian, not just of the flock but of the whole pastoral world. He is not just nature's darling; he is her support.

This Daphnis' fame, moreover, reaches "from here to the stars." Notoriety is not a virtue in Theocritus. There the hero derives his stature from the authenticity with which he speaks in the particular moment. But the Vergilian hero lives through the train of effects which he sets in motion in his world. He is conscious of his own importance in and to that world. In death the Theocritean Daphnis is loved (141); the Vergilian Daphnis, revered. The phrase "usque ad sidera notus" is an epithet associated with the epic hero in Vergil's poetry.[14] In applying it to Daphnis he emphasizes his pastoral hero's ties to the world beyond the woodlands, the dependence of the pastoral peace on a "deus" who presides over a whole civilization. The phrase also points toward Vergil's extension in the second song of the pastoralist's vision in yet another direction, and another one excluded from the Theocritean grove: toward the stars.

Because Vergil has already staged the exchange between Mopsus and Menalcas as an encounter, we expect that Menalcas will "answer" his friend's song with a complementary song of his own. It is Vergil's specific contribution to the amoebean form which he takes over from Theocritus that he superimposes a moral antagonism upon the aesthetic one: now rebirth and regeneration "answer" death and decay; now the good Daphnis "returns" to care for his people. But Mopsus' song and Menalcas' song, like the willow and the olive, the wild nard and the rose, have much in common; each takes its meaning from its relation to the other. We know exile by remembering "otium," and we know "otium" now because we see it through the contrast with exile. Menalcas' song marks not simply a turn but a return, the joyful reactivation of a world temporarily stilled by death.

And, as Menalcas commends his friend's song, we are invited, once again, to see the song as a performance. The lament brings us pleasure, tangible pleasure; it can be set alongside the other sweet things in the herdsmen's world. But Vergil's comparisons point not, like Theocritus', to a sweet *sensation* (the singing of the cicada), but, characteristically, to a sweet *change*. What's sweet here is the moment of passage, when deprivation is turned to gratification:

> Tale tuum carmen nobis, diuine poeta,
> quale sopor fessis in gramine, quale per aestum
> dulcis aquae saliente sitim restinguere riuo.
>
> (45–47)

[Godlike poet, your song affects me like sleeping on the grass when one is tired, or quenching one's thirst in the heat of the day with sweet water from a running stream.]

The pleasures of Vergilian pastoral depend on our knowledge of such deprivations: what it feels like to be tired or thirsty, exiled or bereft of a Daphnis. Menalcas' similitudes anticipate the pleasures his own song will bring even more aptly than they describe those of the one just sung, for his song involves precisely such an answering of fatigue by repose, of thirst by refreshment.

In the second song the pastoral world and its pleasures are reborn. Menalcas announces that he will, with his answering song, raise Daphnis to the stars: "Daphninque tuum tollemus ad astra; / Daphnin ad astra feremus" (51–52). Briefly we stand, with Daphnis, at the threshold of Olympus, marvelling:

> Candidus insuetum miratur limen Olympi
> sub pedibusque uidet nubes et sidera Daphnis.
>
> (56–57)

[All in white, Daphnis stands wondering at the unaccustomed threshold of Olympus; beneath his feet he sees the stars and clouds.]

"Candidus" is the first word of Menalcas' song, as "exstinctum" was of Mopsus'; the pure white radiance of Olympus answers decay in the earthly sphere. If Vergilian pastoral is a world we know, the world of custom, this Olympian world is "insuetum," unaccustomed. And it remains that; we do not linger at this threshold, nor go beyond it. Instead we follow the gaze of the newly deified Daphnis downward, back toward earth. Vergil's image of Daphnis looking at the stars and clouds beneath his feet becomes a point of departure for numerous Renaissance Ciceronian visions of the contemptible world below, but it is no such thing here. On the contrary, as Daphnis extends his gaze downward, the earthly world, in joyful response, "rises up" to meet his gaze:

> *ergo alacris siluas et cetera rura uoluptas*
> *Panaque pastoresque tenet Dryadasque puellas.*
> *nec lupus insidias pecori, nec retia ceruis*
> *ulla dolum meditantur: amat bonus otia Daphnis.*
> *ipsi laetitia uoces ad sidera iactant*
> *intonsi montes; ipsae iam carmina rupes,*
> *ipsa sonant arbusta: 'deus, deus ille, Menalca.'*
>
> (58–64)

[At this the woods and all the countryside, Pan, the shepherds and the Dryad girls, are all possessed by lively joy. The wolf contrives no ambush for the flock nor the nets guile to the deer: good Daphnis loves peace. Even the shaggy mountains hurl their voices to the stars in joy; the very rocks take up the song, and plantations echo it: "He is a god, a god, Menalcas."]

The animation and delight which suffuse this scene are informed by a deeper spirit of tranquility. It is peace that Daphnis brings back to earth: "amat bonus otia Daphnis." And, as so often in the *Eclogues*, peace is defined in terms of a release from aggression. Theocritus asked the hart and the hound to change places (135), but Vergil banishes the hunt altogether from his more pacific pastoral.

Menalcas asks Daphnis to remember his people, to protect them and bring them good fortune:

sis bonus o felixque tuis!
        (65)

It is a fervent plea and it reminds us again that we need such pro-
tection here. We need "good fortune" if we are to enjoy this peace,
for nothing but good fortune separates the happy Tityrus from his
friend Meliboeus, the exile.

As Mopsus remembers "otium" in the world of exile, so here
the memories of exile and deprivation linger on and faintly color
the mood of the pastoral festivities:

> *et multo in primis hilarans conuiuia Baccho*
> *(ante focum, si frigus erit; si messis, in umbra)*
> *uina nouum fundam calathis Ariusia nectar.*
> *cantabunt mihi Damoetas et Lyctius Aegon;*
> *saltantes Satyros imitabitur Alphesiboeus.*
>   (69–73)

[And Bacchus, most of all, will make the feasting merry: before the
hearth when it's cold; at harvest, in the shade. I'll pour new nectar
from the cups—wine from Ariusium; and Alphesiboeus will play
the leaping Satyr.]

The gaiety and the intimacy of this little scene depend on our half-
conscious awareness of other less congenial states without. Vergil's
fireside and noonday shade are not simply, as in their Theocritean
originals, pleasures in their own right.[15] They insulate the cele-
brants from extremes of cold and heat. It is in this sheltered setting
that Alphesiboeus can leap about like a Satyr. (So in the first
Eclogue Tityrus stretches at his ease like one who has all the time in
the world, while just beyond the hedge we see the uncultivated
marshland through which the exiled farmer must make his way.)
And Vergil's continual awareness of what lies beyond the immedi-
ate sphere of activity recalls us to the occasion as it shapes the
setting of this celebration. For his herdsmen the festival itself is an
act of homage—and a prayer for continuity.

The precariousness of this pastoral peace is most forcefully
invoked in the closing lines of Menalcas' song:

> *haec tibi semper erunt, et cum sollemnia uota*
> *reddemus Nymphis, et cum lustrabimus agros.*

dum iuga montis aper, fluuios dum piscis amabit,
dumque thymo pascentur apes, dum rore cicadae,
semper honos nomenque tuum laudesque manebunt.

(74–78)

[These rites are yours for ever, both when we pay the Nymphs our
solemn vows and when we bless the fields. As long as boars prefer
the mountain heights and fish love water, while bees graze on
honey and the cricket eats dew—your honors and name and praises
shall endure.]

Once more Vergil is ringing his changes on a familiar Theocritean
motif—here the series of parallel statements which link an event in
the human world to others in the natural world. Such a yoking
together makes the point that the same rules (rules of conduct,
rules of feeling) govern men as govern nature. But the common
element in Theocritus is never, as here, the idea of duration itself.[16]
For in the Theocritean world time, as such, does not exist. But in
Vergil the crucial question, the one Menalcas asks here, is: how
long? His images do not assume duration; rather they would urge
it into being. They express the pastoral poet's *longing for* "otium."

With his return to the world of the frame, Vergil comes back
to the simpler harmonies of Theocritean pastoral. Now Daphnis'
death has been placed, and the song becomes again a thing of
sweetness, to be placed alongside other songs and other objects.
And, as at the close of the Theocritean idyll, our interest is de-
flected at the close from the subject which has most concerned us
to some new topic, there the frisky goats, here an old amour.
Daphnis' death leaves us with no residue of sorrow:

Mo. *Quae tibi, quae tali reddam pro carmine dona?*
nam neque me tantum uenientis sibilus Austri
nec percussa iuuant fluctu tam litora, nec quae
saxosas inter decurrunt flumina uallis.
Me. *Hac te nos fragili donabimus ante cicuta;*
haec nos 'formosum Corydon ardebat Alexin',
haec eadem docuit 'cuium pecus? an Meliboei?'
Mo. *At tu sume pedum, quod, me cum saepe rogaret,*
non tulit Antigenes (et erat tum dignus amari),
formosum paribus nodis atque aere, Menalca.

(81–90)

[*Mo.* What gift can I give you for such a song—which pleases me more than the whistle of the South Wind approaching, or beaches beaten by a wave, or rivers rushing through rocky valleys?

Me. First I'll give you this fragile reed, the one that taught me my "Corydon Loves Fair Alexis" and "Whose Sheep are these? Meliboeus'?"

Mo. Then you must have this handsome crook, which, for all his asking, Antigenes never had of me—and he was lovable enough in those days. Take it, with its even knots and brass, Menalcas.]

But it is also a Vergilian close. The mood is less buoyant, more subdued, than in the corresponding Theocritean exchange. Again we have the sense of savoring pleasures in their passage and knowing that they are passing from us as we savor them. Mopsus compares his friend's song to the sound made by the wind *as it approaches us* and its pleasures to those we derive from the impact of one thing against another, a wave against the smooth sand or waters against the rocky stones of the valley. He looks back on another love, once all-absorbing, now replaced by the new bond between Mopsus and Menalcas. And finally, the poet commemorates the harmonious resolution of all these contrasts in the staff which he gives his friend, the staff with its symmetrically spaced knots.

This concluding passage affectionately recalls the earlier, Theocritean one at every point; at the same time, it gives those reminiscences a new Vergilian setting and a new meaning. So Vergil commemorates the Theocritean poem in this eclogue as a whole. Once again, as in that first Theocritean *Idyll*, Daphnis' death is placed among the concrete pleasures of the herdsman's world. But as those pleasures themselves are more ephemeral now, so is the world in which they exist. Vergil's Daphnis does not die *in* the pastoral world; his death signals the death *of* that world. Now pastoral, a world of mutual dependency, has not the energies within itself to reassert its order after Daphnis' death. The farmer's peace, the world of "otium," must be secured from without. Nature is helpless, we are all helpless, without Daphnis. And thus it takes a poetic reversal to set things right again. Death must be "answered" by rebirth, sorrow "answered" by rejoicing. This dialectical pattern, introduced by Vergil in his fifth *Eclogue*, becomes the pattern for all subsequent pastoral elegies. And the awareness of contrasting states imposed by this dialectical pattern—the sense, above all, that the pastoral world of peace is enhanced by its proximity to other, hostile worlds—conditions all later visions of pastoral and all later pastoral elegies.

The concluding tenth *Eclogue* also deserves at least a few words here. If the Renaissance pastoral elegist takes the structural pattern of his lament from Vergil's fifth, it is from the tenth that he often takes his image of the elegist himself. The tenth *Eclogue* is not a pastoral elegy, since in the end the love-sick Gallus does not go to his death but simply yields to his passions; however, it is about the degree to which we can place our sorrows in the pastoral world. As in the fifth *Eclogue*, Vergil again takes the first *Idyll* of Theocritus for his point of departure. But in this last eclogue he is less affirmative than in the centrally placed fifth, and we look on pastoral with a new self-consciousness here.

Vergil frames the song in the tenth *Eclogue* with a prologue and epilogue spoken in his own voice rather than with a dialogue between two herdsmen. Now more than ever, as he begins his last song, Vergil presents pastoral as a precious world which must be urged into being:

> *Extremum hunc, Arethusa, mihi concede laborem:*
> *pauca meo Gallo, sed quae legat ipsa Lycoris,*
> *carmina sunt dicenda; neget quis carmina Gallo?*
> *sic tibi, cum fluctus subterlabere Sicanos,*
> *Doris amara suam non intermisceat undam,*
> *incipe: sollicitos Galli dicamus amores,*
> *dum tenera attondent simae uirgulta capellae.*
> *non canimus surdis, respondent omnia siluae.*
>
> (1–8)

[Grant me, Arethusa, this final labor: a little poem, but one that Lycoris herself might read too. There are songs to be sung; and who could deny a song for Gallus? Begin then, and when you glide beneath Sicilian waves may the bitter sea water not mingle his current with yours. Let me sing of Gallus' restless loves, while the snub-nosed goats crop the tender young shoots. We do not sing to the deaf: the forest echoes every word.]

Here again we have that sense—so pervasive in Vergil, so foreign to Theocritus—of a world and a poetic mode conscious of their own limits. This is the last song, and only a little one, the poet says; perhaps other concerns are already pulling us away to the larger world without. But Vergil invites us to linger just a few moments more. And never has pastoral beckoned so invitingly. The listening forest awaits our song. The goats at their feeding offer a soothing background to the human tale of troubled love. A sense of expectancy hangs over the scene—perhaps a sense of urgency as well. Sicilian Arethusa's flight from the river god Alpheus seems even now occurring; her safe emergence on the Sicilian isle, though anticipated, is not yet assured. Again Vergil's pastoral world is presented as the longed-for safe harbor toward which we come through troubled waters, the peaceful island sanctuary in a world of aggression.[17] And the poet, it seems, must make a special plea for this world, now, as his own sojourn in it draws to a close.

In the song which follows, that plea is extended on behalf of Gallus, another "exile," a stranger to pastoral and its comforts. Vergil invites the distracted Gallus, love poet and soldier, into this world. He surrounds him first with Theocritean presences, as if to suggest: so it was once for Daphnis; he found a place here, so too may you. Even Adonis (Vergil reminds his friend) pastured cows by the riverside; so you, Gallus, should not be ashamed in this pastoral company. And, as in the first *Idyll*, various comforters gather about the love-sick hero. But these do not come to taunt Gallus nor to remind him of his passion's fated end. They are, rather, persuasive reminders of the attractions of the Vergilian pastoral world, from the gentle herdsman, Menalcas, wet from gathering acorns in the woods, to the divine Silvanus, "his head crowned with rustic honors, shaking flowering fennel and tall lilies," a splendid incarnation of fertility and grace.

Gallus tries, for a time, to picture himself among the simple Arcadian herdsmen. He imagines himself the hero of a pastoral elegy, his sufferings transformed into a thing of beauty by the herdsman's pipe: "Oh how softly, then, my bones will lie, if you should some day tell the story of my love on your reed-pipes." Or, if not commemorated in death, Gallus imagines that he too might have enjoyed his love in this world:

> atque utinam ex uobis unus uestrique fuissem
> aut custos gregis aut maturae uinitor uuae!
> certe siue mihi Phyllis siue esset Amyntas
> seu quicumque furor (quid tum, si fuscus Amyntas?
> et nigrae uiolae sunt et uaccinia nigra),
> mecum inter salices lenta sub uite iaceret;
> serta mihi Phyllis legeret, cantaret Amyntas.
> hic gelidi fontes, hic mollia prata, Lycori,
> hic nemus; hic ipso tecum consumerer aeuo.
>
> (35–43)

[Ah, if only I had been one of you, a guardian of the flock, or a dresser of the ripe grapes. Surely Phyllis then, or Amyntas—or whosoever were my passion (and what if Amyntas be dark? the violet is dark and so is the blueberry)—would have lain with me among the willows beneath the bending vines. Phyllis would have picked me garlands; Amyntas would have sung for me. Here are cool springs; here are soft meadows, Lycoris; here woods; here with you only time itself would slowly waste me away.]

But "utinam" measures the distance we have travelled from Theocritus. The pastoral is only a might-have-been world for Gallus. Though his words to Lycoris echo the traditional pastoral invitation ("here are oaks and galingale; here sweetly hum the bees about the hives"),[18] it is not really the concrete pleasures of this world that Gallus wants his Lycoris to share with him. He invites her to endure with him the wastage of time; and that wastage, once having been acknowledged (as it never is in Theocritus), will not be denied. Lycoris, Gallus concedes, is not here at all but in the distant Alps where sharp stones may pierce her tender feet. And Gallus himself is engaged in a military campaign. The imagined refuge "inter salices lenta sub uita" yields to a crueler image of containment, "tela inter media" (45), amidst the weapons of war. Though he tries to wish himself back into pastoral, he can see himself only as a huntsman here; Gallus brings with him into this world the destructiveness and intractibility of the warrior. Finally, Gallus dismisses pastoral woods and songs altogether:

> iam neque Hamadryades rursus neque carmina nobis
> ipsa placent; ipsae rursus concedite siluae.

48   (62–63)

[Now, once more, neither wood nymphs nor song itself delights me. Once more, woodlands, away with you!]

And Gallus imagines himself living in a world where, instead of the pleasing alternations of pastoral, harsh extremes of climate might, if not heal his suffering, at least match it. Perhaps the tragic fate which, when Vergil wrote this song for his friend, still lay ahead for the real Gallus (his mad self-deification upon being appointed Prefect of Egypt, his subsequent disgrace and suicide) is not irrelevant to a reading of the tenth *Eclogue*. For it is Gallus' self-preoccupation, his inability to see himself in relation to the things around him, which makes him so out of place in the pastoral world.

But it is Vergil's farewell to pastoral, not Gallus', with which the poem, and the eclogue series as a whole, concludes. The calm self-assurance with which the poet speaks contrasts with Gallus' alternations between rhapsody and despair. Vergil speaks modestly of himself in the third person, modestly too of his pastoral art:

> Haec sat erit, diuae, uestrum cecinisse poetam,
> dum sedet et gracili fiscellam texit hibisco,
> Pierides : uos haec facietis maxima Gallo,
> Gallo, cuius amor tantum mihi crescit in horas
> quantum uere nouo uiridis se subicit alnus.
> surgamus : solet esse grauis cantantibus umbra,
> iuniperi grauis umbra, nocent et frugibus umbrae.
> ite domum saturae, uenit Hesperus, ite capellae.

(70–77)

[This is enough, Pierian goddesses, that your poet sung as he sat and wove a small cheese crate with slender marsh-mallow twigs. You will make it dear to Gallus—Gallus, for whom my love grows greater each hour, as the alder-tree shoots upward in the fresh spring season. Now let us rise. Shadows lie heavy on those who make music, and the shadows are heavy on these junipers. The shadows are bad for our fruits as well. Go home then, my well-fed ones; Hesperus is coming; home with you, goats.]

Yet Vergil's claim for these slender twigs is actually quite extensive. The delicate pastoral basket will yield as much richness as we can discover in it. Gallus, Vergil suggests, might, if he wished, find a great deal ("maxima") to please him here. If Gallus saw love only in its destructive aspect, Vergil proposes the alternate image of his own affection for Gallus, which grows like pastoral's green shoots in spring.

Finally, we must leave this world. Gallus' words have touched (if only lightly) on a despair for which new poetic forms will be needed. There are experiences which only an exile can know, and to chart them the poet must go beyond the pastoral enclosure. Vergil's "surgamus" speaks of eagerness for the larger journey which lies ahead—perhaps also of a fear of lingering too long in the simpler world. But the fruitfulness of that world is richly evoked at the moment of leave-taking. The "saturae" (or "well-fed goats") are summoned here for the last time. The shadows, which receive such repeated emphasis in these last lines, hasten our departure, remind us that we cannot over-extend our stay. We have left the timeless Theocritean world of perpetual noon, and time must eventually carry us out of pastoral altogether. But the shadows speak of homecoming as well as of departure. They promise a peaceful evening to the burning heat of Gallus' day. And thus we submit ourselves to rhythms of the pastoral world—noon and evening, activity and repose, the progress out and the return home—even as we leave that world behind us.

To some the slender consolations which the Vergilian pastoral muse extends to us seem too frail or (perhaps) too facile, particularly when the pastoral reed is set against the harsher and grander music of the epic poem. But if the *Eclogues* are more sanguine than the later verses, the ideal of peace, of home-rootedness, they celebrate and the dangers to it they perceive are Vergil's continuing preoccupations. In the *Georgics* we see that the farmer must toil continuously to sustain that peace which the pastoralist simply enjoys.[19] And in the *Aeneid* that elusive peace, and the awareness of what it means to forfeit it, haunts us still. The first words Aeneas utters (1.94–101) tell of an exile's anguished longing for the land of his fathers. The herdsmen of the pastoral world—Meliboeus, Mopsus and Menalcas—speak from beneath the shelter of the beech tree; Aeneas speaks from the center of the storm. The epic hero's wish that he might have died in battle beneath the ramparts of his beloved Troy carries us into a realm of noble sentiment and heroic self-sacrifice beyond the reach of the pastoralist. Aeneas both defends his homeland and willingly assumes the burden of his exile. The herdsman-farmer does neither. His farm is his only through the goodness of a "deus," a Daphnis. If he loses it, should the god withdraw, he can only look back, like the sorrowing creatures in the fifth *Eclogue*, in wonder and regret. Mopsus' nostalgia for the fertile fields of the "patria," for the world before Daphnis' death, is a purer, a less complex emotion than the epic hero can afford. But Mopsus knows what he has lost, whereas in the *Aeneid* that elusive peace seems somehow to get left farther behind the more arduously it is pursued. In the end we wonder whether "otium," or the art of enjoying it, has not been forgotten. Aeneas' son must learn from others the "good fortune," the happiness, which Tityrus simply takes as his own. In the epic world it is all so much more difficult, more complicated. What the herdsman-farmer knows is how to enjoy what he has been given—and how to mourn what he has lost. As Meliboeus says, "it is enough."

3

Placement and Displacement
Four Neo-Latin Laments

PETRARCH, BOCCACCIO
CASTIGLIONE, SANNAZARO

The pastoral elegies of Theocritus and Vergil are impersonal poems. This is not to say they are poems without feeling. Both, in their different ways, make us care about Daphnis' death and show us why we should care. But we are not invited to look on the herdsmen's songs as expressions of private suffering. The songs are performances, sweet things, rewarded in the currency of the pastoral world with other sweet things. And the songs themselves affirm the sweetness of that world. Fate decrees that the Theocritean Daphnis must die, but Daphnis turns his yielding into an affirmation of life and vitality. When the Vergilian Daphnis dies the whole pastoral world dies with him, but the continuing alternations between "otium" and exile, death and regeneration, assure us that peace will come again.

The pastoral elegies to which we shall next turn are, however, private poems about personal losses—though sometimes general ones too. And the songs these poet-herdsmen sing are not always self-contained; now the elegist's sorrows often spill over into the surrounding world of the frame. There is a loss of a certain kind of poise in some of these Renaissance laments. For the Christian poet an earthly peace as ephemeral as Vergil's "otium" may not be a peace that he can place his faith in; and a world that permits his Daphnis to die may no longer seem either sweet or good. The Christian elegist is more intensely, and more painfully, aware of the limits to which art and nature can console him for loss. And this awareness, though it may cost him the detachment of the classical laments, brings with it a new self-consciousness. The Renaissance pastoral elegy is more intimate, more unsettling and, occasionally, far more affecting than its classical predecessor.

How, then, does the Renaissance Christian poet appropriate this pagan form, as, in the early years of the humanist revival of classical learning, he appropriates other forms from the pagan repertory? What special problems does the pastoral elegy present for him? Superficially, no problem at all. The Christian poet discovers in Vergil's fifth *Eclogue* (and until the mid-sixteenth-century it is almost always Vergil he discovers, not Theocritus) a lament easily converted into Christian terms. Some even suppose Vergil has already done their work for them, among them, the sixteenth-century Spanish humanist Juan Luis Vives. As the fourth, or "messianic," *Eclogue* had (from the fourth century on) been widely read as a prophecy of Christ's birth, so the subsequent eclogue quite naturally becomes a prophecy of His death and joyful resurrection. Vergil, according to Vives' gloss, found the matter for his fifth (as that of his fourth) *Eclogue* in the Sibylline Books, but not understanding its true application, supposed the death to be Caesar's and added certain things of his own to round out the poem.[1] For Vives the herdsmen-singers are no more aware of their true subject than was Vergil himself. But when Mopsus sings of nature's decay at Daphnis' death, *we* understand it as a prophecy of the similar reversal of her accustomed order at the Crucifixion, that reversal described by the gospel writers when they speak of a darkness passing over all the land as Christ is dying on the Cross (see Matt. 27.45). The shepherds who will not lead their flocks to water are the grieving Apostles who will not care for *their* sheep in their grief at the Savior's death. Then, with Menalcas' song, we rejoice in His resurrection. The "otium" Daphnis loves is that Christian peace, that Charity, now brought back to earth and implanted in His Church.

The dialectical pattern of death and rebirth, of death in this world "answered" by a rebirth in the other, is, we have seen, already there in Vergil's fifth *Eclogue*. We might suppose that all a Christian poet (anxious to appropriate this classical form, as others, for his own contemporary purposes) must do is to change a few names. Vives' commentary, first printed in 1539 and often reprinted in Renaissance editions of the *Eclogues*,[2] would help point the way—if any pointing were needed.

Yet, as the following pages of this study will bear out, the Christianizing of the pagan pastoral elegy is not so simple as all that. And to understand why this should be so, we might consider the one part of the fifth *Eclogue* about which Vives has nothing to say: the frame. That he leaves unglossed. It is a simple enough matter to change the name of Daphnis' Olympus to that of the Christian heaven. But it is more difficult to change the whole perspective from which those pagan herdsmen contemplate that other world—and this one too. That is the real challenge. Vives, the allegorist, does not take it up. And we can see why. Almost from the beginning commentators have asked whom Vergil figures under the cover of the herdsman, Daphnis. But what are we to "make" of those sweet exchanges between the herdsmen, of their discussion of who should begin the song and whether here or there? The frame, as later commentators have also discovered, resists the allegorist. Its meanings are not easily extrapolated, thus not easily converted into new meanings: it is simply *here*. Vives ignores the frame. To him it is obviously extraneous, an outer wrapping surrounding the precious matter hidden within. But the frame, we know, is not extraneous. It places the herdsmen's sorrow, suggests what meaning death will have in the inner world of the songs.

The Renaissance poet, unlike the commentator, will not, on the whole, ignore those framing dialogues. They hold out to him, as the Theocritean herdsman once held out to his friend, the attractions of this world, of pastoral itself: "here are oaks and galingale; here sweetly hum the bees about the hives." And should he enter this world, will it then be so simple a matter to move from *here* to *there*? Perhaps not. It is this pastoral landscape that the

Christian elegist must confront, enter and, finally, make his own if he is to truly convert the pagan form into something of his own. The Renaissance elegist does, in the end, lament his Daphnis from an earthly landscape that is at once pastoral and Christian. But that transformation does not come easily or all at once. Particularly in the pastoral elegies of the early humanist poets to which we shall now turn, the conflict between pagan and Christian values and settings is more apparent than their integration.

The Italian humanists of the fourteenth century who revived the pastoral genre saw themselves as the rediscoverers of a literary landscape which had lain unknown and uncultivated since Vergil. They were not, strictly speaking, correct.[3] The *Eclogues*, if not the *Idylls*, were widely read and even imitated by medieval churchmen and scholars.[4] But Petrarch and Boccaccio were right to reserve the honor of recovering the pastoral tradition for themselves, because it is in their eclogues that the pastoral landscape is rediscovered. Their encounter with this landscape is charged with ambivalence. Yet it is this ambivalence which makes their pastoral elegies, flawed performances aesthetically, interesting.

Petrarch's eclogue series, the *Bucolicum Carmen* (1346–49), has as its point of departure the poet's affection for roots, both physical and literary ones. In a letter to his brother Gherardo, Petrarch says that the countryside of his beloved retreat at Vaucluse provided the inspiration for the poems.[5] And on the literary side, Boccaccio enthusiastically announced that now at last his friend had brought to life the long-neglected pastoral genre.[6] Later critics have been less enthusiastic, finding little Vergil here and less nature.[7] I think they are wrong. Beneath the didacticism and the often indecipherable allegory, there is a deep affection here both for the landscape and for the literary tradition that celebrates it. But neither is cherished wholly. Nature remains, as elsewhere in Petrarch's writings, a point of departure; we begin with the countryside but we end with the self.[8] Petrarch uses the eclogue form to explore tensions in his own life, tensions Vergil had explored before him. Once more the central theme is the conflict between "otium" and exile. The difference is that in Petrarch's world it is generally the exile who has the last word. And it is, finally, upon the exile, the wanderer, that the poet's mantle falls—not on Tityrus reclining beneath his beech tree.[9]

Petrarch's second eclogue, a lament for his great patron, Robert of Naples, is a good poem with which to begin our study of the Renaissance pastoral elegy. For in this lament, unsatisfactory as it is—a poem which fails to give full expression to the depths of its own grief—we feel all the more intensely the conflict which is to become so characteristic of the Renaissance pastoral elegy: the conflict between placement and displacement. The poet's wish to place his sorrow *here*, in the landscape of Vergil and Theocritus, now contends against his wish to follow his friend to another greener world elsewhere. As that landscape becomes more compelling, this one seems less so. And the poet may be left, as Petrarch is here, lamenting his loss on a barren and lonely plain. Characteristically, Petrarch's pastoral elegy moves from placement to displacement, from the poet's impulse to set his sorrows in a sympathetic landscape to his acknowledgment of isolation, both from that natural world and the "custos" he has lost.

Petrarch begins by setting the scene for a classical lament. As Vergil mourned Caesar under the name of Daphnis, so he will mourn, under the name of Argus, his own watchful sovereign and patron. (Petrarch reads the fifth *Eclogue* as most Renaissance poets will: Vives' Christian interpretation supplements the traditional one but does not displace it.)[10] Robert is commemorated as the patron of poets and poetry, the guardian of the fertile fields, one whose death threatens the survival of both. In Robert's lifetime Petrarch had indeed already turned him (in his own imagination) into a symbolic "custos" of newly revived pagan rites; he insisted, for instance, that Robert "examine" him on the occasion of his famous coronation with the laurel wreath by the Roman senate. Now, as the poem opens, we see the world of peace over which Robert once presided. This landscape corresponds to the Vergilian frame, though it "contains" the disaster itself as well as the songs which rehearse it. We see from the start in the Renaissance pastoral elegy a blurring of the classical distinction between the world *in* which the herdsmen sing (a world which does not, itself, experience Daphnis' death) and the world *about* which they sing (the world in which Daphnis dies). But, in the beginning Robert has not yet died. All is yet tranquil: well-fed sheep ("saturata") lie at their ease; some herdsmen sleep, others (Petrarch himself perhaps among them) weave leafy garlands. The sun has begun its downward course, but it is still high in the sky. It is easy enough to allegorize all this (and inevitably the reader will allegorize it), but the landscape, saturated with Vergilian reminiscences, is still *here* for us—if somewhat stiffly so:

> *Ideus.* *Aureus occasum iam sol spectabat, equosque*
> *Pronum iter urgebat facili transmittere cursu;*
> *Nec nemorum tantam per secula multa quietem*
> *Viderat ulla dies: passim saturata iacebant*
> *Armenta et lenis pastores somnus habebat;*
> *Pars teretes baculos, pars nectere serta canendo*
> *Frondea, pars agiles calamos. . . .*
>
> $(1-7)$[11]

[Already the golden sun was facing the west, and was driving his steeds to accomplish his downward journey with easy course; nor in many generations had any day witnessed such deep quiet in the groves: here and there the sated flocks were lying, and a gentle sleep possessed the shepherds; some were binding smooth sticks, some were weaving leafy garlands while singing, some were fashioning pliant reeds.]

When a great storm suddenly disrupts this tranquil scene, when black clouds obscure the sun and a towering cypress is thrown to the ground, an allegorical reading becomes inevitable. Doubtless, as Petrarch's later commentators suggest, the particulars of the storm correspond to the circumstances surrounding Robert's death: the sun, eclipsed before its time, is of course Robert himself; the cypress torn from its roots by the storm is the murdered heir, Andrew.[12] We can readily understand why Petrarch chose to figure these sinister events under the cover of allegory. But let us not forget the storm itself. Surely Petrarch expected his readers to see it both ways, to see the storm at once as a figurative description of an event (the King's death) and (on the literal level) as a response to that event. The storm that disrupts the shepherds' peace not only tells us *that* the "custos" has died; as in Vergil's fifth, the disruption tells us how this world responded to their guardian's death, what it felt like in this world when he died.[13] And this is important because we observe that these Petrarchan herdsmen respond to the death of the "custos" in a way quite unlike their Vergilian predecessors. The Petrarchan herdsmen do not give over their accustomed pastoral duties; they disperse:

> . . . *Ingentis strepitu tremefacta ruine*
> *Pastorum mox turba fugit, quecumque sub illa*
> *Per longum secura diem consederat umbra;*
> *Pars repetit montes, tuguri pars limina fidi,*
> *Pars specubus terreque caput submittit hianti.*
>
> (19–23)

[Terrified by the crash of its mighty downfall, soon the crowd of shepherds fled, all that had sat carefree under that shade through the long day. Some made for the mountains, some for the threshold of their safe hut, some hid their heads in caves and the gaping earth.]

When the great tree falls Petrarch's herdsmen all go their separate ways. Now we begin to see death in its peculiarly modern aspect— less as the harbinger of destruction or decay than of isolation.

That sense of isolation comes increasingly to the fore as the lament progresses, and it is expressed in the very act of convocation itself. First the shepherds disperse; then, in the wake of the storm, two gather to rehearse their sorrows. But these two are, significantly, still separated even as they converse. Silvius (who represents Petrarch himself) and Pythias (his Neapolitan friend, Barili) are each sequestered in a separate cave and cannot see one another, "being separated by the small obstruction of a projecting rock and by a leafy branch" (39–40). Again, these obstructions can (and should) be read allegorically: they have their counterpart in the geographical distance which in fact separates the two friends; we can imagine, if we like, an epistolary communion. But that intervening rock and branch are also tokens of a more profound separation which prevents these speakers (as perhaps, for Petrarch, any two speakers) from fully opening their hearts to one another.

All this sets the scene, constitutes the frame. Now Silvius asks his friend to sing of Argus' death and promises he will follow with a song of his own, if he is not overcome by grief. Pythias' song corresponds to Mopsus'; Petrarch makes the association explicit: "Daphnis," says Silvius, "was once sung by shepherds, and now great Argus will be sung by you." And Argus, as Pythias commemorates him, is not unworthy of the comparison. His care for learning, for art, for the welfare of his people—all go together. In such phrases as these we hear distinctly the voice of the classicizing humanist poet:

> Argus, honor of the world! Argus, sorrow of the deserted wood! . . .
> Whither is departed our benefactor, whither the glory of our age?
> . . . Who, I wonder, will with his voice touch wild beasts and oaks
> and stones? Or who will pass away in sweet song the long night?
> Who will affright the wild boars? Who will lay snares for the deer?
> . . . Ah, who will care for the wretched sheep, dipping them in the
> river? . . . Of whom will the sheepstealer in the night be afraid? . . .
> (69–81)

And Argus' accomplishments are even more far-reaching than Daphnis', for in the death of this "good shepherd" we mourn the custodian of Christian virtue as well as of the herdsmen's peace. Now the "custos" has care over the spiritual as well as the physical welfare of his flock.

But, as the song ends and we come back to the mourners, Silvius does not (like Vergil's Menalcas) inquire how he can answer it. Instead he stands poised for departure and Pythias must beg him to remain at all:

> *Effugis! Agnosco. Nusquam sine carmine, Silvi.*
> *Si libet ire, cane; post i, tua damna recense.*
> (105–106)

> [You are departing! I observe it; but not without a song, Silvius. If
> you desire to go, sing; go afterwards, review your own sorrows.]

The amoebean form, the second song answering and perfecting the first, though announced at the start, can no longer be assumed. The sorrows expressed in the first now sadden the listeners too. Pythias must urge his friend to respond in his turn; the latter remains distressed, too distressed perhaps even to respond. Grief is no longer contained within the interior world of the songs; it spills over into the surrounding dialogues. The songs remain performances, not romantic effusions of the heart. But we perform what is in our hearts now, and the sadness remains there after the sounds of the song have died away.

When Silvius does finally "answer" his friend's song with his own, there is no corresponding reversal of mood. The second song, like that of Menalcas, carries the hero heavenward. Here we see, however, how different the same basic pattern can feel. First of all, Silvius describes Argus' apotheosis essentially as a flight, a retreat from this world:

> Postquam pertesum est nemorum longique laboris,
> Irrediturus abit, volucrique per avia saltu
> Evolat in montes. Illinc de vertice summo
> Despicit et nostras curas nostrosque tumultus,
> Regnateque videt quanta est angustia silve;
> Alloquiturque Iovem et viduum commendat ovile.
> Arge, vale! Nos te cuncti, mora parva, sequemur.
>
> (115–21)

[After he became wearied with the groves and the long toil, he has departed, never to return; with winged course he flies forth through trackless ways to the mountains. Thence from the highest summit he looks down and beholds our cares and our confusion, and how great is the distress of the wood that he once ruled. He speaks with Jove and to him entrusts the bereaved fold. Argus, farewell! Brief the delay, we shall all follow thee.]

The earlier separation between the several mourners in this world only prefigures the deeper separation which (we now see) divides all of us in this world from Argus, now in that other world. The "trackless ways" through which Argus journeys toward his lofty mountain top are fitting emblems not only of the distance between those worlds but of the absence of an easy passage between them. Significantly, Petrarch (unlike later Christian elegists) does not celebrate Argus' arrival in the Olympian realm. We feel, not his happiness there, but our unhappiness here, without him. Daphnis with his glance brought peace and gladness back to earth. Argus looks down on a world more distressed than ever. And, if it appears that we need him all the more now, there is no impulse toward a return on his part. Though Argus entrusts the care of his sorrowful flock to Jove, those "trackless ways" do not encourage us to hope that heavenly influences penetrate our world any more than we on our part can gain access to that one. All we can do is wait here in this world—now no longer the herdsman's tranquil homeland but the exile's ravaged land—for the day when we can follow Argus there.

As the two singers go their separate ways, a third herdsman, Ideus, who has been listening to their songs all the while and playing the part of narrator, now comes forward. His final reflections are all Petrarch offers us in the way of a closing frame. And Ideus stands now, not in a pastoral grove or field, but, significantly, alone on a sorrowful shore:

> His dictis, abeunt; patrii Sulmonis ad arva
> Contendit Phitias, silvas petit alter Etruscas;
> Solus ego afflicto merens in litore mansi.
>
> (122–24)

[With these words they depart; Pythias bends his way to the fields of his native Sulmo; the other seeks his Etruscan woods. I alone with my grief remained on the sorrowful shore.]

Petrarch does not give his Ideus, whose role is generally that of spectator, his own voice in the poem. But such a figure, standing as here on the edge, or shore, of the pastoral landscape, becomes a central spokesman in later Renaissance pastoral elegies. Petrarch's Ideus is a descendant of Vergil's Gallus, who also remains, when the pastoral song has ended, alone and unconsoled. But Ideus' solitude and sorrow bear witness to a more profound sense of displacement than that of lover or soldier. His is the exile and grief of the Christian pilgrim in this world. If Vergilian pastoral has the concentric configuration of an island-sanctuary, at the center of which the poet reclines beneath his beech tree, Ideus' position on the shoreline describes his peripheral relation to that consoling world. Such a shoreline, expressive of the larger border which separates this world from the other one, becomes a recurrent geographical feature in later Renaissance laments—from Ideus' lonely shore to the "shores and sounding Seas" of "Lycidas." And, increasingly, the pastoral elegist sings his song from the vantage point of that shoreline. It will be for later elegists to give voice to the largely unspoken sorrows of Petrarch's Ideus.

In Boccaccio's "Olympia" (c. 1361), an eclogue in his own *Bucolicum Carmen*, the conflicts within the mourner's breast take the center stage. Boccaccio's Silvius is torn between his desire for a reunion with his lost child in his own, earthly world and his desire to follow her to a sweeter world beyond all separation. For the Petrarchan elegist the stronger impulse is the one which leads us away from the things of this world. But for Boccaccio's elegist the temptation is rather to remain here, in pastoral. The difference between these two laments is one measure of the difference between the two humanists.

Actually, "Olympia" is not, strictly speaking, a pastoral elegy but a dialogue (in the form of a medieval dream-vision) between a bereaved father and the spirit of his dead child. But Boccaccio uses the dialogue structure to dramatize the conflict between the Christian and the classical, pastoral way of placing sorrow. His poem becomes, in effect, that favorite literary form of humanist poets: a dialogue between a pagan and a Christian. And, of special interest to us, Boccaccio stages the conflict between the two speakers largely as a conflict between two landscapes: the landscape of the classical, pastoral world and a new landscape which now enters the pastoral elegy for the first time, the other-pastoral landscape of heaven.

The perspective of the pagan pastoralist is also the perspective of unenlightened humanity—in this case, of a bereaved father. The father is Boccaccio himself who mourns here (as he tells us in his key to the eclogue)[14] his young daughter who died some years earlier. Boccaccio takes his pastoral pseudonym, "Silvius," from Petrarch; but this Silvius seems more at home in his woodland setting than does his predecessor. We see him first walking in the woods with two servants and we are drawn at once into a scene which is animated, gay, full of descriptive details. Silvius speaks first:

Sentio, ni fallor, pueri, pia numina ruris
Letari et cantu volucrum nemus omne repleri.
Itque reditque Lycos blando cum murmure; quidnam
Viderit ignoro: cauda testatur amicum.

(1–14)[15]

[Unless I am in error, lads, I think the sacred rural gods are rejoicing and the whole wood is filled with the song of birds. Lycos runs back and forth with friendly barking; what he has seen I know not: with his tail he bespeaks a friend.]

There is an element of spontaneous play here in the little dog wagging his tail and in a teasing exchange with a timid servant which follows that is quite foreign to Petrarchan pastoral. There we saw the herdsmen at rest but not at play. Boccaccio's pastoral is a freer, more festive world.

Its affirmations do not, however, go unchallenged. Silvius' walk takes place, not at the pastoral hour of noon, but at night; in that nighttime setting Boccaccio reveals his poem's affinities with the medieval dream-vision. The light, first supposed to be that of approaching dawn, which illuminates the forest and causes the dog to wag its tail is discovered to have a supernatural source. Soon the woods are filled with an unearthly splendor, and Silvius discovers at its center the spirit of his young daughter who has died some years earlier.

Overjoyed to see again the child he has "lost," Silvius urges his servants to prepare a celebration, a festival similar to those rites which Vergil's Menalcas promised to perform in honor of the deified Daphnis. And so begins a strange tragi-comedy:

. . . *altaria surgant*
Cespite gramineo; Trivie mactate bidentem
Candidulam, Noctique pie sic cedite fulvam;
Fer calamos pueris, Terapon, fer serta puellis.

(82–85)

[. . . let altars rise of grassy turf; slay to Trivia a white sheep, and likewise offer a dark sheep to sacred Night; bring reed pipes for the boys, Terapon, bring garlands for the maidens.]

This is not simply a humanist poet's round-about way of describing feelings which might better (or more accurately) have been put in Christian terms. When Silvius calls for these pagan rites, he is invoking the assumption behind the pagan poet's gestures, the belief that his loss will now be made good by some form of restitution in this world. Silvius expects that now his daughter will return to him, either as a member of the pastoral society or, like Daphnis, as its guardian spirit. To criticize Boccaccio's poem for its bold, even outrageous, juxtaposition of pagan and Christian imagery is to fail to see that the whole drama of the poem lies in that juxtaposition of two worlds and two sets of values.[16]

For Olympia has no thought of returning. She dismisses the pagan festival in short order: "We have reed pipes," she says. "We have fit garlands, and if you have such great desire to prepare a holiday, we shall sing notes unknown in these woods" (86–88). The remainder of the poem concerns Olympia's efforts to re-orient her father from the "silvan" to the "Olympian" perspective. She proceeds to sing a hymn in honor of Christ the Savior, tells of his descent to earth, his cleansing of the infected flock, his redemption of the ancient fathers from the world below, and his leading them to their new heavenly home above (86–105).

Silvius, however, refuses to understand. In the pagan's failure to comprehend the Christian salvation, Boccaccio feelingly portrays a father's all too human inability to accept the loss of his child. There is something very moving in Silvius' repeated misunderstandings, which are not as naive as they might appear. Poignantly Silvius extends to Olympia the traditional pastoral invitation by holding out to her the fruits of the Vergilian pastoral world:

> Quas oras, mea nata, refers? quas, deprecor, oras?
> Nos omnes teget illa domus, somnosque quietos
> Herba dabit viridis cespesque sub ylice mensam;
> Vitreus is large prestabit pocula rivus;
> Castaneas mites et poma recentia nobis
> Rustica silva feret, teneros grex fertilis edos
> Lacque simul pressum. Quas ergo exquiritis oras?
>
> (132–138)

[What shores, my daughter, do you speak of? what shores, I pray? Yonder house will shelter us all, and the green herbage offer us quiet sleep, and the turf a table beneath the ilex; and this crystal stream will bountifully supply our cups; soft chestnuts and fresh fruits this rustic wood will bear for us, the fecund flock tender kids and cheese besides. What shores, then do you seek?]

More persuasively, because more concretely, than Petrarch before him, Boccaccio summons those pleasures dear to the world of classical pastoral. The intimacy, the tranquillity, the happy self-sufficiency of that world live again in Silvius' words.

But Olympia rejects the invitation. She counters her father's evocation of the world in which they once lived together with a fuller description of her new celestial home:

> Est in secessu pecori mons invius egro,
> Lumine perpetuo clarus, quo primus ab imis
> Insurgit terris Phebus, cui vertice summo
> Silva sedet palmas tollens ad sydera celsas
> Et letas pariter lauros cedrosque perennes,
> Palladis ac oleas optate pacis amicas.
> Quis queat hinc varios flores, quis posset odores
> Quos lenis fert auro loco, quis dicere rivos
> Argento similes mira scaturigine circum
> Omnia rorantes, lepido cum murmure flexus
> Arbustis mixtos nunc hinc nunc inde trahentes?
> Hesperidum potiora locus fert aurea poma;
> Sunt auro volucres picte, sunt cornubus aureis
> Capreoli et mites damme, sunt insuper agne
> Velleribus niveis claro rutilantibus auro. . . .
>
> (170–184)

> Ver ibi perpetuum nullis offenditur austris,
> Letaque temperies loca possidet. Exulat inde
> Terrestris nebula et nox et discordia rerum.
> Mors ibi nulla manet gregibus, non egra senectus,
> Atque graves absunt cure maciesque dolorque;
> Sponte sua veniunt cunctis optata.
>
> (190–195)

[In a secluded spot is a mountain inaccessible to the weary flock, bright with perpetual light, in which Phoebus first rises from the depths of the earth; on its topmost peak rests a wood, lifting towards the stars lofty palms and likewise glad laurels and never-fading cedars, and olives of Pallas, dear to beloved peace. Who can next describe the manifold flowers, who the fragrance which the soft breeze wafts there, who the streams like silver, bedewing all around with wondrous flood, trailing their winding courses with soft murmur now here now there amid the trees? Golden apples the place bears surpassing those of the Hesperides; there are birds speckled with gold; goats there are with golden horns, and gentle does, and lambs, besides, their snowy fleeces ruddy with bright gold. . . .

There a perpetual spring is sullied with no rain winds, a tempered air pervades the joyous regions. Thence are banished earthly mist and night and discord. There no death awaits the flocks nor sickly old age, and heavy cares are absent and wasting disease and pain; everyone's desires are fulfilled of their own accord. . . .]

Here a new landscape makes its first appearance in the Renaissance pastoral elegy. Let us look at it closely, for we will be seeing it (in various transformations) often again. At first the paradise Olympia describes looks like yet another version of the pastoral one: here too are flowers, flocks, murmuring streams and gentle breezes. But note that while the pastoral landscape is always shown to us in its spring season, here there is no other season but "ver perpetuum." In the pastoral world there is at least the theoretical possibility of the wind and the rain; here not. And that makes a large difference. For if pastoral is a world that can absorb change and suffering, Olympia's paradise is "paradisial" just because it excludes them. Neither the pastoral landscape nor this one approximates that of everyday reality. It is a question of two versions of the ideal: pastoral offers us an idealized image of the quotidian; Olympia's paradise exists, by definition, elsewhere. Hers is a world—that heavenly one—from which change, suffering and, above all, death, have been banished.

This fundamental distinction entails others. Pastoral typically exalts the familiar: Tityrus' *known* rivers, the bees that murmur *as they have always done*. Olympia's world nourishes the exotic, the marvellous: streams like silver, animals bathed in gold (here of course Boccaccio borrows from the atypical, and declaredly so, "pastoral" landscape of Vergil's fourth). Again, where the pastoralist cherishes the discrete object (this pine tree by the spring), Olympia values plentitude itself. There is not one of anything in her world but many flowers, many apples, etc. The pastoral poet does not attempt inclusiveness. It is enough for him simply to point, to allude to the pleasures of his world, thus suggesting we already know them. "Look at this," he says; "come here." So, too, Boccaccio's Silvius: "that house there will shelter us all, and the green grass give us quiet sleep." Olympia, however, describes exhaustively. Like a traveller bringing back a report of a strange, wonderful country—which is, of course, just what she is—she wants to tell us everything, and at the same time she knows she cannot possibly do justice to it all. Her speech registers the traveller's effort to describe the indescribable—to communicate, in short, the otherness of heaven. Her account is punctuated by variations on the "who can tell?" formula.[17] We know what her world is like by knowing what it is *not* like, as in the last lines quoted above.[18]

Behind Olympia's account, as behind Silvius', stands a long literary tradition, a body of conventional motifs and rhetorical formulae. We might term the tradition upon which Olympia draws here, by way of distinguishing it from the pastoral tradition upon which Silvius draws, that of the *locus amoenus*, or "lovely place."[19] While this conventional landscape and the pastoral one have some common roots in the human imagination (as they have some common geographical features), they nevertheless embody two different conceptions of mankind's dream of a "good place." One dream is of a return to a primal homeland, to simple joys and sorrows; the other is of an escape to a fabulous country, a world in which the "perfect moment" is indefinitely suspended. (Dreams, of course, are never altogether pure: the pastoral dream feeds upon a measure of escapism and the dream of the *locus amoenus* is perhaps ultimately related to our indestructible belief that once, long ago, life really was perfect.) The *locus amoenus* need not be a celestial paradise, but it must be in some way beyond our ordinary experience rather than a distillation of that experience. It might be the place where human life is said to have begun—an Eden or a

Golden-Age world; it might be a place where men are said to go after death—a pagan Elysium, the islands of the Hesperides, a Christian heaven; or again, it might be some secluded spot or enchanted island which we come upon in the course of our life's journey—a garden of Alcinous or of Adonis. Olympia's heaven has its antecedents in paradises of all these kinds.[20] Here I am less concerned with the doctrinal implications of such a paradise, or whether its promised happiness prove real or illusory, than with its fundamentally different atmosphere from that which confers life and breath on the pastoral dream. Pastoral is a homeland; the *locus amoenus*, a resort. Pastoral is generally described through the eyes of a native; the *locus amoenus*, through the wondering gaze of a visitor or newcomer. Thus Silvius speaks of a world he knows; Olympia of one newly discovered.

Some such version of this *locus amoenus*, more or less remote from the earthly pastoral world we know, becomes a standard feature of the Renaissance pastoral elegy. Sometimes this "other pastoral" world is a world from which we can, as from the threshold of Vergil's Olympus, come back to this world. Sometimes that return is made with considerable difficulty. For as heavenly pastures grow greener, earthly ones fade. The sweet, familiar world in which the elegist was wont to place his sorrow becomes a barren ground, and he is left unconsoled, looking toward those greener fields elsewhere.

This is what happens in Boccaccio's lament. Gradually Silvius comes to realize, if not quite to accept, that his daughter has indeed left him; and the place where she is must necessarily be a more perfect world than his own. We do not *feel* that it is more perfect, however; nor does Silvius take much comfort in the fact that Olympia is happier where she is. The Christian "consolation" is experienced here mostly as human loss. Olympia has, to be sure, won the debate. But in imaginative terms she loses it. The heavenly world she describes is not, finally, very compelling. One reason for this is that Boccaccio fails us where Dante (but so few others) succeeds: he fails to make his heaven seem compelling on its own terms. It is a more perfect (and hence, as I have suggested, a less perfect) earthly world, not really a different world. We have little sense in Olympia's speeches of the spiritual realities which presumably lie behind the physical appearances she describes, little sense that the sweetness of her world is of an entirely different order from the pastoral sweetness. One wonders whether the consolations which Olympia holds forth to her father are not less compelling to the poet himself than the tangible sweets of Silvius' world which he describes so well.[21]

Olympia has, nonetheless, won the debate. She disappears from sight and all sweetness seems to depart with her. Now Silvius sees his old world, once so dear to him, with changed eyes. The sympathetic landscape of pagan pastoral yields to the sorrowful terrain of the Christian pilgrimage in this world:

> Quo tendis? quo, nata, fugis, miserumque parentem
> Implicitum linquis lacrimis? Heu! cessit in auras
> Ethereas, traxitque simul quos duxit odores.
> In mortem lacrimis ibo ducamque senectam.
> Vos, pueri, vitulos in pascua pellite: surgit
> Lucifer et mediis iam sol emittitur umbris.

(280–85)

[Whither are you going? Whither, daughter, do you flee, and do you leave your wretched father overwhelmed in tears? Alas! she has vanished into the heavenly breezes and has drawn with her the fragrance which she brought. With tears I shall go to death and drag out my old age. You, lads drive the calves to pasture: Lucifer rises and now the sun is sent forth from the midst of the shadows.]

Here it is Lucifer, not Hesperus, and morning shadows rather than evening ones, which urge the herdsman homeward. This inversion of the Vergilian close reminds us that the Christian herdsman will return to the world of toil and suffering, not to the serenity of pastoral repose.

Thus in the end we leave Silvius very much where we left the Petrarchan elegist: alone on the solitary shore, bereft at once of the consolations of pastoral and of those surer, perhaps, but less tangible consolations of the other world. "Olympia," a poem over half of whose lines are devoted to the celebration of the other world, reserves its strongest emotions for the things of this world—its attachments and the pain of losing them.

Here let us pass over almost 150 years so that we may set alongside these laments by Petrarch and Boccaccio a neo-Latin pastoral elegy by a humanist of a very different stamp from either— Baldassare Castiglione. In "Alcon" (1506) the elegist of those earlier Christian laments is transplanted to a secular setting. Yet, despite the magnitude of the change and its important implications, Castiglione's elegist might well be called the spiritual descendant of those earlier ones, for he is heir to their ambivalent feelings about the pastoral world and its consolations. Though Iolas is not torn between a "pagan" pastoral vision of peace and a Christian other-worldly one, he too experiences loss in its personal, and problematic, aspect; he too sings his song from the lonely shore ("solo in littore"); he too is drawn to the consolations of the pastoral world, and yet, in the end, finds them unavailing. Castiglione's poem is one of the most moving of Renaissance pastoral elegies. And it moves us, in part, because the peace which it envisions so intensely is a peace located irrevocably in the past. Castiglione's elegist looks, not forward to the other-pastoral world he might yet gain, but back on the perfect world and perfect friendship he has lost.

Even more than Petrarch or Boccaccio, Castiglione records a private loss. For his is just that: grief at the death, not of some mythical hero, nor for his country's father, nor even any blood relation; it is the death of a friend Iolas mourns. The bond does not inhere in nature; it is freely chosen and thus the most personal of all. Renaissance elegies are more often written for princes than for friends, but this latter subject perhaps best realizes the special potentialities of the Renaissance mode. Matteo Falcone was the companion of Castiglione's student days in Milan, and the intellectual bond between two humanists equally enamoured of the classical past is no small part of the friendship commemorated in this neo-Latin lament. At the time of his death Falcone was serving in the poet's household in Mantua as tutor to his younger brother. Castiglione thus reverses the usual relation of the elegist to his subject, in which we pay our debt to the departed "custos." Now the elegist, not his subject, is the "lord." He has no debt to pay; he is freed from even the slightest suspicion of flattery. His sorrows are thus all the more his own and all the more irremediable. In a letter he wrote to his mother shortly after his friend's death, Castiglione says, "there was no one in the world who knew my whole mind so entirely as he did."[22] Here it is not the support of an entire civilization but that *alter ego*, that ideal Renaissance friend who alone can penetrate the barriers of our own selfhood, we miss. This is the loss that cannot be healed, for there is no replacing him. And it is this private loss that Castiglione mourns again unconsoledly in the pastoral elegy he wrote for Falcone in the following year.

As with Petrarch and Boccaccio, the elegist's own real and pressing sorrows again will not be contained within the lament but penetrate the outer world of the frame. Castiglione effects this change differently, though, by transferring material originally included in the lament to that outer world. His frame, a narrative passage which sets the scene for Iolas' solitary song, takes its first words from the first words of Mopsus' song in Vergil's fifth:

> *Ereptum fatis primo sub flore juventae,*
> *Alconem nemorum decus, et solatia amantum,*
> *Quem toties Fauni et Dryades sensere canentem,*
> *Quem toties Pan est, toties miratus Apollo,*
> *Flebant pastores. . . .*
>
> (1–5)[23]

[For Alcon taken away by the fates in the first flower of his youth, the meadow's ornament and lovers' comfort, whom so often the Fauns and Dryads heard sing, whom so often Pan, so often Apollo admired; for Alcon the shepherds wept.]

Vergil's "exstinctum," however, has become "ereptum," thus marking at the very outset of the poem our more acute sense of deprivation here, the elegist's feeling that his dear companion has been literally snatched from his grasp.

It is this feeling that the rest of the poem explores. Castiglione does not oppose the sorrows of this world to the peace of the world hereafter. It is the gulf between past happiness and present sorrows he feels so keenly; it is to that past world his thoughts keep returning. Like Vergil's, Castiglione's pastoral world seems the dearer to us because we know how vulnerable it is. Castiglione recreates the Vergilian landscape, not now as the farmer's beloved homeland but as a setting for the perfect intimacy which he and his friend once enjoyed. He recalls how they used to lie at their ease, "escaping the hot sun of a long summer's day in the soft shade," while hills and valleys gave back the echoes of their songs (71 ff.). Gallus' Lycoris, we see, is only a spectator in this world, not the object of the herdsmen's devotions. For Castiglione celebrates an ideal of mutuality. From their tenderest years he and Alcon lived as one ("viximus una"); together they endured the heat and the cold; together tended their flocks. Why, then, asks Iolas, "since thou art gone has life been left to me?" (82).

In the most moving passage of the poem, Iolas re-creates his own state of mind at the time of his friend's death. Ignorant of the loss he had already incurred, the poet was in Rome expecting a visit from Alcon, "fondly fashioning idle dreams" of a hoped-for reunion. That imaginary reunion, described so tenderly here, takes place only ostensibly in Rome, as the longing it revives is occasioned by a more distant separation than that between Rome and Mantua. In his friend's imagined journey from the inhospitable rocks and hills of Mantua to the fertile fields of the Roman countryside, Castiglione transports us by slow degrees from the world of his present suffering and isolation back to the pastoral world of perfect unity before death. As the two friends reach out toward one another, the gap between past and present is, at least for the moment, closed:

'Haec ego rura colam celeberrima; tum meus Alcon
Huc veniet linquens colles, et inhospita saxa,
Infectasque undas, et pabula dira veneno,
Molliaque inviset prata haec, fluviosque salubres.
Occurram longe, et venientem primus amicum
Agnoscam; primus caris complexibus ora
Impediam; excutient hilares nova gaudia fletus
Sic tandem optato laeti sermone fruemur,
Aerumnasque graves, olim et transacta vicissim
Damna referre simul, rursusque audire juvabit:
Tum veteres sensim fando repetemus amores,
Deliciasque inter pastorum, et dulcia ruris
Otia. . . .

Hic umbrae nemorum, hic fontes, hic frigida Tempe,
Formosum hic pastor Corydon cantavit Alexin.
Ergo ades, o dilecte puer: te pascua et amnes
Expectant. . . . '

(105–117; 125–127)

[I shall dwell in these glorious fields; then my Alcon will come hither, leaving the hills and the unfriendly rocks, the pestilential waves, and herbs reeking with venom, and he will visit these soft meadows and wholesome streams. I shall run to meet him from afar; I shall be the first to know my friend as he comes; I shall be the first to smother him with loving embraces; our new joys will force out tears of happiness. Thus at last we shall happily enjoy long wished discourse, and we shall delight in telling over in turn the heavy sorrows and hardships once passed, and in hearing them again. Thus as we speak, we shall gradually resume our old loves, and amid pastoral delights, and the sweet repose of country life, we shall pass our lives in untroubled peace. . . .

Here are woodland shades, here springs, here cool vales, here the shepherd Corydon once sang his beautiful Alexis. Then come, thou dearly beloved youth; the pastures and streams await thee. . . .]

The sense of a dear, familiar world slowly coming into view is wonderfully captured here in the poet's gradual reconstruction of the Vergilian landscape. As the two friends first approach one another from a distance, then meet, embrace and gradually resume their former loves, so the atmosphere of the Vergilian world bit by bit steals over us. First the soft meadows ("mollia prata"); then the pleasure of remembering a time of sorrow in a time of joy (so much a part of the Vergilian pastoral experience); then "otium" itself; and finally, with the traditional pastoral gesture of invitation ("hic umbrae nemorum, hic fontes"), we have arrived: *here* Corydon sang for his Alexis, *here* Iolas too shall sing for his Alcon. Thus a literary as well as a private gulf has been bridged in this passage— or rather, the pleasures of the personal encounter are not really separable from those of the literary one, the encounter of the humanist poet with the classical heritage. The joy of a double reunion animates these lines.

Iolas, as he reaches with outstretched arms to embrace the friend who is no longer living, recalls to us earlier elegists, particularly Silvius in "Olympia," for he too reaches out as if to grasp one who will not, cannot, be so apprehended. And, as in that poem—though here it is back into the past we reach, not toward heaven—the impulse is ultimately frustrated. There is no return to the world of "otium." Iolas' dreams do not change anything. Like Gallus' (whose fantasies of peace these also recall), Iolas' reveries are brought to a close by the sudden intrusion of the bitter, present reality. It was only a dream, and even as he was dreaming it, his friend already lay dead. The poet was not there to lay the body on the bier, shed tears over the grave, not there to perform the due rites of death (90–104; 130–131). His sorrows were not soothed by those ceremonies, and the poem itself becomes another unconsummated rite. Iolas' sorrows are not placed; the tomb which he erects for Alcon in his imagination remains an empty one (139 ff.).

Castiglione's pastoral landscape, his sunlit Vergilian world, is a world surrounded by darkness. There is a passing reference here to Alcon "walking gladly in the shade of Elysium" (95), but of the Christian faith in the life hereafter as a sufficient "answer" to human mortality we have no sense.[24] The metaphysical underpinnings of Castiglione's lament are essentially pagan. He revives and intensifies "Moschus"' contrast between the returning vegetation and the finality of human life, superimposing upon that original constrast the Catullan one between the sun which sets to rise again and our own lives which rapidly hasten toward their destined end:

> Vomeribus succisa suis moriuntur in arvis
> Gramina, deinde iterum viridi de cespite surgunt;
> Rupta semel non deinde annectunt stamina Parcae.
> Adspice, decedens jam Sol declivis Olympo
> Occidit, et moriens accendit sidera coelo;
> Sed tamen occiduo cum laverit aequore currus,
> Idem iterum terras orienti luce reviset.
> Ast ubi nigra semel durae nos flumina mortis
> Lavere, et clausa est immitis janua regni;
> Nulla unquam ad Superos ducit via, lumina somnus
> Urget perpetuus, tenebrisque involvit amaris.
>
> (54–64)

[Cut down by the plow the grasses die in their fields, then again spring up from the green sod; but the Fates join not together again the threads once they are broken. Behold, the declining sun now sinking in the heavens is setting, and as it dies, kindles the stars in the sky; still, when it has bathed its chariot in the western waves, it will revisit the lands with orient light. But when once we have bathed in the black waters of cruel death and the door of that relentless realm has been shut, no way leads ever to the upper light, everlasting sleep overwhelms our eyes, and enshrouds us in bitter darkness.]

Most Christian elegists soften "Moschus"' contrast when they invoke it: we die like the grasses, but if not (like them) reborn here, we are reborn elsewhere. Castiglione holds out no such assurance. On the contrary, his version of this classical motif intensifies the sense of darkness closing in upon us with death and emphasizes the impossibility of any remittance.[25]

The darkness of the "everlasting sleep" which awaits us all and the darkness of his present life together frame Iolas' vision of pastoral sweetness. That sweetness exists only in the past; at the end of the dream and the end of the poem the elegist awakens to his present sorrows and exchanges the sweet world of pastoral for the reality of continued bitterness:

> Et tumulo moestae inscribent miserabile carmen:
> 'Alconem postquam rapuerunt impia fata,
> Collacrimant duri montes, et cositus atra est
> Nocte dies; sunt candida nigra, et dulcia amara.'
> (151–54)

[. . . and with downcast mien they will inscribe upon the tomb this mournful verse: 'Since the wicked fates stole Alcon away, rough mountains are weeping, and day has been overcast with dark night; the white has turned to black, and the sweet to bitter.']

Readers of Castiglione's *Book of the Courtier* will be reminded of that work as they read this lament for past happiness. They may recall particularly Castiglione's description at the beginning of the second book (a metaphor for approaching old age) of the old man sailing out to sea, who keeps his eye fixed on the ever-receding shoreline of the bright world he has left behind him, until "scuddling across that stormy sea . . . [he is] finally shipwrecked upon some reef.''[26] The world of the courtiers at Urbino is itself such a bright haven of innocence and sweetness as the old man looks back upon. And Castiglione's pastoral world—one which, like the world of his courtiers, values ease, but more than that, intimacy, and which also delights in its rediscovery of antiquity—is another such bright haven. Like the wayfarer's harbor and the courtier's world at Urbino, this one too is destined to be swept away by stormy seas of time, to be recaptured only in our imaginations.

The final lines of Castiglione's lament, which exchange the sweet world for a bitter one, revise the classical form in another sense too. Now the epitaph which the elegist asks to be inscribed upon the tomb refers us, not to Daphnis or Alcon, but to the mourner, Iolas. It is his state we most concern ourselves with here and with which the poem concludes. In all three of these humanist laments—in Petrarch's, Boccaccio's and in Castiglione's—we hear, with increasing clarity and assurance, the voice of the private man. None of these speakers is altogether at home in the pastoral; Petrarch is the least, Castiglione the most, at ease here. None of the Renaissance poets can say with the Theocritean herdsman: ''I am that Daphnis who herded here his cows, and watered here his bulls and calves.'' Yet the loss of one kind of poise is the gain of another. As sorrow isolates the mourner from his world, from pastoral and its consolations, it also intensifies his sense of himself. These elegists insist upon the autonomy and validity of feelings which cannot be altogether contained within the assurances of the classical form. Their individual voices begin to break down the impersonality of that form, to penetrate the frame, to violate to a greater or lesser extent the detachment of the classical laments.

Petrarch, Boccaccio and Castiglione all ask themselves whether there is a place for their own subjective feelings of grief within the consoling world of classical pastoral. That sweet world attracts them, but it cannot entirely accommodate their sorrows. Each is left standing on a lonely shore, left looking elsewhere. In Jacopo Sannazaro's ''Phyllis,'' we have an example of a quite different approach, one we shall see again in French and English pastoral elegies. Instead of bringing his private suffering to the landscape of classical pastoral, Sannazaro brings that world to the Christian shore—brings, that is, the classical convention home to his own Naples. Here along the Neopolitan coast, among its busy fishermen, we place our sorrows again in a sweet objective world which is also *our own* world. The transferal of the conventional pastoral motifs to the novel setting of the seashore in Sannazaro's *Piscatory Eclogues* (1526), the substitution of fishermen for shepherds, and the closeness with which this setting is observed, permit us to see the pastoral world with fresh eyes and fresh delight. Sannazaro recaptures the vitality and the "hereness" of Theocritus.[27]

Indeed the *Piscatory Eclogues* are, appropriately, the first Renaissance poems to reveal more than a passing acquaintance with the *Idylls* (not printed till the late fifteenth century.)[28] While Renaissance critics generally formulate the contrast between Theocritean and Vergilian pastoral as one between primitivism and sophistication, or crude literalism and weighty allegory,[29] and thus obscure the real differences between the two modes, the poets themselves are often more acute in their perceptions. What Sannazaro takes from Theocritus here are the qualities which most distinguish his art from Vergil's: the tendency to record experience as a series of disjunctive impressions; the freedom from comparisons both literal and figurative; the greater authorial detachment; and most importantly, the association of pastoral sweetness with vitality rather than tranquility. What is less congenial to Sannazaro in Theocritus, and what he does not bring to his own pastorals, is the complementary awareness, which gives an edge to the Theocritean sweetness, that, for all that vitality, we are still victims— victims of nature in us, and, in the end, of fate.

"Phyllis" is the most untroubled of pastoral elegies. It is the lament, set in a framing dialogue, of the fisherman, Lycidas, for the girl he was to have married. Various contemporary women have been suggested as its *real* subject, but nothing in the poem itself invites us to penetrate its smooth surface, to discover actual sorrows behind fictitious ones. Here we are far removed from the personal, introspective mode of the Christian laments considered thus far. Sannazaro's seashore, the shore from which this Christian elegist too looks toward another world, is anything but lonely.

The Christian shore has itself become a sweet world populated by fishermen going about their varied activities. And this shore, elsewhere a setting for the elegist's frustrated desires, is here the starting point for an unprecedented imaginative journey in which, through the transforming medium of the sea, the boundaries between this earthly world and the next are dissolved.

The first word spoken by the fisherman, Lycidas, sets the mood for the whole poem, a mood of wonderment rather than grief:

> *Mirabar, vicina, Mycon, per litora nuper*
> *Dum vagor exspectoque leves ad pabula thynnos,*
> *Quid tantum insuetus streperet mihi corvus et udae*
> *Per scopulos passim fulicae perque antra repostae*
> *Tristia flebilibus complerent saxa querelis,*
> *Cum jam nec curvus resiliret ab aequore delphin*
> *Nec solitos de more choros induceret undis.*
>
> $(1-7)$[30]

[I marvelled, Mycon, as recently I went wandering along the neighboring shores and spying out the agile tunnies at their feeding, for what reason the raven should be calling after me more than his wont, and why the dripping wild-fowl, huddled everywhere along the cliffs and in the caves, were filling the sad rocks with their querulous complaints, while neither was the arching dolphin springing out of the sea nor leading his wonted band through the waves as is his custom.]

Sannazaro, like other Renaissance elegists we have seen, allows the sorrowful subject of the lament to "spill over" into the exterior world of the frame. But, unlike them, he does not permit it to have any unpleasant consequences for that world. If formal detachment is less absolute than in the classical laments, emotional detachment is maintained. A more desperate grief would not pause to ask itself these questions about nature's altered appearance. It would know that its own sentiments were, as a matter of course, reflected on the surface of nature's world. But Lycidas does pause. And if he will answer his own questions in the subsequent lines (the raven calls, the fowl are crying because it is the anniversary of his Phyllis' death), meanwhile he has time—and we with him—to savor these lovely images for their own sake. The raven calls after us, as does the wild fowl wet with sea-water; while in the absent dolphin, cavorting in the waves or leading his wonted band of followers, Lycidas evokes nature's whole realm of custom. With Lycidas we wander leisurely along the shore, observing with him the varied activities of this landscape (or seascape) *before* we need to know what sets those activities in motion. When we do learn the occasion, moreover, it is distanced from us in another way, by being a commemorative rather than an immediate one: it is the anniversary of Phyllis' death.

Nor is the surrounding world of the seashore wholly taken up with sorrowful recollections. Lycidas and the sea-birds remember Phyllis; but near-by another fisherman is setting out his nets to dry in the sun. Once more it is noon and the day's activities are invoked in their momentary suspension. Now is the moment, urges Mycon, to sing of Phyllis' death. "Begin," he says to his friend. We wait expectantly, sweetly suspended, as the seashore stretches forth its soft sand for the singer and the raging waves cease their murmuring (31–32; 42–43).

The song which follows is less a lament for the departed Phyllis than a lively imaginative journey in pursuit of her. Sannazaro's Lycidas does not just stand on his lonely shore with arms vainly outstretched. He asks father Glaucus (in a passage which recalls several Theocritean ones)[31] to turn him, too, into a fish, that he may follow his beloved Nymph beneath the waters of death:

> Quos mihi nunc, Divae, scopulos, quae panditis antra,
> Nereides? quas tu secreti litoris herbas,
> Glauce pater, quae monstriferis mihi gramina sucis
> Ostendes nunc, Glauce, quibus tellure relicta,
> Ah miser, et liquidi factus novus incola ponti
> Te sequar in medios mutato corpore fluctus
> Et feriam bifida spumantia marmora cauda? . . .
>
> Me miserum, qua te tandem regione requiram?
> Quave sequar? Per te quondam mihi terra placebat
> Et populi laetaeque suis cum moenibus urbes;

Nunc juvat immensi fines lustrare profundi
Perque procellosas errare licentius undas
Tritonum immistum turbis scopulosaque cete
Inter et informes horrenti corpore phocas,
Quo numquan terras videam.

(44–50; 69–76)

[What reefs now, Goddesses, what caves, daughters of Nereus, do you reveal to me? What herbs, father Glaucus, from a hidden shore, what grasses now with magic juices, Glaucus, will you display to me, through which (ah, wretch!) having left the land behind, and made a new inhabitant of the watery sea, with transformed body I shall follow you in the midmost waves and beat the foaming surface with forked tail. . . .

Wretched as I am, in what region shall I seek you out at last? Or where shall I follow you? For your sake once the land was pleasing to me and crowds and cheerful cities with their walls; now it is my pleasure to wander the borders of the vasty deep and to roam freely over the stormy waves mingled with crowds of Tritons and amid the monsters of the rocks and rude-shaded seals with fearful forms, where I can never see land.]

Sannazaro's piscatory elegist, as he roams freely through the waves, becomes a type of intrepid Renaissance explorer—eager to see new worlds however threatening, eager, above all, for the experience of change itself. Nothing is alien to him, not even the world after death, for which these stormy seas (that now perhaps contain the spirit of his departed Phyllis) become a metaphor. We smile at the exuberance of the fantasy; but the fantasy is fed by the buoyant optimism of the poet himself. Unlike his Theocritean predecessor, the enamoured Cyclops of the eleventh *Idyll*, this underwater explorer does not summon his roving fantasy home unconsummated. There is no harsh awakening from the dream, as that which called Castiglione's elegist from his imagined reunion back to the reality of solitude. More than those of "wishful thinking," Sannazaro's lines convey the pleasures of an imaginative journey realized.

As among strange underwater forms, Sannazaro deftly navigates, too, among conflicting theologies. In this Protean world beneath the sea, pagan and Christian images of the life after death meet and merge. Lycidas draws freely upon both traditions as he addresses the spirit of his departed Phyllis:

> *At tu, sive altum felix colis aethera, seu jam*
> *Elysios inter manes coetusque verendos*
> *Lethaeos sequeris per stagna liquentia pisces,*
> *Seu legis aeternos formoso pollice flores,*
> *Narcissumque crocumque et vivaces amaranthos,*
> *Et violis teneras misces pallentibus algas . . .*
>
> (91–96)

[But you, whether you in felicity dwell in the high Aether, or now among the Elysian shades and venerable bands of Lethe pursue the fish through the crystal streams, or whether you pluck unwithering flowers with your lovely hand, narcissus and crocus and immortal amaranth, and blend the delicate seaweed with pale violets . . .]

Sannazaro is vague about the location of this other-worldly pastoral paradise. Doctrinally as well as geographically, he prefers to leave it open, to have it both ways: "sive . . . seu . . . seu." We cannot imagine Petrarch or Boccaccio being so blithely unconcerned about the location, or the doctrinal foundation, of the other-pastoral world. Yet Sannazaro's paradise establishes its own poetic authority. Here immortal amaranth blooms alongside delicate underwater flora. And through this world rich and strange—half-pagan, half-Christian, associated, above all, with the transforming powers of the sea—we are borne gently back toward earth.

Like Vergil's Daphnis, then, Sannazaro's Phyllis becomes the custodian of life in this world:

> *Aspice nos mitisque veni; tu numen aquarum*
> *Semper eris, semper laetum piscantibus omen.*
>
> (97–98)

[. . . look down on us and gently come to us; you shall be ever the godhead of the waters, ever a happy sign to fishermen.]

But Sannazaro's claims for the custodian of his fishermen's world are considerably more modest than Vergil's. Phyllis is a force for graciousness or gentleness ("mitisque veni"), not for goodness. Sannazaro's fishermen know neither larger comforts nor larger deprivations.

In the closing, as in the opening frame, the fishermen remember Phyllis' death—can recall it just because it interferes so little with their peace. There is no need here (as in the first *Idyll*) to insulate death within the interior world of the lament. The elegist's concluding "surgamus" balances easily the claims of the mourner against those of his friend who now returns to his fishermen-comrades and the labors of the day:

> Sed quoniam socii passim per litus ovantes
> Exspectant poscuntque tuas ad retia vires,
> Eia age jam surgamus. Ego haec ad busta sedebo;
> Tu socios invise, escas nam quaerere tempus
> Et tibi nunc vacuae fluitant sine pondere nassae.
>
> (126–30)

[But since your joyful comrades await you everywhere along the shore, and ask for your strength at the nets, come now, let us rise. I shall remain by this tomb; you pay your comrades a visit, for it is time to seek out your bait and now your empty weels are floating weightless.]

The fishermen's traps are floating empty; the day's catch is still to be made. The sun is still high in the sky ("nox obscuras jam distulit umbras / Necdum permenus caelum Sol . . ."). The lament has not stolen any time away from the activities of the day, any more than death itself impinges here upon our lives. It is a serene conclusion to a poem which never leaves serenity far behind, never, throughout its various metamorphoses, loses itself in sorrow.

The pastoral elegy reaches the height of its popularity among the neo-Latin humanist poets of the early sixteenth century. Before turning to various developments in the vernacular tongues (where we will again be looking closely at a number of individual poems within the convention), we might step back for a moment and attempt a somewhat broader overview of the convention in its most "conventional" phase. A collection of neo-Latin pastoral poetry published in mid-century, *Auctores Bucolici*,[32] reveals the pastoral elegy to be a highly popular form. Most of the thirty-eight poets represented here (the collection includes the early bucolic songs of Petrarch and Boccaccio as well as contemporary works) employ the form at least once. In his comprehensive survey of neo-Latin pastoral, W. Leonard Grant provides us with a useful catalogue of this body of poetry, brief summaries of some sixty-two neo-Latin pastoral elegies, or as he prefers to call them, *epicedia*.[33] The majority of neo-Latin laments are by Italian poets, but the convention is represented in France, Germany, Holland, England and (in one instance) Portugal. The first poem cited by Grant (who reserves for separate treatment the earlier eclogues of Petrarch and Boccaccio) is Giovanni Pontano's "Meliseus" (c. 1490). The convention enjoys its greatest popularity during the first half of the sixteenth century, is still thriving through the latter half of that century, and then gradually declines in popularity during the seventeenth, with the usual time lag as we move from Italy to the other European countries. Milton's "Epitaphium Damonis" (1639) comes, like "Lycidas" among the vernacular laments, at the end of a tradition.

The first impression we are likely to have in reading these neo-Latin laments is that of greatly increased bulk. When we are told in Pontano's "Meliseus," for instance, how meadows, woods, fields, valleys, rocks, hills, trees, birds of various kinds, cows, goats and more, all weep at Ariadna's death, it is something of a surprise to turn back to Vergil (or Theocritus) and realize how little we see there of such display, how delicately the "pathetic fallacy" is introduced. The first *Idyll* is 152 hexameters (of which about 35 are devoted to the description of the goatherd's cup); Vergil's fifth is 90; Pontano's "Meliseus" is 248; Vida's "Quercus," a pastoral elegy on the death of Pope Julius II, is 539 hexameters. One of the chief attractions of the classical pastoral elegy for these Renaissance poets is, of course, the transferal of the subject from its original setting to the world they know. But they are rarely as restrained as Sannazaro in their evocations of that world. And, as the landscape becomes increasingly crowded, we are apt to lose the very thing we want: the sense that we are "here," in this particular place, "beneath the elm."

If few of the neo-Latin elegists can create a landscape as inviting as the one in which Sannazaro places his lament for the fishing-maid Phyllis, few give us a mourner whose sorrows affect us as do those of Castiglione's Iolas. But the direction of many neo-Latin pastoral elegies is toward that greater concentration on the figure of the mourner and his private sorrows which we have already seen in "Alcon." It is difficult to draw sharp distinctions between these neo-Latin laments and the vernacular ones which gradually supersede them. Not infrequently, the neo-Latin laments are as personal as, or more personal than, their vernacular equivalents. This is worth pointing out because it is the opposite of what one might expect. Perhaps it is just because these neo-Latin poems are to a greater extent coterie poems that they *can* be more personal. For here the poet speaks in a special language which he and his audience share with the poets of antiquity. His audience, so to speak, already knows him, knows the passages to which he alludes, knows the world in which he places his sorrows. To such an audience one speaks more intimately. In the "Epitaphium," Milton addresses a particular community; in "Lycidas," he speaks to all of us.

Our attention is focused more narrowly now on the mourner and his private sorrows in several ways. One of them is by severing the lament from a pastoral sequence. In Theocritus and Vergil sorrow is only one of a succession of moods, and the lament participates in the affirmations of the pastoral sequence as a whole. Petrarch and Boccaccio retain the form of the eclogue series, but, by opening up the pastoral world to include a wide variety of new subjects, they weaken its unity. The sixteenth-century pastoral elegists take this process a step further by freeing the lament from a pastoral series altogether. The Renaissance elegy is, most often, an occasional piece, bound not to the pastoral series but to the subject that calls it forth. It might (and generally does) take its place eventually among the poet's other eclogues, but would not be read in this setting by its first readers. It might, rather, according to the custom of the time, take its place among the funeral obsequies, perhaps even be pinned to the hearse itself, and thus become, in a literal sense, a gift to the deceased rather than to the listening herdsmen. Thus it is to the particular occasion, not the impersonal form, to the world of sorrow rather than that of sweetness, that many Renaissance pastoral elegies belong. When a lament is still bound to a pastoral sequence, as are Sannazaro's "Phyllis" and Spenser's "November" eclogues, we feel the difference. Sannazaro's lament and Spenser's are two very different poems, but both preserve the detachment of the classical pastoral elegies: both present suffering as a mood which takes its place among other moods.

The greater subjectivity of neo-Latin Renaissance pastoral elegies, compared to their classical predecessors, is reflected, too, in the frequency with which they superimpose the figure of the melancholy Gallus upon the structure of the fifth *Eclogue*. The fifth is the all-important model for the Renaissance poet—but this is, after all, an elegy without an elegist. Mopsus describes a whole world mourning, not a particular man. But the Renaissance elegist, especially if he is lamenting the death of some personal friend or loved one, wants a mourner at the center of his stage. So he often begins his poem as Castiglione in "Alcon" and Basilio Zanchi in his "Meliseus" begin theirs, with a description of a solitary mourner lamenting his loss, disconsolate while all of nature flourishes around him.[34] Then, as the mourner begins *his* song, we are presented once again with the familiar themes from Vergil's fifth: the lament of nature, the eulogy of the deceased, the apotheosis. But it is this melancholy herdsman, not the sweetly contentious Mopsus from the opening frame of Vergil's fifth, who presents them to us.

A Christian consolation is the rule among these neo-Latin pastoral elegies, but it is not inevitable. Petrarch and Boccaccio struggle with the conflict between the earthly pastoral world and the other-pastoral one; its greener pastures make those of our world fade by comparison. The Christian consolation can be introduced perfunctorily in the sixteenth-century Latin laments—without necessarily changing anything. These poets will also frequently invoke "Moschus"' contrast between the returning vegetation and the finality of our life in this world. The idea that we, the strong and the wise, live but a brief space in the sunshine of this world while the vegetation annually renews itself, is sometimes presented more forcefully than is the assurance that we die to be reborn elsewhere.

"Moschus"' contrast enters the Renaissance pastoral elegy with the publication of the *Greek Bucolic Poets* by Aldus in 1495. But of Theocritean influence on the Renaissance pastoral elegy we see much less. Sannazaro, we have seen, knows Theocritus and knows him well, but this is exceptional. The explanation lies partly in Renaissance misreadings of Theocritus (the tendency to look on the *Idylls* merely as a primitive ancestor of the *Eclogues*); it lies partly in the greater accessibility of the Vergilian texts (when Renaissance men read Theocritus, they read him most often in very "Vergilian" Latin translations);[35] and it lies in the greater accessibility of Vergil himself. Vergilian pastoral—an island of tranquility in a sea of warfare, a world conscious of its own pleasures and of its own limitations—appeals strongly to the imaginations of Renaissance poets. The Theocritean mixture of extreme literalism and extreme artificiality, the absence of any commentary on what this world is, where it is, or why it matters to us, is more difficult to assimilate.

The Renaissance pastoral elegy is, above all else, a series of variations on Vergil's fifth *Eclogue*, and its favorite subject is, accordingly, the royal patron. If we catalogue the neo-Latin laments mentioned in Grant's survey we find a few, like "Alcon" or the "Epitaphium Damonis," written in honor of friends (four of Grant's sixty-two poems may be classified in this category); we find some written for professional colleagues, scholars, physicians and the like (six poems); others, like Pontano's "Meliseus," are written for family relations (eleven poems); but the largest single group (twenty poems) are those which honor a king or a noble patron. What better tribute to a Renaissance sovereign than to commemorate him as Julius Caesar himself was once commemorated by the greatest poet of antiquity!

Thus, by the mid-sixteenth century the pastoral elegy has become an extremely popular form. And by the close of the century the convention seems clichéd enough to be burlesqued. Marco Publio Fontana, who wrote a serious pastoral elegy in 1574 for a fellow poet, composed another one later in his career on the death of a friend's pet goat. The poem is worth a brief consideration here, for there is no better way to discover which features of a convention are considered the "conventional" ones than to see which are parodied. "Caprea" begins with the usual invitation: the grieving poet calls the surrounding pastoral (or in this case, caprial) world "here," to mourn this loss with him:

> *Aeriae rupes, et vos juga plurima circum*
> *Dissita, sola feris sedes fidissima capris,*
> *Huc rigidas praebete aures, huc, stantibus ornis*
> *Dum dulcem capream, dum lamentamur, adeste.*
>
> *Si vos, si propriae subrepta ob pignora, cautes*
> *Lustraque capripedum nudis gemuere sub antris;*
> *Quos ipsum Finum, qui sensum et mollia servat*
> *Viscera, censetis gemitus fudisse, tenellam*
> *Ut vidit capream, quam vestra in valle repertam*
> *Detulerat Licidas, crudeli tabe jacere!*
>
> $(1-10)^{36}$

[Lofty crags, and you, many ridges scattered round about, where alone the wild goats are safe, turn here your stoney ears, be present here while I lament a sweet she-goat to the tall ash trees.

If you, her own rocks and haunts, have groaned in the empty caves for your loved one snatched away, what groans do you think Finus himself, a man of both sense and tender feelings, poured forth when he saw his tender little she-goat, whom Lycidas found in your valley and carried down—saw her lying in cruel gore?]

Nature grieves for her darling, but the goat's master, a man of tender feelings, grieves more. After a description of the she-goat's innocent life and her death (attended by all the Muses) before her prime, we follow Finus' pet to heaven, where the familiar features of the other-pastoral landscape come into view:

> *Et nunc Elysiis tendens per gramina campis*
> *Propter aquae rivum, gelidave sub arboris umbra,*
> *Mollis ubi venris aspirat amaracus auris,*
> *Ipsa tuo capiti violas, et lilia nectit.*
>
> $(40-44)$

[And now, as she browses in the grass of the Elysian fields, along a river bank, or under the cool shade of a tree, where the scent of the soft marjoram is borne on spring breezes, she weaves a garland of violets and lilies for your head.]

Still grieving, Finus recalls his pet in days of former happiness, recalls her presence alongside him at the dinner table, urges Pan to leave his Arcadian haunts for these and the shades to bring his "caprea" back to him. That is not to be: she has entered the realm of perpetual night from which there is no return: thus Fontana conflates Christian and pagan images of death. The mourner is comforted, however, by the thought that his pet may now become a constellation in the heavens, whence she will look down on her pastoral world and, like Daphnis, bring us good fortune:

> Sic olim missurus erit, cum Juppiter imbres
> Signa dabit, caelo exoriens manifesta sereno.
> (85–86)

[Thus when Jupiter threatens rain, she will give warning, rising clear in a calm sky.]

The mourner commands a tomb to be built and an inscription engraved upon it. The poem concludes with the poet's address to his sorrowful friend, in which he recommends to him the sweetness of his own pastoral retreat:

> His mihi juncta domus, spatioso limite molles
> Circumstant horti: hic curis oblivia duco;
> Hic studiis, caeloque fruor laetatus aperto:
> Dum tu, quae servant tibi plurima, Fine, penates
> Rura petis; pluresque simul cum moenibus urbes
> Te proprium accipiunt repetita ad limina civem.
> (98–103)

[My home is close by, surrounded with tender gardens in a broad enclosure; here I cover my cares with forgetfulness; here I happily enjoy my studies and the clear sky. Meanwhile, you, Finus, seek the country places which your own home (or private wealth) makes available to you; and, when you return to their gates, many walled cities accept you as one of their citizens.]

From the traditional excursions into both a Christian and a pagan afterworld, we come back "here" at the close, back to pastoral, with the reminder, too, that this is a privileged existence: Finus will soon be returning to the city. It would be useful to have a full catalogue of these neo-Latin pastoral elegies, and of their various internal conventions. But Fontana's delicate little lament—half burlesque, half a tender evocation of the "sweet world" (both literary and literal) shared by two fellow humanists—tells us much that we might learn from such a catalogue.

4

"Et in Arcadia Ego"

SANNAZARO, TRISSINO, TASSO

Returning homeward from his travels, Don Quixote comes upon a familiar meadow and calls out enthusiastically to his friend Sancho:

> This is the meadow where we fell in with those gallant and gaily bedecked shepherds and shepherdesses who were endeavoring to imitate and restore the Arcadia of old, a novel idea and an inspired one; and if you approve, Sancho, I would suggest that, at least for the time that I have to live in retirement, we likewise turn shepherds. . . . Together we will roam the hills, the woods, and the meadows, now singing songs and now composing elegies, drinking the crystal water of the springs or that of the clear running brooks or mighty rivers. . . . song will be our joy, and we shall be happy even in our laments . . . [1]

This meadow and the way of life it sustains, which Don Quixote finds so attractive, had been discovered (or, we might better say, invented) some two hundred years previously by Jacopo Sannazaro. Sannazaro's Latin *Piscatories* started a minor fashion of their own; but it was his earlier Italian prose-poem, the *Arcadia* (1502, 1504), which fired the imagination of an age, establishing both the model for Italian pastoral and a definition of the genre with which all later pastoralists, whether or not they subscribed to it, would have to contend. Sannazaro's herdsmen (like Vergil's) call their world Arcadia; but for all its Vergilian reminiscences, this golden world is no more Vergilian than it is Greek. It has its own distinctive atmosphere, one which Don Quixote defines precisely when he says, "here we shall be happy even in our laments." For the Arcadians are never happier than when they are lamenting; they are happy in the lament itself. What Sannazaro bequeaths to the pastoral tradition (and particularly to the pastoral elegy) is the pleasure of nostalgia, of a sorrow divorced from any actual object.

The whole *Arcadia* might be viewed as one extended pastoral elegy, punctuated at intervals by love laments, narrative passages and other traditional forms, but held together by the sustained note of sweet lamentation, by a sorrow whose sources are various but finally unimportant. Death is no more unsettling here than in the world of Sannazaro's fishermen. But where in the *Piscatories* the poet denies death its power to disturb us by placing it in the familiar world of Neapolitan fishermen, in the pastoral romance he dissipates grief by dissolving it in a more distant and less substantial realm. In his *Arcadia* the scenery is always lovely and always the same. We do not find here those precise references to objects in the landscape through which other pastoral elegists (and Sannazaro himself elsewhere) chart the inner landscape of feeling. In *Arcadia* it is not so much "a clear sky one day, rain the next" as perpetual haze. The sunlight bathes everything here in an even light; this is a calm, we might say a static, world; scenes characteristically compose themselves as tableaux.[2] We might suppose the narrative passages which link one tableau (one eclogue, or pair of songs) with another would confer on this romance a larger dramatic interest than is customary in pastorals, but they only serve to emphasize how little dramatic development there is here; everything in Sannazaro's Arcadian world works against it. The varieties of the emotional climate are as limited as those of the weather. We find the same basic situations (the sorrows of love or those of death) rehearsed again and again. This is a literary climate the twentieth-century reader is likely to find less congenial than the sixteenth- or seventeenth-century one. But if we will take Sannazaro's world for what it is, without demanding that it satisfy needs or deal with emotions it does not really pretend to deal with, we may find that this pastoral world has its own charms. We may be able to say, with those earlier visitors to these meadows, "how beautiful! how sad!" That is the sort of emotional response Sannazaro invites from us. And we may see too, just beneath the surface of this Arcadian melancholy, the figure of a youthful poet: he is not weeping but is rejoicing in the discovery of his powers, rejoicing to see just how much he can "make" of sorrow.

And it is a good deal. In the twelve "chapters" of the *Arcadia* (each composed of a verse and a prose section) the pastoral elegy makes three separate appearances, and the first of these includes the double-lament contained in the fifth prose and fifth verse sections. Sannazaro looks to a different model on each of these occasions—to the late Roman poet, Nemesian, to Vergil, to "Moschus," and to his own friend, the poet Pontano. But all these pastoral elegies (except perhaps the last of them, which is a telling exception since it is recited after the hero has left Arcadia and returned to his native Naples)[3] might be considered as the separate verses of a single stream of lamentation running through the Arcadian landscape and surfacing at various intervals. To sample these waters at any one place is to know the flavor of the whole stream. Here is a draught, from the opening section of the eleventh *Eclogue*:

> Piangi, colle sacrato, opaco e fosco,
> e voi, cave spelunche e grotte oscure,
> ululando venite a pianger nosco.
> Piangete, faggi e querce alpestre e dure,
> e piangendo narrate a questi sassi
> le nostre lacrimose aspre venture.
> Lacrimate voi, fiumi ignudi e cassi
> d'ogni dolcezza; e voi, fontane e rivi,
> fermate il corso e ritenete i passi.
> E tu, che fra le selve occolta vivi,
> Eco mesta, rispondi a le parole,
> e quant'io parlo per li tronchi scrivi.
>
> (4—15)[4]

[Weep, sacred hill, thick-shadowed and dark;
  and you, ye hollow caves and grots obscure,
    making your clamor, come to weep with us.
Weep you, ye beeches and hard and rugged oaks;
  and weeping tell these rocks

our bitter lamentable fates.
Pour out tears, ye rivers, stripped and drained
of every sweetness; and you, ye springs and streams,
arrest your courses and hold back your steps.
And you who live hidden away amid the woods,
unhappy Echo, answer to my words;
and what I speak, write it upon the trunks. . . .]

Sannazaro is a connoisseur, if not of suffering itself, of the gestures of sorrow. The elegist's customary role of chief mourner has been exchanged for that of master orchestrator of the general grief. What interests Sannazaro is not what the mourner feels, or why, but the way his feelings penetrate and color the world around him. Grief insinuates itself into hollow caves and dark grottoes; it is a kind of solvent, turning hard things (like rugged oaks) into soft ones. The "pathetic fallacy," which, as we have seen, is used sparingly if at all in the classical pastoral elegy, is everywhere in evidence here. For it is this poet's desire to diffuse his human feelings through the whole inanimate world. Sannazaro's verse form enhances these effects. Instead of the unobtrusive, flexible hexameter (or some vernacular equivalent to that classical meter, standard in pastoral), Sannazaro appropriates from the Petrarchan lyric tradition a wide variety of stanzaic forms, even inventing some new ones. The hexameter, in which the single line is the metrical unit, forces us to focus on one thing at a time; Sannazaro's rhyming verses, and particularly his favorite *terza rima*, in which one line is always flowing into the next with no break in the momentum, are used to brilliant effect, enhancing our sense that one object, one sensation is always dissolving into another one.

We do not ask why we should weep; Sannazaro does not mention the subject of the lament, Massilia, until the twentieth line of the poem. When he does, he refers to her indirectly and uses two metaphors rather than one, thus further distancing the event itself: "The learned Egeria and the Theban Manto / death has rapt away with sudden rage." This is all the attention Massilia herself receives in the poem. In the prose section preceding it we are told that the speaker in both, the melancholy shepherd Ergasto, is lamenting the death of his mother. This has caused some confusion among critics, for "Massilia" sounds rather like "Masella," Sannazaro's own mother. Is Sannazaro himself the mourner Ergasto? Then why does he elsewhere figure himself in *Arcadia* as Actio Sincero, the Neapolitan visitor among the shepherds? These questions have no proper answers. For Sannazaro's approach is to blur identities. It is not that his Massilia represents *all* mothers, as Vergil's Daphnis was all our support or Castiglione's Alcon is the type of all friends; it is rather that he wants the effect of one identity, or one response, dissolving into, merging with another one.

In Sannazaro's laments there is no appeal to an alien world (of African lions or beasts of the forest) which must be persuaded by the force of the elegist's emotions to enter part way into his human world. For nature is, so to speak, already there, already humanized by myth:

> *O Filomena, che gli antichi guai*
> *rinovi ogni anno, e con soavi accenti*
> *da selve e da spelunche udir ti fai;*
>> *e se tu, Progne, è ver c'or ti lamenti,*
> *né con la forma ti fur tolti i sensi,*
> *ma del tuo fallo ancor ti lagni e penti;*
>> *lasciate, prego, i vostri gridi intensi,*
> *e fin che io nel mio dir diventi roco,*
> *nessuna del suo mal ragione o pensi.*
>> (46–54)

[O Philomel, you who renew each year
  your ancient woe, and with your gentle notes
    from forests and from caverns make yourself heard;
and if it be true of you, Procne, that now you lament yourself,
    nor were your senses taken from you with the form
      but still for your fault you moan and are penitent,
leave off, I pray you, your piercing lamentations
    and until I am become hoarse in my speech
      let no one speak or think of her own evil.]

It is not the birds Sannazaro appeals to but the metamorphosed heroines of the classical myth.[5] His Filomena and Progne belong to the same community of refined and gentle feelings as his Arcadians. And they can put aside their own "ancient woes" for these present ones, can so readily enter into the speaker's own sentiments, because it is essentially a mood, and not an event, they are invited to share.

In the fifth Arcadian prose chapter Sannazaro's preference for mood and gesture over action, his tendency to reduce (or even eliminate) emotional tension, to dissolve pastoral sorrow in pastoral sweetness, are all apparent. Significantly, in this lament, which is indebted to Vergil's fifth via Nemesian, it is the gathering itself, the convocation about the hero's grave, which now becomes the focal point of the whole poem. That motif is not at all prominent in the fifth *Eclogue*, where Vergil simply asks that leaves be scattered on the ground and shade drawn over the fountain (40) at Daphnis' grave. But the late Roman poet Nemesian, in "Meliboeus," conflates that passage with the description of the woodland gods, adorned with fruit and flowers, who converge about the sorrowful Gallus in the tenth *Eclogue* (24–27). Thus the funeral rite is joined to the pastoral offering. Sannazaro (and after him many later Renaissance pastoral elegists) finds the combination irresistible. To Sannazaro the association of melancholy *feelings* and sweet *things* is particularly attractive; he expands Nemesian's account considerably. Each of these graveside visitors seems to vie with the preceding one in the abundance of his or her offering; their baskets are overflowing; sorrow is literally buried in sweetness here:

> Ecco che il pastorale Apollo tutto festivo ne viene al tuo sepolcro per adornarti con le sue odorate corone. E i Fauni similmente con le inghirlandate corna, e carichi di silvestri duoni, quel che ciascun può ti portano: de' campi le spiche, degli arbosti i racemi con tutti i pampini, e di ogni albero maturi frutti. Ad invidia dei quali le convicine Ninfe, da te per adietro tanto amate e riverite, vengono ora tutte con canistri bianchissimi pieni di fiori e di pomi odoriferi a renderti i ricevuti onori.
>
> (27–33)
>
> [Look how the shepherd god Apollo all festive is coming to your sepulchre to give you ornament with his sweet floral crowns; and

likewise the Fauns with garlands on their horns and laden with woodland gifts are bringing them to you, each as he is able: from the fields the grains, from the vines the clustered grapes with all their tendrils, and ripened fruits from every tree: in emulation of whom the Nymphs who dwell nearby, so much loved and revered by you of old, are all of them coming now with their white baskets full of flowers and fragrant fruits, to requite you the honors they received.]

Sannazaro's offerings are both ampler and less specific than Nemesian's. Instead of "laurel," his Apollo brings "sweet floral crowns"; instead of "honey," the nymphs bring "baskets of flowers and fruits."[6] What Sannazaro makes us feel is the fulsomeness of the gesture itself.[7]

In a passage like this one the optimism that is always close beneath the surface of the Arcadian melancholy is particularly palpable. In the piling up of pastoral sweets the occasion itself seems to have been left behind. Death sets the Arcadian melancholy in motion; it brings the Nymphs and Fauns to the convocation; having done that it can be dismissed. Death exists in Sannazaro's pastoral world to be transcended, transformed, like the gravesite itself, into an object of beauty.

Sannazaro's pastoral world assimilates everything to itself—even the world beyond its borders. In the lovely assumption song in the fifth *Eclogue* Androgeo is transported to a paradise which, for all its "otherness," seems but an extension of the one we know here:

> altri monti, altri piani,
> altri boschetti e rivi
> vedi nel cielo, e più novelli fiori;
> altri Fauni e Silvani
> per luoghi dolci estivi
> seguir le Ninfe in più felici amori.
> Tal fra soavi odori
> dolce cantando all'ombra
> tra Dafni e Melibeo
> siede il nostro Androgeo.
>
> (14–23)

> [*Other mountains, other plains,*
>   *other woods and rills*
>   *you see in heaven, and a fresher flower:*
>   *other Fauns and Sylvans*
>   *through pleasant summery spots*
>   *pursue the Nymphs in happier loves.*
>   *So amid soft odors*
>   *sweetly singing in the shade*
>   *between Daphnis and Meliboeus*
>   *our Androgeo sits . . .*]

Sannazaro's "altri . . . altri" suggests "more" rather than "different." His "fresher" flowers and "happier" loves seem to breathe the same air as those here on earth. Nymphs and fauns frequent both worlds; in both we recline in the soft shade and pursue the same pleasures—the pleasures of song and of love. And, most important of all, in both earthly and the heavenly realms, pagans and Christians sit side by side. For as he dissolves traditional distinctions between *here* and *there*, Sannazaro dissolves conflicts between pagan and Christian attitudes toward death. As "il nostro Androgeo" happily takes his place between Vergil's Daphnis and Nemesian's Meliboeus, the poet announces his assimilation of the Christian form to the classical one. As in the neo-latin "Phyllis," we are struck by the effortlessness with which it has been done. We must be careful in describing just what has been achieved here, lest we make it seem to be something more (or other) than what it is. Sannazaro can place his Androgeo alongside the Vergilian Daphnis so easily because there is so little awareness in his poem of anything that might keep the two figures apart. There is no more sense of Christian other-worldliness here than there is a "pagan" recognition that death entails any real suffering, any real privation, in *this* world. Sannazaro's integration of pagan and Christian motifs operates on an aesthetic level, not, like Spenser's or Milton's, on a deeper moral level as well.

In the *Arcadia* sorrow is essentially something out of which to make music; and Sannazaro's muse proclaims, above all, the transforming power of the song. His fifth *Eclogue* concludes appropriately with the traditional assertion that its subject will live on in song, not only in his song but (with this poet's characteristic amplification) "through diverse shepherds in a thousand other sampognas and a thousand verses." And the eleventh *Eclogue* concludes with an even prouder boast:

> Ove, se 'l viver mio pur si prolunga
> tanto, che, com'io bramo, ornar ti possa,
> e da tal voglia il ciel non mi disgiunga,
> spero che sovra te non avrà possa
> quel duro, eterno, ineccitabil sonno
> d'averti chiusa in così poca fossa;
> se tanto i versi miei prometter ponno.
> (154–60)

> [Whereupon–if my life be yet prolonged
> so far that I can adorn you as I wish,
>   and Heaven not disjoin me from such will–
> that harsh unwakable and eternal sleep
> I trust will not have power over you
>   to keep you close, within so narrow trench:
> if thus such promise my verse have power to make.]

Here the pastoral pipe is not so much an instrument for placing sorrows as for transcending them. Recalling once more the legendary descent of Orpheus, Sannazaro suggests that the elegist's song might yet win that longed-for release from death. The wish is thrice qualified: if he should live so long; if heaven should permit it; if his verses should have such powers. Yet the qualifications only seem as spurs to the poet's imagination. His spiraling terza-rima lines acknowledge limitation only to rise above it. This passage is the strongest statement, in any pastoral elegy I know, of the elegist's power to transcend death through his song—we might say, to deny it. For in this Arcadia we are not happy in spite of sorrow, or happy because we have placed our sorrow within nature's cyclical course; we are happy here, as Don Quixote says, in the act of lamentation itself.

It is not difficult to understand the attraction Sannazaro's *Arcadia* had for later generations of poets and of mourners both. I suspect the temptations these pastoral elegies hold out to us are temptations which every mourner has at some moment in his suffering experienced. One way of dealing with loss is to confront it head-on. The opposite way is to allow oneself to become so absorbed in the gestures of grief that the loss itself becomes unreal to us. Probably most mourning involves some mixture of the two responses. We want to *know* what has happened to us; we also want to be able to forget—and both these activities are part of what Freud would have called the "work" of mourning.[8] Perhaps especially for the funeral poet, just because he deals with mourning as a ritualistic act, the temptation to use words as shields *against* the pain rather than as the means of exploring it (of giving pain a name) is always present. And again, I suppose that most funeral poems do both these things, and sometimes do both at the same time. Theocritus lets nature's sympathy for Daphnis roll over us in comforting waves at the very moment he makes us acknowledge just how little that sympathy can ever change anything. Perhaps we need the soothing capacity of words most when we are using them to probe the wounds of grief. The point I want to emphasize here is that in using the sweetness of pastoral to deny the power of death, Sannazaro is not doing something radically new with the convention; he is rather emphasizing one side of it at the expense of the other, complementary, side. Here it is *all* sweetness and light; Daphnis' death seems introduced just to allow Mopsus the opportunity to "raise him to the stars."

Yet in speaking of Sannazaro, words like "temptation" and "denial" seem inappropriate: his Arcadian laments are so innocent of a knowledge of pain that must be put behind us; there is so little awareness here that there might be real sorrows we might be tempted to run away *from*. The grief which brings the love-sick Actio from Naples to Arcadia is as insubstantial as those of the herdsmen-singers he encounters there. But for later Renaissance poets, where sorrows may be quite real, the seductions of this Arcadian retreat may be less innocent and its consolations less consoling.

Sannazaro's Arcadia, a far-away world where all our sorrows are sweet ones, is rediscovered and recolonized by Renaissance pastoralists, particularly by Italian poets, throughout the sixteenth century. We have a nice example of how the Arcadian atmosphere permeates Italian pastoral in a lament by the humanist poet Giangiorgio Trissino. Trissino, an ardent believer in the doctrine of imitation, composed both an epic and a tragedy according to the "rules" of Homer and Aristotle respectively. When he came to pastoral he chose to follow the Theocritean rather than the Vergilian model (as was customary). And he defended his choice in his Ars Poetica, *Le Sei Divisione della Poetica* (1550). Trissino praises Theocritus for his adherence, not only to the themes and setting appropriate to the herdsmen's world, but also to the rough speech of actual rustics. But he admits that in his own pastorals he has not taken this path;[9] and indeed these betray a very different affiliation.

Trissino's "Dafne," a lament for the prelate Cesare Trivulzio (c. 1527), is not a particularly effective or inspiring poem. But it is worth considering briefly here because it reveals so clearly the various cross-currents of influence present in Renaissance pastoral. "Dafne," particularly in its opening and closing passages, is a narrow imitation of the first Theocritean *Idyll*, the sort of thing we would expect from a humanist poet of this school. And yet, it is when Trissino is following Theocritus most closely (in fact almost word for word), in the framing dialogue, that we feel the Arcadianate atmosphere most strongly, as it infuses this "Theocritean" exchange with its own colors:

> Tirse   Soave è il fischio de i fronduti Pini,
>   Mossi dal vento ne l'ardor del giorno,
>   Ma più soave è 'l suon de le tue canne.
>   Tu suoni così ben, che'l primo onore
>   Si dona a Pan, e a te si dà il secondo.
>
> Batto   Pastor, più dolce è 'l tuo cantar soave,
>   Che 'l mormorio, che fan di pietra in pietra
>   L'acque, che scendon da i sassosi colli. . . .
>
>   (1–8)[10]

[*Tirsi*: How soothing is the whispering of the fringed pines, moved by the wind in the heat of the day, but more soothing is the sound of your reeds. You play so well that, if Pan receives the first prize, the second goes to you.

Batto: Shepherd, your sweet singing is more soothing than the murmur that the waters make when they fall from the rocky hills and move from stone to stone.]

Trissino clearly has his eye on the elements out of which the Theocritean scene is composed. But a softer sweetness suffuses the air. Instead of particular sensations (the whispering in the pines, the water splashing), Trissino describes the wind moving through the fluttering pines, the water moving from stone to stone. Vergil would have given us the play of light against shade or of waters against the stones, not the sense of flow we have here. Trissino's whispering pines and murmuring waters, with their soothing sounds, belong to the world of Sannazaro's *Arcadia*.

And, as we enter into the lament itself, we see that Trissino continues to break down the Theocritean sense of the distinctiveness of things. Notice, for instance, that insentient woods and fields follow the beasts in lamenting his Dafne's death:

> La morte di costui pianseno i lupi,
> Et i leoni, e gli aspidi, e le tigre;
> Piansenla i boschi, le campagne, e i colli.
>
> (78–80)

[For his death the wolves wept, and the lions, and the serpents, and the tigers; the woods, and the fields and the hills wept for it.]

I suspect that for Trissino the difference between a mournful creature and a mournful tree is a difference in degree, not kind. We scarcely notice this extension of the lament into the insentient realm of nature because, within the Arcadian world, everything can—and does—feel just what we are feeling.

As sorrowful beasts yield imperceptibly to a sorrowful countryside, so life yields imperceptibly to death. Trissino's Dafne clings less ardently to life than his original. Indeed he welcomes his death:

> Fortuna avversa, e voi feroci mali,
> Che circondato la mia vita avete,
> Prendete pur di lei l'ultima spoglie,
> Che gran gloria vi fia, se armati, e forti

Vincete un uomo disarmato, e infermo;
A me fia grazia uscir di tanti affanni.
(115–120)

[Adverse fortune, and you, fierce afflictions, which have surrounded my life, take from it even the ultimate spoils; and may it be a source of great pride to you if, armed and strong, you can conquer a man unarmed and weak; to me it will be a joy to leave behind so many troubles.]

Trissino's Dafne does retain something of his predecessor's pride and self-containment. But the note of weary resignation is new—and more harmonious with a world in which it seems sweet to die and sweet to sing of death.[11] Here we can speak only of tendencies. Trissino gives us, not a consistent picture of what it means to die or to sing of death in the pastoral world, but several different impressions, one set on top of the other. Yet it is just these dissonances which are most revealing, as we see the Theocritean model yielding to the softer (but here more persuasive) influence of Sannazaro.

If we turn to Italian pastoral in the age of the counter-Reformation we find Tasso continuing in the tradition of Sannazaro. But the Arcadian dream seems more distant now and the dream itself less vital. In "Il Rogo Amoroso" (1588), a long funeral poem which incorporates elements of the pastoral elegy along with other forms of obsequy, Tasso conveys his own longing for repose, or "ozio," far more forcefully than he does the consolations of the Arcadian world. Written during the final years of Tasso's life, a period of physical as well as continuing mental instability for the poet, the "Rogo" reflects Tasso's own anguished search for the asylum he was never to find.

Although this quasi-pastoral dialogue takes place on the banks of the Roman Tiber, Tasso sets the scene in the opening frame—a dialogue between Aminta (the poet's friend and patron, Don Fabio Orsini) and Tirsi (Tasso himself)—for a dreamy Arcadian lament. As the poem opens we see Aminta mourning the death of his beloved mistress: "Piangea dolente e sospiroso Aminta. . . . piangea Corinna in lacrimoso canto."[12] ("Full of sorrow and sighs, Aminta wept. . . . he wept for Corinna in a tearful song.") Once more the sorrowful subject penetrates the outer frame, but, as generally in the Italian pastoral elegy, without disturbing the atmosphere of sweet tranquility. From far away Tirsi hears the "soave note" and comes to his friend's side. His first words are telling: "Non perturbi il mio venire / le dolcissime tue voci canore" ("Do not let my presence interrupt the extraordinary sweetness of your melodious words"). The interlocutor's function here is to keep the sweet sounds coming, not to interrupt them with words of consolation.

And, as in other Italian laments, the sweet song, with its melancholy refrain, meets no more resistance here from nature than from man. Grief diffuses itself in ever-widening circles, as nature (not deaf to the song) takes up the human melody and gives us back the echo:

> E ne 'l pianto canoro i sette colli
> rispondevan Corinna, e il tosco fiume
> risonava Corinna, e i chiari fonti
> Corinna, più lontano i verdi boschi,
> Corinna mormorâr l'ombrose valli;
> tal che ninfe e pastor quel suon deluse
> gioiosa no ma dolorosa imago.
>
> (12–18)

[And to the tuneful weeping the seven hills responded, "Corinna," and the Tuscan river gave back, "Corinna," and the clear fountains, "Corinna," and farther away the green woods and the shady valleys murmured, "Corinna"; so that the sound (an image of sorrow, not of joy) deceived the nymphs and the shepherds.]

Tasso, we notice, is more self-conscious than Sannazaro or Trissino about the way human feelings insinuate themselves into nature. He feels compelled to remind us that the nymphs and shepherds are deceived when they suppose the woods and waters themselves are speaking, to remind us that some of pastoral poetry's special effects depend, after all, on illusions.

Various other mourners, following Tirsi, gradually converge about Aminta's riverbank where a "rogo" (or "funeral pyre") honors the memory of the dead Corinna. Each mourner makes an appropriate offering to her spirit: Mercury presents his wings,

Diana her arrows, and so on. Aminta and Tirsi themselves present the two halves of a Vergilian pastoral elegy, Aminta taking up the lament and Tirsi following with the consolation. Tasso, like Trissino, follows his classical source closely, and again it is the minor changes which are the most revealing.

Tasso's happier pastoral world over which Corinna presided before her death is, like Vergil's, a cultivated world. But this landscape is considerably more removed from nature:

> Corinna dimostrò ne i rozzi boschi
> qual fosse gentilezza e cortesia,
> e insegnò prima a le selvagge ninfe
> a figurar con l'ago i fiori e l'erba
> e i dipinti augelletti e i vaghi cervi
> con le ramose corna, e i capri e i pardi;
> tal che le sue vittorie ella dipinse
> e i suoi propri trofei spiegò ne l'oro
> cara a Dïana e cara anco a Minerva.
>
> (45–53)

[Corinna showed what gentleness was, and courtesy, in the rough woods; and she first taught the savage nymphs how to draw flowers and grass and painted little birds and pretty harts with branching horns and goats and leopards with the needle; so she—dear to Diana and dear also to Minerva—pictured her victories for them and displayed her own trophies in gold.]

Corinna and her nymphs prefer to contemplate themselves hunting in the embroidered images of art than to pursue the pleasures of the hunt itself. There is a quality of self-absorption here, of enervation, which belongs neither to Vergil's pastoral nor Sannazaro's.

Tasso envisions a different sort of peace from either of those poets—envisions, ideally, a world of repose. This emerges most clearly in a passage from Tirsi's answering song, which echoes that of Vergil's Menalcas. There, we recall, nature responds to the glad news of Daphnis' assumption by ceasing her usual acts of aggression: the wolf contrives no ambush for the flock nor sets snares against the deer. And the vision of "otium" restored culminates with Menalcas' affirmation: "amat bonus otio Daphnis" ("good Daphnis loves peace"). Tasso echoes that line with his "amat

Corinna l'ozio," but then he adds a curious interpolation of his own:

> Ama Corinna l'ozio e l'ozio è in cielo:
> ma la Fatica s'ange in su le porte
> de 'l tenebroso inferno, ove dolente
> sta fra la schiera d'infiniti mali.
>
> (105–08)

[Corinna loves leisure, and leisure is in heaven. But Toil torments herself at the gates of the shadowy underworld, where she grieves among the throng of innumerable evils.]

This sudden apparition of Fatica (or "Toil") writhing below at the gates of Hell has no precedent in the tradition and seems oddly out of place amid the usual scenes of other-pastoral delights. Tasso, it would appear, feels compelled to remind us (or remind himself) that there can be no peace until its opposite is first put away. But why fatica? why toil? Because Tasso's "ozio" has traveled a good distance from its original source in the Vergilian "otium": this is a peace opposed not to warfare but to work; it is, in short, leisure. Vergil envisions a pastoral world freed from aggression, so his herdsman-farmer can sing his songs and cultivate his fields. Tasso's vision betrays the weariness of an older and a more embittered poet; it is a release from labor, from the world of "fatica" altogether, for which he yearns.[13] And yearns for unrequitedly. Tasso's longed-for "ozio" seems continually to elude him. Here it exists only in heaven with the dead Corinna. And if only *there*, that is not because the ideal is itself a spiritual one. Tasso's "ozio" should not be equated with the unearthly peace for which Petrarch's elegist and (to a lesser extent) Boccaccio's yearn—no more than with the "otium" Vergil's herdsmen enjoy. This is essentially an ideal freedom from pain. When Tasso places it in heaven, with Corinna, he does not so much refine it as suggest its inaccessibility.

For the world of blissful repose and quietude Tasso describes is a world he will never enjoy. We feel indeed that we too are looking at the ideal from the outside now. But, as the poem progresses, we realize there is another landscape that makes a greater claim on us, demands that we believe in it if not desire it. The

"Vergilian" pastoral elegy has concluded with the usual exchange of gifts; other offerings are committed to the funeral pyre; but still Aminta remains disconsolate. Then, toward the end of this long narrative poem, the mourner takes up another motif from our convention: the demand that nature turn her order upside-down in sympathy with his sorrow. But the reversals Aminta calls for go beyond the usual pastoral ones in the degree of violence they entail:

> Tenebre, o voi che le serene luci
> m'ingombraste repente,
> coprite il cielo e i suoi spietati lumi,
> e minaccino sol baleni e lampi
> d'ardere il mondo e le celesti spere;
> stiasi dolente ascoso il sol ne l'onde,
> tema natura di petpetua notte.
> Tremi la terra, ed Aquilone ed Austro
> facciano insieme impetüosa guerra,
> crollando boshi e le robuste piante
> svelte a terra spargendo; il mar si gonfi,
> e con onde spumati il lido ingombri;
> volgano i fiumi incontro i fonti il corso.
>
> (586–98)

[You, darkness, who suddenly hid from my sight those orbs serene, cover the heavens and their pitiless lights, and let only lightening bolts and flashes threaten to burn both heaven and earth. Let the sun remain in mourning beneath the wave, and let nature fear an everlasting night. Let the earth tremble, and the North Wind and South Wind make fierce war against one another, felling the trees and scattering on the ground the strong, slender plants. Let the sea swell up and with spuming waves engulf the shore. Let rivers turn in their courses back toward their springs.]

This vision of cataclysmic destruction is far removed from those playful inversions of nature's order commanded by the Theocritean Daphnis, and equally remote from Vergil's vision of a world turned upside-down, where death is associated with barrenness, a failure of life. Tasso's vision of order overthrown is full of energy—of a baroque, stylized sort. Indeed all the vitality we miss in his pastoral landscapes seems to find its outlet here. For Tasso the pastoral Arcadian world, however seductive, is finally an illusion, a dream-world which (unlike Sannazaro's) lacks the necessary energy to sustain itself. When we awaken from the dream we find ourselves, significantly, in the world upside-down. This landscape, with its irrational violence, is the "real" world for Tasso, the real setting of his grief. This world, not the pastoral one of wished-for "ozio," is *here*.

Three Laments for the Royalty of France

MAROT, SCÈVE, RONSARD

The common feature of French pastoral poems is their intimate relation to the French court.[1] Where Italian pastoralists take the age-old dream of peace to a distant Arcadia, the French celebrate the stability (or relative stability) of their own homeland, an "otium" guaranteed by the Valois kings and queens to whom their eclogues are addressed.[2] Too often in these eclogues the courtier's voice drowns out the shepherd's and freedom is forfeited to flattery.[3] But not always. And sometimes a poet uses pastoral forms (and particularly the pastoral elegy) to explore anew the relationship between that guardian "custos" and the humbler world which depends on him for sustenance. In this chapter I will discuss three French pastoral elegies—for a queen mother, a prince and a king—which, in quite different ways, turn to advantage the conjunction of royal subject with pastoral setting.

The association between French pastoral poetry and the court begins with France's first pastoral poem, and first pastoral elegy: Clement Marot's lament for the queen mother, Louise of Savoy (1531). Marot's poem was highly praised at the court of Francis I when it was first presented and was still recalled in the days of the Pléiade poets as a model reincarnation of a classical form. Now at last (to paraphrase Du Bellay) had the tradition of Theocritus in Greek, Vergil in Latin and Sannazaro in Italian been translated into the French tongue and brought home to the French country[4]—

brought home indeed to its very heartland, its royal family. In bringing the pastoral elegy to France, Marot not only domesticates it (as Sannazaro had, for instance, in the neo-Latin "Phyllis"): he nationalizes it. In eulogizing his queen mother he eulogizes her realm, and in mourning her death he tells us what her countrymen have *all* lost. Marot's Louise, like Vergil's Daphnis, loves peace; and, like him, she stands for a peace larger than any leisure we may find in a private Arcadian world; it is our peace she loves, or (in the language of the Christian pastoralist) that of her sheep. "Et n'oubliez," says the poet to nymphs bearing offerings to her grave, "force branches d'Olive, / Car elle estoit la Begere de Paix." ("And do not forget many olive branches, for she was the shepherdess of peace" [239–40]).[5]

Marot expands the pastoral frontier, moreover, without sacrificing pastoral "hereness." Indeed, his lament conveys throughout an effect of considerable intimacy. This has to do, in part, with its female subject, and Marot's lament for Louise should be compared to Pontano's lament for his wife and Spenser's for Dido. But the intimacy we feel here has (like Spenser's) a second source: it is rooted in the earnest sincerity of the Christian moralist. To the concrete pleasures of the sweet world are now joined (and very nicely joined) the equally concrete duties of the Christian worker in this earthly mold. Marot's characteristic tone is well illustrated in the following passage, where the poet recalls how Louise would gather the young "shepherdesses" of the realm about her (the daughters of the French nobility, that is) and lecture them on the dangers of "oysiveté":

> Lors que Loyse en sa Loge prospere
> > Son beau mesnage en bon sens conduysoit,
> > Chascun Pasteur, tant fust il riche Pere,
> > Lieu là dedans pour sa Fille eslisoit.
> Aulcunesfois Loyse s'advisoit
> > Les faire seoir toutes soubz ung grand Orme,
> > Et elle estant au millieu leur disoit:
> > Filles, il fault que d'ung poinct vous informe;
> Ce n'est pas tout qu'avoir plaisante forme,

Bordes, trouppeaux, riche Pere et puissant;
Il fault preveoir que Vice ne difforme
Par long repos vostre aage florissant.
Oysiveté n'allez point nourrissant,
  Car elle est pire entre jeunes Bergeres
  Qu'entre Brebis ce grand Loup ravissant
  Qui vient au soir tousjours en ces Fougeres!
A travailler soyez doncques legeres!
  Que Dieu pardoint au bon homme Roger!
  Tousjours disoit que chez les Mesnageres
  Oysiveté ne trouvoit à loger.

(65–84)

[When Louise in her thriving abode managed her excellent household with discretion, every shepherd, however rich a father he might be, chose a place for his daughter there. Sometimes Louise would see fit to have them all sit under a great elm and being in their midst, she would say to them: "Daughters, I must inform you on one point. It is not everything to have a charming figure, lands, flocks, a father rich and powerful; you must take care lest through long idleness vice disfigure the bloom of your life. Do not encourage indolence, for this is worse among young shepherdesses than among the sheep is that big ravening wolf which always comes at evening to these thickets. So then be alert to work; may God pardon good Roger: he always said among good housewives indolence found no place."]

Here is yet another version of pastoral vitality: the royal matron expounding to her young charges the virtues of the active life, as described in the parable of Christ the good shepherd in John X. We will notice that Marot explicitly banishes from his pastoral world "indolence" ("oysiveté" here, "ozio" there)—the very thing that for Tasso constituted its chief attraction. This moralizing strain in an evangelical poet is one the reader may associate with the not-very-pastoral eclogues of Mantuan. But in Marot at least, Christian didacticism does not vitiate pastoral sweetness: the two are harmonized in the poet's tone of innocent, even clumsy, sincerity. Marot clothes the moralist's call to work in the pastoral metaphor of nourishment ("oysiveté" makes poor food for shepherdesses).[6] And he softens the sermon by couching it in the form of a mother's tender admonitions to her daughters. Still, this is a call to work.

The landscape in which Marot places his queen mother is a work-a-day world of simple pleasures and simple activities. In the opening frame, which once more recalls the Theocritean one,[7] Marot's herdsmen itemize for us the pleasures of their grove ("ces plaisirs excellens") in a matter-of-fact way, without embellishment. The Arcadian languorousness has disappeared: the little stream rushes ("bruyant") along its course.

Marot remembers Sannazaro's Arcadia, but he concretizes and demythologizes it as he brings it home to France. His Philomel and Procne are, or may be understood to be, simply weeping birds, not metamorphosed maidens:

> Sus Arbre sec s'en complaint Philomene;
>   L'aronde en faict cryz piteux & tranchans,
>   La Tourterelle en gemit & en meine
>   Semblable dueil; & j'accorde à leurs chants.
> (125–28)

[In the withered tree Philomena complains, the swallow utters piteous and piercing cries, the turtledove moans and shows like sorrow, and I am in accord with their songs.]

Marot remembers too Sannazaro's bountiful offering of flowers at the grave of the Arcadian Androgeo; but here again he particularizes and nationalizes. His flowers are emblems of the varied beauties of the royal realm, which now, at their queen mother's death, converge about the Valois grave. And we notice that in itemizing Sannazaro's fulsomeness, Marot turns the offering into a catalogue.[8] He asks us to see, not the lavishness of the gesture, but the flowers themselves, as they are presented one by one:

> Portez au bras chascune plein Coffin
>   D'herbes & fleurs du lieu de sa naissance,
>   Pour les semer dessus son Marbre fin,
>   Le mieulx pourveu dont ayons congnoissance!
> Portez Rameaulx parvenus à croissance,
>   Laurier, Lierre & Lys blancs honnorez,
>   Rommarin vert, Roses en abondance,
>   Jaulne Soulcie & Bassinetz dorez,

> *Passeveloux de Pourpre colorez,*
>   *Lavande franche, OEilletz de couleur vive,*
>   *Aubepins blancs, Aubefains azurez,*
>   *Et toutes fleurs de grand beaulté nayve!*
>   (225–36)

[Let each one bring in her arms a basket filled with herbs and flowers from the place of her birth, to scatter them upon her smooth marble tomb, the finest that we have knowledge of. Bear bouquets that are full blown: laurel, ivy, and glorious white lilies, green rosemary, abundant roses, yellow marigold, and golden crowfoot, coxcombs colored purple, lovely lavender, carnations of bright hue, white hawthorns, blue hawthorns, and every flower of great natural beauty.]

Thus it is Marot who first brings together the traditional funereal convocation about the grave with the equally traditional pastoral inventory of sweets. In transferring the conventional recital of pastoral pleasures ("here are oaks and galingale, here sweetly hum the bees . . . ") to a specific locale within this landscape, the grave-site, the elegist says in the most emphatic possible way: here too are sweet things—or, perhaps rather, here too sweet things can be *brought*. For the singer of the lament must extend himself somewhat further than the herdsman of the frame: the latter need only point; the former must bear the flowers to the grave, bring life's vitality to the scene of death and suffering. We may be surprised to realize that the catalogue of flowers has not been a part of our convention all along; it seems so succinct an expression of the pastoral elegist's way of seeing things. All the elements were indeed there before this; but it is perhaps appropriate that they are brought together, fused in a new *topos*, in Marot's lament for Louise. For as Marot places one bright, clear shape alongside another, we have a particularly strong sense of the "hereness," the palpability, of this mourner's world.

Indeed Marot takes pastoral "hereness" about as far as one can take it—takes it even *there*, beyond the threshold of heaven itself. His other-pastoral landscape emerges as an ideal domestic paradise where the queen-mother is entertained by her own favorite pet parrot!

> *Tous Animaulx plaisans y sont compris,*
> *Et mille Oyseaulx y font joye immortelle,*
> *Entre lesquelz volle par le pourpris*
> *Son Papegay qui partit avant elle.*
>
> (209–12)

[Every pleasant animal is found there, and a thousand birds give immortal joy, and among them about the place flies her parrot, which departed before her.]

In reading such passages as this, we may wonder whether the tone of artless naiveté, which Marot appropriates from the Theocritean herdsmen, is a tone deliberately assumed by this poet or is not rather his natural voice. I suspect that for Marot pastoral simplicity is something too closely allied to a very non-Theocritean moral earnestness to be in any sense "put on."

Marot's association of the pastoral world with the larger royal realm will be taken up again, and complicated, by later French pastoralists. Less congenial to them, however, is his infusion of this courtly realm with the humble didacticism and matter-of-factness of the Christian moralist. It remains for later generations of English Protestant poets to revive Marot's association of pastoral sweetness with Christian virtue. And it remains for them to inform Marot's Christian pastoral landscape with what it hardly contains here: a sense of the precariousness of that earthly peace.

Returning from Italy in 1536, Marot stopped in Lyon, where he was entertained by the poets of that city, foremost among whom was Maurice Scève. Scève would certainly have remembered Marot's lament for Louise when he composed (earlier in the same year) his own French pastoral elegy for her grandson, the Dauphin.[9] But Scève is heir to another tradition, one, we have seen, which Marot finds less congenial than the Lyonnais poet: the Italian one. In "Arion," one of the most curious and appealing of Renaissance pastoral elegies, Scève blends the courtly subject of Marot with the lyricism of the Italians to create a pastoral landscape wholly his own, a theatre for the poet's melancholy introspection. Scève's is the first pastoral elegy (unless we include Vergil's tenth *Eclogue*) to use the form to explore its own resources, particularly the resources of the Arcadian tradition. Scève is the first to ask whether this landscape, this literary tradition, *can* console us. Milton will ask the question again—ask it more insistently and answer it more affirmatively.

In "Arion" the pastoral landscape takes on a new complexity of surface. The sweet world is no longer a simple one. The intricacies of the poem begin with the way its royal subjects are introduced into the pastoral (or piscatory) setting. The elegist, Arion, represents the king, Francis I, who here mourns the premature death of his young son and heir. But Arion is also the Arion of the Greek legend, the lyrist who (according to the Ovidian version of the myth),[10] having been thrown overboard by sailors, was rescued by a dolphin which became so enraptured with the poet's song that he carried him on his back safely to the shore. The application of this myth to Scève's poem begins with the punning association of the dolphin of the legend with the dauphin lamented here. A further parallel is discovered in the events of the young prince's life: had he not also "rescued" a poet (Francis was a practitioner as well as a patron of the art) when, in return for his own imprisonment, he "allowed" his father to be freed from his Spanish captivity after the latter's defeat at Pavia? Thus the father laments the death of the "dolphin" who formerly ransomed him from death.[11] This allegory, as will be easily imagined, is not without its embarrassments for Scève; descriptions of the dauphin as the studious and sober prince do not sit well with descriptions of his aquatic adventures. But the real function of the Ovidian allegory is to transfer the whole subject from the actual world of the court to a marvelous, mythological realm. As Arion on his sorrowful shore looks back on what he has lost, the pastoral presents itself to his imagination as an exotic fantasy world, a world he alternately gathers about himself and dismisses.

Scève's poem is not really about the dauphin's death; it is not about the relation of the ruler to his people in the sense that Vergil's lament for Caesar, or Marot's for Louise, or Ronsard's for Henry II, is about that relation. What the elegist grieves for concerns us little more here than in the fictional world of Sannazaro's Arcadia. The subject is only the poet's point of departure, and the mourner Arion is not really the king but Scève himself. His true theme is not a public but a private one: to explore the ways in which the imagination responds to loss. What happens, the poet asks, when we place our sorrow in the fictive pastoral setting? Is this a healing or perhaps rather a destructive world? Where does the Arcadian melancholy finally lead us?

As the poem opens, with the unhappy Arion standing at the sea's edge, "Dessus le bort de la Mair coye, et calme,"[12] nature once more gathers round expectantly to hear the poet's song. But Scève sets the stage for a conventional pastoral lament only to frustrate our expectations. The accustomed sounds will be heard no more, Arion tells his marine listeners:

> Qu'escoutés vous Dieux de la mer patente,
> Tourbe marine autour de moy attente?
> Qu'escoutés vous,ô vous monstrueux poissons?
> Attendés vous les accoustumés sons
> De ceste Lyre enrouée, et ja casse?
>
> (5–9)

[What are you listening for, Gods of the open sea, marine herd attentive about me? And what are you listening for, oh you monstrous fish? Are you waiting for the accustomed sounds of this lyre, which is hoarse and already broken?]

And yet, this attentive world is not so easily cast off. Arion's very gesture of dismissal creates in its wake a whole train of new attractions:

> Attendés vour desormais qu'elle face
> A vour Tritons delaisser leurs doulsaines,
> Et oublier aux lascives Seraines
> Harpes, et Lutz, et chansons deceptives,
> Pour tousjours estre entour moy intentives?
> Prenés, Tritons, vous coquilles tortues,
> Tournés en Mair par les undes batues.
> Et vous aussi Seraines ennemies
> Des riches nefz, rendés les endormies,
> Et laissés cy languissant sus la rive

Arion plain de douleur excessive.
Laissés le errer dessus la moiste sable
Pleurant sans fin sa perte irrevocable.

(10–22)

[Do you, Tritons, expect that henceforth it (his lyre) will compel you to put down your conch shells, leaving harps, lutes and deceptive songs to the lascivious Sirens, to be always attentive about me? Tritons, take up your twisted shells, turned in the sea and buffeted by waves. And also you Sirens, enemies of rich ships, put them to sleep, and leave here languishing on the shore Arion overflowing with grief. Leave him to wander on the moist sand, weeping without end for his irrevocable loss.]

The consolations of pastoral are presented in a peculiarly seductive light here. Arion's lyre is aptly compared, first to the Triton's shell, twisted and turned by the sea's waves, and then to the siren's song, which lures rich ships from their appointed courses. Like both of those, Scève's own pastoral song, the poem itself, is highly polished, seductive, but also wayward, indeed, tortuous.

And, as Arion takes up the lament, we see again that melancholy has its own attractions, though what we termed self-absorption in Sannazaro and Tasso might better be called introspection here, as it takes its coloring from the highly speculative cast of this poet's imagination. His grief leads Arion into ever more intricate spirals of thought:

Et que je scay estre cy assemblés,
Cuydants, en vain, que ma Lyre provoque
Mort à pitié, ou bien que je revoque
Des bas enfers vostre espoir long temps mort,
Espoir pour qui mort avec luy me mord.
O vain desir des mortelz, et fragile,
Voulenté fraisle, inconstante, et agile.

(32–38)

[And whom (the marine herd) I know to be assembled here, hoping, in vain, that my lyre might provoke pity from Death, or else that I might release from the underworld your hope long since dead—hope for the one who, dead, consumes me with him. Oh vain and unstable desire of mortal man, with his frail, inconstant and ever-turning will.]

So here on his sea-shore the elegist turns and turns again, invoking one version of the pastoral and then another.

But the affirmations of pastoral seem reserved for the past, as in the passages where Arion recalls the dauphin's Spanish captivity and his joyful progress home again. So the father recalls how, at his son's departure, he skirted the swirling waters of the shore, calling "Dolphin," and again "Dolphin," while mountains and echoing shores took up the cry. And recalls how, at his release, nature joined in the celebration, bearing her "dolphin" home again with a splendid marine escort:

> Lequel laissant la grand Mair occeane
> Vint desiré en sa Mediterrane
> Accompaigné de meints divers Poissons,
> Qui autour luy gettoient meints joyeux sons
> De leurs clerons, trompettes et buccines,
> Tant que les boys et les roches voisines,
> De leurs doulx chants par tout retondissoient,
> Et près, et loing hautement remplissoient
> De l'haulte Mair les grands undes salées,
> Plaines, Marests, et umbreuses vallées.
> Vous, Dieux marins, sourtistes des abismes.
> Et vous, ô monts, elevastes vous cymes,
> Pour veoir venir le triumphant arroy
> Où il venoit coronné comme Roy.
>
> (93–106)

[The longed-for (Dolphin), leaving the open sea, entered his own Mediterranean accompanied by many kinds of fish, who swimming about him gave off many joyful sounds from their clarions, trumpets and whelks, so that the woods and the neighboring rocks reverberated with the sweet songs everywhere; near and far proudly they filled the great salt waves of the high sea, the plains, the marshes and the shady valleys. You, sea gods, arose from the depths; and you, oh mountains, raised up your crests, to see the triumphant procession approaching, as he came crowned like a King.]

Here Scève invokes the traditional progress of the pastoral (or piscatory) elegy—from nature's decay to her joyful rebirth, from separation to reunion, exile to "otium"—as with the dauphin's return a new era of European peace ("presque au monde expirée") is ushered in. But Scève presents it all as an exuberant fantasy, a *tour de force* of the imagination. It is only, he suggests, within the fiction of the Ovidian myth that the traditional pastoral sympathies between man and nature can be summoned.

For, as Arion returns to his present sorrows, the whole mythological allegory slips away and the poet is left alone with his grief. His present sorrow is one too deep for nature to share. Like Gallus, Arion banishes the pastoral woodlands; but with those woodlands now go all the attendant consolations—the various creatures, the little birds, the rivers that were wont to pause in their downward courses—which have found a place for themselves in these literary woods since Gallus' day. Scève dismisses the whole Renaissance tradition of pastoral consolation:

> Plus ne feras venir de toutes parts
> Tygres, Lyons, Cerfz, Ours, Dains, et Liepars
> Autour de moy, et les Loups ravissants
> Joindre aux Brebis et aux beufs, mugissants.
> Plus ne feras retarder le discours
> Au cler Phebus, et aux fleuves leur cours,
> Aux oyselets laisser leurs verds buissons
> Pour escouter tes armonieux sons. . . .
>   Or allés donc, Allés mes brebiettes.
> Plus ne lairrés la pasture des champs,
> Pour escouter mes soulacieux chants. . . .
>   Retirés vous donc, ô fiers animaulx
> Non congnoissants l'abisme de mes maulx.
>   (173–78; 194–96; 211–12)

[No more will your sounds (those of his lyre) summon from all parts tigers, lions, deer, bears, does and leopards about me, or hungry wolves alongside sheep and bellowing oxen. No more will you make clear Phoebus slow his discourse or the rivers their courses, or the little birds leave their green thickets to listen to your harmonious sounds. . . . Away with you now, go, my little sheep. No more leave off your feeding in the fields to hear my comforting melodies. . . . Retire, then, you fierce animals, ignorant of the depth of my suffering.]

Arion prefers in the end the way of withdrawal rather than renewal; and this too, we realize, is a "pastoral" way—a way chosen by Renaissance pastoralists if not by classical ones. His melancholy shore recalls the bleak seashore on which other Christian elegists before him have stood, contemplating man's frailty and the vanity of his earthly desires. But Arion's gaze, directed, not outward toward the shores of a more perfect world, but inward on his own emotions, suggests other sources for his melancholy: those Arcadian groves where Italian poets sighed for unrequited loves or wept for lost ones. In Arion's sea-shore the restless *contemptus mundi* of the Christian elegist is united with the languorous self-absorption of the Italian elegist. Here Scève leaves his Arion, looking for companionship neither to the sweet, animated world around him, nor to that more distant peace elsewhere, but to the "doulx languir" within:

> Donc pour plourer une si grande perte
> J'habiteray ceste terre deserte,
> Ou ce mien corps de peu, à peu, mourra,
> Et avec moy seulement demourra
> Pour compaignon sus ceste triste rive,
> Ung doulx languir jusqu'à la mort tardive.

(223–228)

[To bewail then so great a loss, I will live in this deserted country, where my body, little by little, will waste away. And the only companion to stay with me on this sad shore will be a sweet languor leading at last to a lingering death.]

And now Scève acknowledges that the ultimate end of this pastoral retreat, of the Arcadian "doulx languir," is death. Here, on Arion's deserted shore, the tradition of Arcadian lamentation, of "sweet sadness," which began with the exuberant songs of Sannazaro's herdsmen, has its end. It is to death the siren's songs are calling us; that is the final temptation. The sheltered pastoral world can lead us out of sorrow; but this retreat (we see more clearly now), as it involves us more deeply in ourselves and leads us away from the object of our suffering, away from a concrete world of things, may lead us finally to death itself.[13]

Marot is not embarrassed to dress his queen mother in humble shepherd's weeds; they do not compromise the simple dignity with which his poem invests her. Scève transfers his royal subjects to a mythological realm, where they speak to us primarily as figures of his own imagination, not as rulers. Ronsard's approach is unlike both these. First he creates a purified (in some respects, a restricted) pastoral landscape; then he asks his kings and queens, not whether they will condescend to play the parts of herdsmen, but whether they are fit to enter into the world he has created for them. More often than for living kings and queens, however, this ideal setting becomes in Ronsard's poetry the resting place of dead ones, reminders of a more perfect past.

Several years before he composed his long pastoral poem, the *Bergerie*, Ronsard had already made the association between a sanctified pastoral world and a royal gravesite. The "Ode, aux cendres de Marguerite de Navarre" (1555) places Margaret's death in an idealized classical landscape. Ronsard's pastoral world is classical in a rather special sense. It is not a particularly Vergilian landscape, but one in which classical nymphs and dryads and Vergilian reminiscences confer an air of sanctity. These classical presences exist in a world that is better than, purer than, and infinitely remote from, the one we know. It is to such a landscape that Ronsard transports Margaret, to a landscape of sweet herbs, fountains and flowers, where Naïades gather beneath the moon to play melodious songs on their flutes. His imitation of the Vergilian series of comparisons for Daphnis takes us away from the farm, with its vineyards and its herds of cattle, toward the open countryside:

> *Comme les herbes fleuries*
> *Sont les honneurs des prairies,*
> *Et des prez les ruisselets,*
> *De l'orme la vigne aimée,*
> *Des bocages la ramée,*
> *Des champs les bleds nouvelets,*
>
> *Ainsi tu fus, ô Princesse,*
> *Ainçois plustost, ô Deesse,*
> *Tu fus certes tou l'honneur*
> *Des Princesses de notre âge . . .*[14]

[As the flowering grasses are the honor of the plains, and of the meadowland the streams, of the elm the cherished vine, of the groves the green arbors and of the fields the wheat, so were you, oh Princess, rather, oh Goddess, you were truly all the honor of the princesses of our age . . .]

Indeed Ronsard banishes from Margaret's gravesite the herdsmen's very sheep:

> *Dites à vos brebites:*
> *"Fuyez-vous-en, camusettes,*
> *Gaignez l'ombre de ce bois;*
> *Ne broutez en ceste prée,*
> *Toute l'herbe en est sacrée*
> *A la Nymphe de Valois."*
>
> (67–72)

[(Shepherds,) tell your little sheep, "Away from here snub-nosed ones; take the shade of the woods, but don't graze in this meadow. All the grass here is sacred to the Nymph of Valois."]

Ronsard's pastoral is a world of holy innocence, calm and inviolate. The poet who composed one of his most eloquent laments for some venerable trees about to be felled for lumber,[15] pleads on behalf of the uncivilized forest rather than the cultivated farm. The only figures who inhabit this landscape are classical nymphs and dryads, creatures of a purer world, and the spirit of that other nymph, Margaret herself. Living kings and queens, as much as herdsmen and their sheep, would disturb this peace.

In the *Bergerie* Ronsard permits his holy pastoral world, the gravesite of a vanished age of innocence, to reverberate against the less-than-perfect one of political reality—with telling effect. The *Bergerie* is a series of eclogues, written for recital in the manner of a masque, and was probably performed in the spring of 1564 at Fontainebleau with real princes playing the parts of Ronsard's shepherd-singers. Thus the court poet dresses up his courtiers as shepherds, and puts in their own mouths the words which tell them how they ought to act. The message which emerges from this "play" is not without its ironies for the youthful speakers. The occasion of the courtly festival is the coming of age of the young monarch, Charles IX; and the center of the piece ought, therefore, to be the fourth eclogue—announcing the new "golden age" which is about to dawn. But the retrospective cast of Ronsard's pastoral vision keeps calling us—and those young princes so inadequate to the great tasks confronting them—backward. The thematic center of the piece becomes instead the second eclogue, a pastoral elegy for the old king, Henry II. And the whole eclogue series becomes an extended dirge for the old order which has died, rather than a celebration of the new one about to be inaugurated.

In the first shepherd's song we look back over the events of the past four years since Henry's death in 1559, years of intermittent but continuing religious civil war—warfare which would indeed tear the realm apart for the next thirty years. From the royal (and here, the pastoral) perspective, the Huguenots are the ravaging wolves; it is they who upset the established order of nature and devastate the farmer's fertile fields. The *Bergerie* is a plea—and a fervent one—to the young monarch about to assume his throne, that he be a second Daphnis, that he watch over his people and bring back a reign of peace. Yet, as we contemplate in this first song the unsettled world around us, we find ourselves looking backward, to the peaceful world we have lost, not to the promised reincarnation. And in the second song Ronsard puts into the mouth of another of his royal celebrants a full-scale lament for the old order which these too-frivolous courtiers have themselves helped to destroy.

Though only four years past, Henry's age emerges in Ronsard's lament as infinitely remote, an ideal golden age of innocence which we can hardly hope to recover. Ronsard's technique is necessarily just the opposite of Marot's. He does not want to familiarize Henry, but to distance him, to show us and his shepherd-singers how far they have departed from that ideal. So we see little here of Henry's specific accomplishments, little local color. Henry lived, not in the French landscape we know, but, like Margaret of Navarre, in a purer, antique world. He was what the vine is to the elm and the grape to the vine. Henry was a second Daphnis—that is, a second Caesar:

> Ce fut ce Henriot qui remply de bon-heur
> Remist des Dieux banis le seruice en honneur,
> Et se monstrant des arts le parfait exemplaire,
> Esleua iusqu'au ciel le gloire militaire.
>
> $$(15–18)^{16}$$

[This was the Henriot who, filled with prosperity, restored to honor the worship of the banished gods, and while showing himself the perfect exemplar of the arts, raised military glory to the sky.]

Ronsard's version of the gravesite rites is more "classical" than Vergil's own: here are no French nymphs bearing local gifts but pagan funeral games set to the music of the shepherd's pipe:

> Sois proprice à nos voeux: ie te feray d'yuoire
> Et de marbre vn beau temple au riuage de Loire
> Où sur le mois d'Auril aux iours longs & nouueaux
> Ie feray des combats entre les Pastoureaux
> A sauter, à luter sur l'herbe nouuellete,
> Pendant au prochain Pin le prix d'vne musette.
>
> (69–74)

[Be propitious to our vows. I will build thee a fair temple of ivory and of marble on the bank of the Loire, where in the month of April, when the days are long and new, I will have contests between the shepherd boys, in leaping, in wrestling on the fresh grass, while there hangs on the nearest pine the prize of a pipe.]

Henry, Ronsard suggests, belongs to that purer, antique age, that (above all) vanished age.

Like some other Christian elegists, Ronsard makes more of his departed saint's new life *there* than of our regeneration *here*. When Henry departs this world he takes (like Boccaccio's Olympia) its loveliness with him. But again we feel, as we have felt (perhaps somewhat uneasily) in several of these "Christian" Renaissance laments, that the sweetness of that other world is conceived as well as expressed in earthly terms. This is a sweetness everlasting but not otherwise radically different from the one we know—despite the reiterated "autres . . . autres." Or would *like* to know: for Ronsard (like Tasso) makes us feel the remoteness or, in his case, the *pastness* of the ideal world, but not (any more than Sannazaro) its otherness:

> *O Berger Henriot, en lieu de viure en terre*
> *Toute pleine de peur, de fraudes & de guerre,*
> *Tu vis là haut au Ciel, où mieux que parauant*
> *Tu vois dessous tes pieds les astres & le vent. . . .*
>
> *Où tu es, le Printemps ne perd point sa verdure,*
> *L'orage n'y est point, le chaud ny la froidure,*
> *Mais vn air pur & net, & le Soleil au soir*
> *Comme icy ne se laisse en la marine choir.*
>
> *Tu vois autres forests, tu vois autres riuages,*
> *Autres plus hauts rochers, autres plus verds bocages,*
> *Autres prez plus herbus, & ton troupeau tu pais*
> *D'autres plus belles fleurs qui ne meurent iamais.*
>
> (41–44; 57–64)

[Shepherd Henriot, instead of living on an earth full of fear, of deceit and of war, thou livest up yonder in Heaven, where better than before thou beholdest beneath thy feet the stars and the wind. . . . Where thou art, the springtime never loses its verdure, storms do not exist there, nor heat nor cold, but a pure and clear air, and the sun at evening does not, as here, allow himself to sink into the sea. Thou beholdest other forests, thou beholdest other shores, other higher rocks, other greener groves, other grassier meadows, and thou pasturest thy flock with other fairer flowers that never die.]

Henry's heaven is another version of Ronsard's ideal, golden-age landscape of unadulterated purity and calm[17]—a refuge, perhaps, not so much for the Christian saint as for the poet's own imagination.

The rites about the grave of Henry II have been completed; and the next eclogue in the *Bergerie* sequence begins with another shepherd's passionate inquiry whether that "bel âge doré . . . [de] pure innocence" will ever return again. Subsequent verses assure us that it is indeed about to be reincarnated in the new reign of Charles IX. But the *Bergerie* as a whole testifies to its author's better foresight, for everything in it associates that "bel âge doré" with the virtues of an age forever past. And while the poet appears to be flattering his royal actors, associating them with their ideal, "pastoral" selves, he is actually doing just the opposite: pleading that they too look backward, recover, if they can, the virtues of that earlier age. We do not expect that these Valois princes will correctly interpret the drama the poet has created for them. And so, in yet another sense, this pastoral celebration becomes, not a festival, but a lament, a pastoral elegy for France itself, which takes on a subtle irony as it is delivered by the unwitting rulers themselves.

6

Placing Sorrow in a Christian Landscape

SPENSER, SIDNEY,
AND THE LATER SPENSERIANS

In giving this large term "Christian pastoral" a somewhat restricted application in these pages, in reserving it for the poetic settings of the English laments to which we shall now turn, I mean to underline a point made earlier, but one central to my analysis of all these pastoral elegies: it is the whole setting in which the poet places his sorrow, and particularly this earthly setting (the world in which he lives, the world in which the poet sings) that consoles us here, not simply the doctrinal resolution of that sorrow to which he may or may not come in the end. And it is in English pastoral poetry that this earthly landscape becomes truly a Christian landscape, a place (to borrow the vocabulary of a later English pastoralist) charged "deep down things" with the grandeur of God. The English Renaissance poet does not come to this world like the Italian traveler, primarily to be soothed, nor like the French one, to mourn his country's loss. He may come for those things too; but first of all, he comes here to make sense out of suffering and death. The landscape to which this English pastoralist comes is, above all, a moral landscape. Marot, we have seen, had already modified the pastoral world along these lines by turning the sweet Theocritean grove into a setting for busy Christian workers. But that landscape becomes a far richer world as it is recolonized and reinterpreted by the larger poetic imaginations of Spenser and Milton.

To insist upon the primacy of this earthly setting for the pastoral elegist is not to deny the fuller consolations he may find elsewhere or their significance for the shape of his song as a whole (the movement from *here* to *there* and back again). It is rather to suggest that—at least in poetry—*that* imagined world follows *this* known one: it takes its color from the color of our earthly dreams, answers our human desires. Thus, in our pastoral elegies, Christian earthly settings will yield Christian images of the life hereafter; while other earthly settings yield other images of bliss, however nominally Christian these may be. If we hesitate to label "Christian" those heavenly pastures where the spirits of the dead recreate themselves (or repose) in Sannazaro's pastoral elegies or in Tasso's or perhaps in Ronsard's; and if we feel, on the other hand, that the "Christian" consolations granted other Renaissance pastoral elegists (as Petrarch and Boccaccio) are not, finally, very consoling—so strenuously do they deny the consolations of this earthly world; yet, when we come to Spenser and Milton, we know that "Christian" is the right name, the only name, both for those heavenly pastures and for these earthly ones. And *those* console because they answer now to needs which are felt (and in part realized) in *these*.

Spenser begins his poetic career as he ends it, with a pageant of the twelve months. And in the youthful songs of the *Shepheardes Calender* (1579), as in those last, uncompleted cantos of "Mutabilitie," the lively spectacle of the changing seasons helps us place more painful mutations in our own lives. The association of changing human states with changes in nature's world is, we know, as old as the pastoral tradition itself. "Clear sky one day, rain the next," said the Theocritean herdsman to cheer his unhappy friend: fluctuations in our human feelings are as much the rule as fluctuations in the weather. But Spenser wants to bring (we might say, needs to bring) these parallel fluctuations into some larger harmony. And he discovers that harmony by stepping backward to the point where the pattern underlying nature's changes is revealed : the pattern, that is, of seasonal alternation. In the *Shepheardes Calender* the carefree uncertainties of the Theocritean universe are sacrificed for the assurances of design. By casting his eclogue series in the novel form of a calender of the months, Spenser builds the association of human cycles and natural ones into the very structure of his pastoral universe.

Now rebirth follows death, rejoicing follows sorrow, as surely as November yields to May. Spenser's "November" eclogue, to which I now turn, thus enforces to a degree unique among Renaissance pastoral elegies the traditional sympathy between the human and non-human worlds, a sympathy which has its deeper justification here in Spenser's profound sense that human life and nature's life both flow from the divine order of things, that we are truly bound together in "natures kindly course." The pastoral sympathy becomes the expression of a deeper, Christian sympathy. Yet just because we do see God's virtue working itself out in this earthly soil, we long more intensely now to see that virtue, not just *here* but *there*—at its source, where our soul has its true home.

But "November," like the other months of the *Calender*, is set in this earthly world, and it is with its cyclical rhythms that we begin and end. The opening verses of the framing dialogue between the shepherds establish the basic pattern of seasonal alternation and link the naturalistic cycle to the human one. As we made mirth in May, so now we must grieve in November:

> *Thenot:* Colin, *my deare, when shall it please thee sing,*
> *As thou were wont songs of some iouisauance?*
> *Thy Muse to long slombreth in sorrowing,*
> *Lulled a sleepe through loues misgouernaunce.* . . .
>
> *Colin:* Thenot, *now nis the time of merimake.*
> *Nor* Pan *to herye, nor with loue to playe:*
> *Sike myrth in May is meetest for to make,*
> *Or summer shade vnder the cocked haye.*
> *But nowe sadde Winter welked hath the day* . . .
> (1–4; 9–13)[1]

The death of Spenser's Dido, then, will be set in this dying November world; and in Colin's song, "November"'s song, we mourn the death of May and the whole May world. E. K., Spenser's mysterious annotator, tells us that in the figure of Dido

Spenser represents "some maiden of great bloud."[2] She is otherwise unidentified. And best she remain so; for in the figure of Dido Spenser represents both the gentlest, most delicate flowerings of the human spirit and the largest cosmic forces of light and life. Dido, Thenot says, is "the greate shepehearde his daughter sheene: / The fayrest May . . . that euer went" (38–39).[3] She is identified with the sweet, short-lived blossoms of spring—

> The fayrest floure our gyrlond all emong,
> Is faded quite and into dust ygoe.
>
> (75–76)

and, as the song unfolds, with the easy, unstinting generosity of nature herself:

> She, while she was, (that was, a woful word to sayne)
> For beauties prayse and plesaunce had no pere:
> So well she couth the shepherds entertayne,
> With cakes and cracknells and such country chere.
> Ne would she scorne the simple shepheards swaine,
>   For she would cal hem often heme
>   And giue hem curds and clouted Creame.
>   O heauie herse,
>   Als Colin cloute she would not once disdayne.
>   O carefull verse.
>
> (93–102)

This scene of pastoral hospitality, with Dido at its center, reminds us of Marot's image of Louise at the center of her circle of shepherdesses. And, as E. K. points out, Marot's poem is Spenser's immediate source here. But we do not feel that the literary echoes are fundamentally sustaining in "November," as they are, for instance, in Castiglione's or Milton's pastoral elegies. The reminiscences of Marot remain superficial; for it is not that others have been here before us that makes this landscape so dear. It is that this is Nature's world, and God's. Dido and her landscape owe less to specific literary sources (Renaissance or classical) than to the common Renaissance heritage of traditional Christian imagery and ways of patterning experience.

Dido, the May flower, is also the emblem of the Christian law of Kinde—that kinship which, binding all nature's creatures together, brings with it kindliness. At the maiden's death this whole moral order threatens to come undone. And thus Spenser brings to the pastoral elegy's scene of nature's sympathetic grief a sense of larger dislocation. Yet, as so often in our convention, traditional sympathies are reaffirmed even as they are turned "upside-down"; and here nature shows her kindliness once more as she mourns Dido's death:

> Ay me that dreerie death should strike so mortall stroke,
> That can vndoe Dame natures kindly course:
> The faded lockes fall from the loftie oke,
> The flouds do gaspe, for dryed is theyr sourse,
> And flouds of teares flowe in theyr stead perforse.
>> The mantled medowes mourne,
>> Theyr sondry colours tourne.
>>> O heauie herse,
>> The heauens doe melt in teares without remorse.
>>> O carefull verse.
>
> The feeble flocks in field refuse their former foode,
> And hang theyr heads, as they would learne to weepe:
> The beastes in forest wayle as they were woode,
> Except the Wolues, that chase the wandring sheepe.
>
> (123–36)

It is a peculiarly tender scene, its tenderness perhaps accentuated by the sweetness of the verse form, whose rhymes return in diminishing intervals as we approach the final, short refrain line: here too the evidence of order works to cancel the message of disorder. Spenser follows Marot in banishing the wolves (who howled, as we recall, at the first Daphnis' death) from his scene of grieving nature. He does not want (anymore than Marot) a hyperbolic sorrow to invite our wonder—or perhaps our disbelief. He wants us rather to feel that *of course* nature (a kindly nature, at once intimate and grand) will weep for us. But there is more even than this. For Spenser need not, of course, have mentioned the wolves at all; or he might, like Marot, simply have told us they abstained from the general sorrow.[4] But Spenser's wolves do more than abstain; they introduce a note of active malignancy. They suggest that, at least on the fringes of this kindly, Christian world, all may not be well, all may not be kindly. Spenser does not make much of these wolves. But they are there; and they and their shadowy forms are related to other intimations in the poem of a sorrow which threatens to go out of all bounds, beyond the alternations of May and November. Those darker possibilities are, in their turn, answered only by the final, triumphant vision of a stable world beyond the perpetual alternations of this earthly one.

But the Christian pattern of death and resurrection is not superimposed on the naturalistic one of growth and decay only at the poem's conclusion; it is there all along. In Dido's death, in the fading of that May flower, we mourn from the very start all our deaths—and Adam's sin which first brought death into the world. Indeed, throughout the poem Spenser moves with breath-taking ease from images of Dido as queen of country cheer, dispensing cakes and cream to Kentish shepherds, to intimations of a universal darkness:

> Shepheards, that by your flocks on Kentish downes abyde,
> Waile ye this wofull waste of natures warke:
> Waile we the wight, whose presence was our pryde:
> Waile we the wight, whose absence is our carke.
> The sonne of all the world is dimme and darke:
>   The earth now lacks her wonted light,
>   And all we dwell in deadly night,
>   O heauie herse.
>
> (63–70)

It would be interesting to know whether Spenser read Vergil's *Eclogues* as he read other works of classical antiquity: in Christianized form. Might he have seen, for instance, Vives' gloss on the fifth *Eclogue*, with its interpretation of Daphnis' death as a prophesy of the death of Christ and its reminder of the sun's eclipse at the Savior's death? Very likely he would have. But Spenser would *in any case* have seen Dido's death, and all our deaths, in Christian terms, as types of that death; he would, in any case, have superimposed upon the naturalistic pattern of decay and regeneration the Christian pattern of suffering and spiritual renewal. What is important for us to recognize here is that Spenser does *not* do what the allegorist does: he does not translate the naturalistic event into the spiritual one. In the passage I have just quoted we could not (and should not attempt to) distinguish the death of the woman, Dido, which makes the day seem like night to us, from, on the one hand, the dimming of the sun's light as May yields to November, or, on the other hand, the grand, sacrificial death of the Son himself. The point is that for Spenser Dido's death implies all these things; and Dido herself is the beloved maiden, the May flower and the type of Christ.

Or, is all these up to a point. For the maiden and the May are not, finally, one. And the acknowledgment of separateness (traditional, we know, in the pastoral elegy) comes with a special shock here just because the two have been so closely united in that kindly order which is, ultimately, God's order. Spenser makes the most of the shock. For, as he invokes the pastoral elegy's traditional distinction between the returning vegetation and the finality of human life in this world, he cuts away all the instances of nature's renewal—the sun in its diurnal course, all the different kinds of herbs and trees whose green leaves return again in the spring—everything but the one thing, the flower, most associated with Dido herself. And now he invokes that association once more, and most poignantly, as he qualifies it:

> Whence is it, that the flouret of the field doth fade,
> And lyeth buryed long in Winters bale:
> Yet soone as spring his mantle doth displaye,
> It floureth fresh, as it should neuer fayle?
> But thing on earth that is of most availe,
>   As vertues braunch and beauties budde,
>   Reliuen not for any good.
>   O heauie herse,
> The braunch once dead, the budde eke needs must quaile,
>   O carefull verse.
>   (83–92)

What is painful here is not simply the recognition (as we saw it elaborated, for instance, in Castiglione's "Alcon") that nature's living things revive in the following season while we do not; it is the sense of being so much a part of nature's world—belonging to her flourishing realm as branch and bud belong, being indeed the thing on earth "that is of *most* avail," just because we *are* virtuous— and still being cut off from nature's consolations.

With the recognition of our unique frailty as humans, "November" begins its descent into despair. And at the bottom of that descent, the narrator, in what has been up to now an impersonal lament, cries out in his own voice, Spenser's voice:

> O trustlesse state of earthly things, and slipper hope
> Of mortal men, that swincke and sweate for nought,
> And shooting wide, doe misse the marked scope:
> Now haue I learnd (a lesson derely bought)
> That nys on earth assuraunce to be sought:
>   For what might be in earthlie mould,
>   That did her buried body hould,
>   O heauie herse,
> Yet saw I on the beare when it was brought
>   O carefull verse.

(153–62)

"Yet saw I on the beare when it was brought." There is the naked fact. Pastoral and its consolations seem to slip away from us as the narrator and his subject (death itself) come into sharper focus. In this stanza (which has no equivalent in Marot's lament) we hear once more the voice of the Christian wanderer in this world. It is a recurrent voice in Spenser's poetry, along with other voices. Now suddenly all the activities of the pastoral world seem misplaced, purposeless. For our end lies elsewhere: there "nys on earth assuraunce to be sought." Like Vergil, Spenser asks not how sweet a world? but how long-lasting a one? For him, however, the eternal oscillations of the *Calender*, of "otium" and exile, are not, finally, enough.

Yet from this mutable, cyclical world we may be granted a vision of the world beyond all change. The vision of that stable order follows immediately upon the speaker's outcry in the preceding stanza and it answers his despair: *here* is no assurance, but *there* is. It is the inevitable answer, the answer we have seen elsewhere—in Petrarch, Boccaccio, Sannazaro, Marot and Ronsard. Yet we have also seen that this same answer, this by now highly conventional account of *other* groves and *other* streams, is presented with considerable range of feeling and thus means something quite different to each one of these poets. Spenser's version of the Christian answer is in several respects unique and is, I think, compared with others we have seen thus far, uniquely moving. This is so for several reasons. First, Spenser's reversal is won, not simply declared. It is presented as a glorious victory (re-enacting Christ's great victory) in the eternal combat of the soul against the forces of death and darkness. Spenser's reversal, then, is not the denial of death we have seen elsewhere, but the active conquest over it. Here we must first descend to hell and break those deadly bonds before we can ascend to heaven. And the victory is an affirmation of pastoral vitality as it is an affirmation of life itself. It is a liberation, a breaking of bonds, a triumph of light over darkness, which catches up and confirms the earlier images in the poem of alternation between May sunshine and November darkness. Now pastoral light and freedom are translated to a higher sphere:

> But maugre death, and dreaded sisters deadly spight,
> And gates of hel, and fyrie furies forse:
> She hath the bonds broke of eternall night,
> Her soule vnbodied of the burdenous corpse.
> Why then weepes Lobbin so without remourse?
>   O Lobb, thy losse no longer lament,
>   Dido nis dead, but into heauen hent.
>   O happye herse,
> Cease now my Muse, now cease thy sorrowes sourse,
>   O ioyfull verse.

(163–72)

Spenser's pastoral muse thus traces the traditional epic progress and wages in miniature the traditional epic battle between good and evil: we look from the humble pastoral fields down to hell and up to heaven. What is remarkable is that the grandeur and sweep of that epic journey seem so effortlessly contained within the slender pastoral form. There is an epic gravity at moments in the *Shepheardes Calender* just as there is a pastoral sweetness in the *Faerie Queene*, and neither seems out of place. We feel no tension, no strain, here, I suppose, because Spenser himself evidently feels none: to him it is only natural to perceive in the simple world of the English herdsmen the working out of God's grand design. Indeed, that design may be more visible in these open fields than elsewhere.

This brings us to the other important point about Spenser's handling of the conventional reversal. He presents it, not only as a victory for Dido herself, but as a vision, a moment of seeing—for the narrator, for us—a vision which answers the non-seeing, the aimlessness, the missed marks of the preceding stanza. Now the narrator says joyfully:

> I see thee blessed soule, I see,
> Walke in Elisian fieldes so free.
> O happy herse . . .
> (178–80)

So many heavenly groves in Renaissance pastoral elegies have been defined as unseen worlds, places inaccessible to us. But what Spenser's poem grants us, its consolation if we will, is precisely a vision of that otherwise unseen world.

It remains an *other* world, no mere extension of this one— hence our joyfulness. Dido's "fields ay fresh [and] grass ay greene" are not in any earthly pastures. For here death is a freeing of the spirit, a release of the soul from the "burdenous corpse," a release from the world of alternation. We know the pleasures of this earthly world in "November"; but we also know that the pleasures Dido now enjoys are those "that mortall men do misse" (196). It is, in short, a Christian heaven, and the fact is only underlined for us when Spenser calls these fields *Elisian*. He does not have to tell us (as Milton will) that this is the name he gives to a Christian paradise; it would not occur to us that it could be anything but that.

The vision of that paradise is, however, but a vision, a *moment* of seeing: the fact of separateness remains. And the following line gives voice to the longing that still remains unfulfilled: "Might I once come to thee (O that I might) . . ." That is not to be—at least not yet.

The final lines of the poem bring us back to the alternations of the *Calender*:

> Ay francke sheheard, how bene thy verses meint
> With doolful pleasuance, so as I ne wotte,
> Whether reioyce or weepe for great constrainte?
> Thyne be the cossette, well hast thow it gotte.
> Vp Colin vp, ynough thou morned hast,
> Now gynnes to mizzle, hye we homeward fast.
>
> (203–08)

We do indeed have an impression of mixed emotions as we read these last lines, and of mixed origins too. Typically in the concluding frame the herdsmen draw back from the greater emotional intensity of the lament. Spenser's version of this withdrawal combines two different traditions. There is, on the one hand, the classical return to the sweet world of pastoral, the affirmation of nature's on-going vitality, the exchange of gifts. Sannazaro, Marot (Spenser's immediate source here), and Ronsard are among the Renaissance pastoral elegists who continue that tradition. But we have seen—in Petrarch, in Boccaccio, and (in a secularized form) in Castiglione and Scève—a very different kind of withdrawal at the song's close: the elegist's return to a landscape of suffering and isolation, a landscape whose vitality seems more depleted for the poet's glimpse of greener pastures elsewhere. Spenser's "doolful pleasaunce" expresses a mingling of these two responses. He retains the exchange of gifts: the song itself is one; it *has* brought joy to the herdsmen: Thenot makes his presentation in turn; his little goat (like its distant Theocritean ancestor) recalls us to nature's world. These herdsmen, moreover, are not left standing on a lonely shore; like their Vergilian predecessors, they have a home to return to. Sorrow, Thenot suggests, has run its course; the lament has been placed in the sweet world of pastoral once more. But sadness still lingers in the damp November air here, and home, perhaps, is but a shelter from the storm. We know, as the cycle of "iouisaunce" and "sorrowing" comes round full circle, that we will weep again in another November. There is joy in the return because we have been granted from these pastoral fields a vision of the world beyond this one, a vision which gives meaning to the pastoral cycle of decay and regeneration. There is sorrow mixed with the joy because, having seen a vision of "fields ay fresh [and] grasse ay greene," one returns with difficulty to the world of change.

The "doolful pleasaunce" Thenot feels here is a recurrent emotional state in Spenser's poetry; its mingling of moods is something we come to associate particularly with the endings of his poems.[5] And the vision of an order underlying the alternations of this world below the moon, the vision granted to the herdsman-poet in "November," is the same vision for which a less sanguine poet ardently prays in the very last line Spenser wrote of the *Faerie Queene*:

> When I bethinke me on that speech whyleare,
>   Of Mutability, and well it way:
>   Me seemes, that though she all vnworthy were
>   Of the Heav'ns Rule; yet very sooth to say,
>   In all things else she beares the greatest sway.
>   Which makes me loath this state of life so tickle,
>   And loue of things so vaine to cast away;
>   Whose flowring pride, so fading and so fickle,
> Short Time shall soon cut down with his consuming sickle.
>
> Then gin I thinke on that which Nature sayd,
>   Of that same time when no more Change shall be,
>   But stedfast rest of all things firmely stayd
>   Vpon the pillours of Eternity,
>   That is contrayr to Mutabilitie:
>   For, all that moueth, doth in Change delight:
>   But thence-forth all shall rest eternally
>   With Him that is the God of Sabbaoth hight:
> O that great Sabbaoth God, graunt me that Sabaoths sight.
>
> (VII, 8, i–ii)

These two stanzas are built around the same opposition, between the cyclical alternations of the *Calender* and the steadfastness of Eternity, that we have seen in "November," the opposition which makes Thenot, who belongs to both worlds, feel a "doolful pleasaunce" at the poem's end. It is the same opposition, but Spenser's way of seeing things has changed. In the sweet world of the *Shepheardes Calender*, that "flowering pride, so fading and so fickle," is for all its transience still very dear to us. And, if this ephemeral world does indeed "in Change delight," we too delight as well as grieve with the shepherds at those changes. For what is made visible to the herdsmen of the *Shepheardes Calender*—the operations of the divine will working through "nature's kindly course" in this mutable world—may be less apparent in the dark and tangled woods of the *Faerie Queene*. And the vision granted to the pastoral poet, that of a world beyond all change (that "Sabaoths sight"), is the same vision yearned for but unrealized in the final cantos of the epic poem. For Spenser (as for Milton) the pastoral field is not so much a secluded spot on nature's map, a "hideaway," as a place from which we *can* see—see the moral order which underlies and makes sense of our human suffering.[6]

Most of the English pastoral poetry composed in the late sixteenth century (and there is a great deal of it) follows the Spenserian model: local in setting, naive in diction, frequently didactic in its ends. But Sidney goes another way; and indeed it may be that his "Dicus" (*Old Arcadia* 75), and not Spenser's "November," is the first English pastoral elegy. Here as elsewhere the two greatest poets of their age appear to have proceeded independently of one another and to have pursued different paths.[7] Where Spenser brings the pastoral elegy home to a Christian, English landscape and bends his eclogue series into the cyclical form of a farmer's almanac, Sidney follows Sannazaro (and Montamayor) back to the exotic Arcadian fantasy-world, where he sets his eclogues down, in clusters of several poems each, to mark the divisions between the "acts" of a romantic narrative. Yet Sidney follows Sannazaro (as recent criticism has suggested)[8] in a spirit of sceptical inquiry; and the apparent deviation of his pastoral poems from the main line of the English convention comes to seem less real as we engage them more deeply. Many of these Arcadian eclogues are taut and probing in a way that sets them quite apart from Sannazaro's. There is an insistent quality to the Arcadian music now, a seriousness with which the poet questions his world that is more reminiscent of Spenserian gravity than Sannazaro's ebullient optimism. If Dicus' lament, set in a quasi-pagan landscape, cannot be called a Christian poem, Sidney nevertheless uses the form to ask questions other Christian poets (and particularly other English ones) are asking. His poem is an expressive statement of the Renaissance elegist's desire to *be* expressive, to make himself heard, and of his sense that he can no longer take that expressiveness for granted. Making music out of grief is not so easy for Sidney as it was for Sannazaro, even in (or perhaps especially in) Arcadia.

"Dicus" is modeled on Sannazaro's eleventh Arcadian eclogue (discussed above), and Sidney sets his song in the same spiraling terza-rima verses. The occasion for the lament is the presumed death of the Arcadian king Basilius. But again, as with Sannazaro, the occasion is no more than an occasion. (Here, in fact, it later turns out that the king has not actually died; that is not important.) What is important, once again, is what the poet can "make" of his suffering. Sidney begins where Sannazaro began, seeking to insinuate his human feelings and human words into the non-human world around him:

> Since that to death is gone the shepheard hie,
>   Who most the silly shepheard's pipe did pryse,
>   Your dolefull tunes sweete Muses now applie.
>
> And you ô trees (if any life there lies
>   In trees) now through your porous barkes receave
>   The straunge resounde of these my causefull cries:
> And let my breath upon your braunches cleave,
>   My breath distinguish'd into wordes of woe,
>   That so I may signes of my sorrowe leave.
>
> (1–9)[9]

The "porous" Arcadian tree trunks are still there; but we are conscious now of the pressure the elegist must exert if he would penetrate their bark. Sidney pauses to inquire if there really is any life (any sympathy for human suffering) in trees. There may be, but we have to work for it here; and it is this sense of the effort involved—to penetrate those barks, to make oneself heard—that Sidney's lament conveys so forcefully. "Dicus" registers the pressure with an almost physical intensity, as the elegist seeks to leave some mark, some imprint of his sorrow, on his world. No longer can the elegist's voice glide smoothly (as Sannazaro's did) over the surface of things: it must "cleave" the branches of the trees if nature is to know and share its sorrows. Nor are the sounds of this elegist's voice blurred together: Sidney represents his human breath (in what may well be a conscious revision of Sannazaro's mode) as "distinguish'd" (like the separate blows of the hammer) into separate "words of woe." Like Spenser's, but unlike Sannazaro's, Sidney's pastoral elegist feels, and feels acutely, the distinctions as well as the sympathies between the human and nonhuman worlds.

Feels them, indeed, more strongly than Spenser. As the poem continues, the possibility that nature may be deaf to the poet's human song becomes increasingly real. And as it does, the sense of pressure intensifies. Sannazaro's gentle sighs will not serve this elegist: he must fill the woods with "roaring" if he wants his complaint to echo even to the heavens:

> O Echo *all these woods with roaring fill,*
> > *And doo not onely marke the accents last,*
> > *But all, for all reach not my wailefull will:*
> One Echo *to another* Echo *cast*
> > *Sounde of my griefes, and let it never ende,*
> > *Till that it hath all woods and waters past.*
> *Nay to the heav'ns your just complayninges send . . .*
> > (31–36)

The complaint may be just, but will it be heard? Sidney gives us (and gives us wonderfully) the elegist's wish to make his voice heard, to have his sorrows shared, rather than (like Sannazaro) the desire realized. For, as he puts it some lines later in the language of pastoral, perhaps there is no longer any *place* for the poet's sorrows in this world:

Alas, me thinkes, my weakned voice but spilleth,
The vehement course of this just lamentation:
Me thinkes, my sound no place with sorrow filleth.
                              (97–99)

"Non canimus surdis," said Vergil at the beginning of his tenth *Eclogue*, "respondent omnia silvae" ("we do not sing to the deaf; the woods echo our every word"). The knowledge that the echoing woods are *here* is, in the simplest sense, what the pastoral elegy—or at least the classical pastoral elegy—is all about. But the Renaissance elegist is, for the various reasons we have analyzed in these pages, less sure of that fundamental sympathy. Dicus' "roaring" expresses the fear that the listening woods may no longer be attentive to his cries. His poem questions the sweetness and serenity of the classical laments as well as those of Sannazaro. Dicus' insistent "roaring" should be set, not only against the soft sighs of the Arcadian shepherds, but also against the self-containment of the original Daphnis, who bears his bitter love deep within himself until he is ready to take leave (in sweet, measured terms) of his world. Sidney's Dicus lacks Daphnis' restraint as he lacks his assurance of belonging (in a very concrete, immediate way) to his world. His poem is about the Renaissance elegist's loss of that classical poise. There is music to be made here too, out of this elegist's more violent encounter with less penetrable rocks and trees. But it is another kind of music, one that looks forward to the "hideous roar" and harsher cadences of "Lycidas" as much as back to the easier sighs with which Sannazaro's herdsmen disburden themselves of their sorrows. Milton will give us both the "roaring" and the assurance that we are, for all that, still bound (as Spenser knew he was bound) to nature's wheel.

But in "Dicus" we feel increasingly estranged from nature. We notice, for instance, a telling shift in emphasis in Sidney's version of the *topos* contrasting nature's annual renewal with human mortality. Now it is mind that sets us apart from nature, and as much apart in life as in death. For as we must sink below her then, so now we proudly rise above her:

The filthy snake her aged coate can mende,
  And getting youth againe, in youth doth flourish:
  But unto Man, age ever death doth sende.
The very trees with grafting we can cherish,
  So that we can long time produce their time:
  But Man which helpeth them, helplesse must perish.
Thus, thus the mindes, which over all doo clime,
  When they by yeares' experience get best graces,
  Must finish then by death's detested crime.
We last short while, and build long lasting places:
  Ah let us all against foule Nature crie:
  We Nature's workes doo helpe, she us defaces.
                                                    (82–96)

We may teach nature how to perpetuate her kind, but the instinctive sense of being a part of that kindly course, even as we are distinguished from it, is absent here; and in the last lines of this stanza the human and nonhuman worlds are coupled only in their mutual antagonism.

With Sidney's proud image of men's minds, "which over all doo clime," his poem too climbs beyond the bounds of pastoral. For Spenser, we said, such boundaries do not exist: pastoral is the place from which the larger pattern—of the Calender and, beyond that, of God's providence—becomes visible. But Sidney must go, feels he has to go, outside this pastoral world in order to make sense out of things. In the last stanza of the poem he dismisses the pastoral woodlands and, with them, the fluid attenuated rhythms of the opening stanzas. The melancholy Arcadian singer makes way for the Christian moralist, who speaks now on behalf of a whole society and voices his complaint in the impersonal terms and heavy, alliterative, end-stopped cadences we associate with the English pageant and morality-play tradition rather than Arcadian romance:

Justice, justice is now (alas) oppressed:
  Bountifulness hath made his last conclusion:
  Goodnes for best attire in dust is dressed.
Shepheards bewaile your uttermost confusion;

> *And see by this picture to you presented,*
> *Death is our home, life is but a delusion.*
>
> (118–23)

So, in the end, Sidney shares with the English pastoral elegist the need to make sense out of death, as he shares the Italian poet's wish to make something sweet of it. If he cannot penetrate Arcadian trees and rocks, if they may no longer be sympathetic to his song, there are other melodies and others who may have ears to hear them. There is more than one way of making music out of suffering. But in "flying higher," may we not sacrifice the consolations peculiar to pastoral—the intimacy, the sweetness, the sense of *hereness*? This is the question with which the poem ends:

> *. . . But ah; my Muse hath swarved,*
> *From such deepe plaint as should such woes descrie,*
> *Which he of us for ever hath deserved.*
> *The stile of heavie hart can never flie*
> *So high, as should make such a paine notorious:*
> *Cease Muse therefore: thy dart ô Death applie;*
> *And farewell Prince, whom goodnesse hath made glorious.*
>
> (136–42)

Sidney's pastoral elegy is not so much an exercise *in* the convention as a highly self-conscious and critical exploration of its resources. In this respect its closest relative among the poems we have discussed here is perhaps Scève's "Arion." In both these laments we feel the speaker is more concerned about the possibility of sharing his feelings (whatever they may be) than about the particular occasion for his grief. And both are acutely aware how hard it is to share their feelings, how hard now to create that sympathetic listening world of nature in which the lament might be *placed*. Yet these two poems—straining the pastoral bonds of sympathy to their extreme limit, stressing all that distinguishes man and nature and makes his feelings hard to share—remind us all the more forcefully that for the Renaissance pastoral elegist, as for his classical predecessor, the great issue is the issue of *communication*. The modern poet, or the Romantic one, cares more about finding words than about sharing them. We speak *sotto voce*, no more seeking to be heard than feeling the need for it. But if we turn inward in our grief, the Renaissance elegist still looks outward—looks to some larger world that, as it shares his suffering, helps him resolve it. He is less sure, however, than his classical predecessor that the echoing woods are there. Sidney's poem dramatizes with great force the elegist's efforts to make himself heard, using words almost as physical counters to beat against a now-receptive, now-resistant nature. So his words, still seeking that sympathy, seeking to make their impact felt, now beat against the branches of the trees, now "roar" against the heavens; spill themselves and then gather together again; reach out to some wider world beyond the woodlands, collapse in upon themselves and finally cease.[10]

The ten years following Sidney's death in 1586 mark the height of the pastoral elegy's popularity in England, with Sidney himself, the flower of the Elizabethan world, untimely plucked, its chief subject. Of the seven tributes to Sidney in the "Astrophel" volume (1595) three, including Spenser's contribution,[11] fall within the range of the Renaissance convention, while two more allude to it intermittently.[12] Indeed it is difficult to write a funeral lament in these years without alluding to the pastoral elegy convention.[13] This can be attributed in part to the prestige of Spenser, echoes of whose "November" eclogue are heard continually in all these laments. It has to do also with the spirit of the age itself. England in the last decade of the sixteenth century is particularly receptive to the pastoral, and perhaps especially to the pastoral elegist's way of seeing things. Men might still be mourned, as Sidney is, under the aspect of a flower. To simplify is not yet to distort, but to clarify the nature of the ideal. And, at the same time, there is a consciousness of this simpler world's passing. The years following the Armada victory are years in which men see themselves as living at the end of an era. The great Elizabethans (Sidney, Raleigh, Walsingham) are dead; the death of Elizabeth herself is imminent. Nostalgia is in the air, as palpable as the breath of the plague which swept through London in the summer of 1592.

Thomas Nashe captures the spirit of these years in the opening song of his pageant, *Summers Last Will and Testament* (1592)—and captures it, significantly, in the language of the pastoral elegy:

Fayre Summer droops, droope men and beasts therefore:
So fayre a summer looke for neuer more.
All good things vanish, lesse then in a day,
Peace, plenty, pleasure, sodainely decay.
  Goe not yet away, bright soule of the sad yeare;
  The earth is hell when thou leau'st to appeare.

What, shall those flowres that deckt thy garland erst,
Vpon thy graue be wastfully disperst?
O trees, consume your sap in sorrowes sourse;
Streames, turne to tears your tributary course.
  Goe not yet away, bright soule of the sad yeare;
  The earth is hell when thou leau'st to appeare. [14]

Like the pastoral elegist, Nashe achieves intensity by appealing to simple things—"Peace, pleasure, plenty"—while reminding us that these universal blessings are, like the summer season itself, among the most ephemeral of life's gifts. Like the pastoral elegist, he celebrates a world where men and nature are linked in bonds of sympathy and love. When summer droops, men and beasts droop with her, while trees and rivers shed human tears. Yet, as he celebrates this harmony, Nashe also, like the pastoral elegist, laments its passing. The famous line, "brightness falls from the air," even as it draws together once more human and nonhuman kinds of beauty, identifies both with the intensity of a setting sun. In the death of the famous Elizabethan player, Will Summers, Nashe invites us to mourn the passing of a whole era, an era whose virtues are summed up in the luminous and elusive "brightness."

The pastoral elegist, too, mourns the passing of that "brightness." But, as time goes on, the vision of an ideal sympathy between man and nature fades. In the years between 1595 and 1637 (the year in which Milton writes "Lycidas") we can trace the gradual decline of the pastoral elegist's way of seeing things and the consequent decay of the convention itself. New ways of looking at death and mourning are emerging—ways which cannot be contained within a pastoral landscape (however spacious or various that landscape may be) but will eventually demand new settings, new poetic forms. It is not one particular change in attitude which makes the pastoral elegy seem obsolete, but a whole complex of changes. Nor is the form necessarily abandoned when it becomes outmoded; a poet may work around it. But it is certain that when Milton comes to the pastoral elegy in 1637 he comes to a form that is already passé, if not yet an anachronism.

The Renaissance pastoral elegies we have considered in these pages differ widely from one another, both in subject matter and in tone. Some elegists bring their sorrows home; others take them to a distant Arcadian world. But always the interest of the poem centers on the *encounter* between the elegist and the landscape. We do not know precisely what feelings the poet will bring to this encounter, or what he will take from it. What we know is that he will come *here*: he will ask himself how nature may, or may not, sympathize with his sorrow, what he, in turn, can share with her, and what he must bear alone. As the convention declines, however, the center of interest shifts gradually away from this encounter between the poet and the landscape. The setting may still be there, but it becomes a backdrop; it is not *here* that we place our sorrows.

We begin to sense the change in the eclogues of Michael Drayton. Drayton is very much interested in the pastoral landscape, but he is interested in it for its own sake, not as a setting for his sorrows. Drayton is the most accomplished of the Spenserians, and the first (1593) version of his lament for Sidney is closely modeled on Spenser's "November." The lament of nature, the protestations of grief are all there; but they have become perfunctory. More appealing to this poet than pastoral suffering is pastoral sweetness; but the two seem altogether unrelated. Drayton's description of the decking of the grave with flowers is charming, quite without a trace of melancholy, and so are the framing dialogues. Here, for instance, is the closing passage:

> But now the sunne beginneth to decline,
>   And whilest our woes been in repeating here,
> Yon little elvish moping Lamb of mine,
>   Is all betangled in yon crawling Brier.
> (152–55)[15]

The little lamb entangled in the brier catches our eye; one feels that the poet has had his eye on her all along.

When Drayton revises this eclogue in 1606, he does two things: he heightens this pastoral sweetness, and he adds several new non-pastoral stanzas on contemporary issues, condemning, for instance, Sidney's detractors who now threaten the future of English poetry. And as he rehearses one of the favorite themes of his day, assuring Sidney of his poetic immortality in the ringing language of the Shakespearean (and Draytonian) sonnets, he leaves the pastoral landscape far behind:

> And learned Shepheard, thou to time shalt live,
> When their false Names are utterly forgotten,
> And Fame to thee Eternitie shall give,
> When with their Bones their Sepulchers are rotten.
>   (101–04)[16]

When he wants to say something serious, of immediate concern to his audience, the elegist increasingly goes outside pastoral. Drayton does not dismiss pastoral, but (as in his later poem, *The Muses Elizium* (1630), he relegates it to the realm of play. What Drayton has to say about Sidney's death is not something he can say within the pastoral landscape.

William Basse also wrote a pastoral elegy for Sidney,[17] but when he comes to write a lament on the death of Prince Henry in 1613, pastoral no longer seems the appropriate vehicle:

> Not (like as when some triviall discontents
> First taught my raw and luckless youth to rue)
> Do I to Flockes, now, utter my laments,
> Nor choose a tree, or streame, to mourn unto:
> My weightier Sorrow now (Dear Sir) presents
> These hir afflicted features to your view. . . .[18]

The pastoral elegy has, of course, been thought a "weighty" enough form in which to lament a prince's death in the past, but now the idea of addressing oneself to a tree or a stream seems faintly absurd; for, the implication is, these things have nothing to do with the "real," political world. The listening groves and streams are but fictions; when the poet wants to show us his true "afflicted features" he must unmask. The notion that pastoral serves only for the "trivial" experiments of youth is now accepted simply at face value.[19]

And in William Browne's eclogues (1614) we have all the Spenserian mannerisms—the archaic diction, the rusticity, many of Spenser's own phrases, the association of alternating moods and alternating seasons—everything but the sense that all this serves some purpose. When a convention is dying, its formulae are often preserved intact. No current of fresh emotion flows through such lines as these:

> Vnder an aged Oke was Willy laid,
> Willy, the lad who whilome made the rockes
> To ring with ioy, whilst on his pipe he plaid,
> And from their maisters wood the neighbring flockes:
> But now o're-come with dolors deepe
> > That nye his heart-strings rent,
> > Ne car'd he for his silly sheepe
> > Ne car'd for merriment.[20]

And, in the only original passage in the poem, the poet admits as much:

> Tis not a Cypresse bough, a count'nance sad,
> A mourning garment, wailing Elegie,
> A standing herse in sable vesture clad,
> A Toombe built to his names eternitie,
> > > Although the shepheards all should striue
> > > > By yearly obsequies,
> > > And vow to keepe thy fame aliue
> > > > In spite of destinies
> That can suppresse my griefe:
> > All these and more may be,
> Yet all in vaine to recompence
> > My greatest losse of thee.
>
> Cypresse may fade, the countenance bee changed,
> A garment rot, an Elegie forgotten,
> A herse 'mongst irreligious rites bee ranged,

A toombe pluckt down, or else through age be rotten:
    All things th'vnpartiall hand of Fate
        Can rase out with a thought,
    These have a seu'rall fixed date
        Which ended, turne to nought.
Yet shall my truest cause
    Of sorrow firmly stay,
When these effects the wings of Time
    Shall fanne and sweepe away.

(pp. 214–15)

Here the pastoral elegy and its various internal conventions (the mournful herdsman, the grave decked with flowers) are only empty forms. The pastoral sympathy may be there (as "all these and more may be"), but it does nothing to ease the poet's grief. It is there, but, compared to the reality and permanence of his feelings, it is unreal, ephemeral. We should take care to distinguish the sort of dismissal of the convention we see here in Browne's lament from those more passionate dismissals we have seen elsewhere: Gallus' angry rejection of the pastoral woodlands in which he has sought to place his love and failed; Arion's withdrawal from the marine herd which has gathered expectantly about him; Dicus' castigation of nature for her indifference to his complaint. All those dismissals ring with the poet's sense of his betrayal: he has come to the pastoral world, asked for its sympathies, and received less than he wished for. Browne has not really made that poetic journey. He goes through all the forms, simply as forms, and then acknowledges they don't mean very much to him. The note of betrayal is, significantly, absent here.[21]

Increasingly the funeral elegist wants to express truths about loss other than those which a pastoral setting, no matter how modified, can contain. To simplify is, of course, also to distort; it is, then, to be false to the complexity of actual experience. The pastoral elegist assumes that the problem of loss is fundamentally simple. Death itself, however unsettling, is for him still part of the known order of things, is "something understood." But to the metaphysical poet death presents itself as a puzzle, a paradox which he must solve by the ingenuity of his own wit. This is the attitude which has gained ascendency by 1637; this is the setting in which "Lycidas" is embedded in *Justa Edovardo King*. The difference between the pastoralist's view of death and that of the metaphysical poet is nowhere more apparent than when the poet himself denies it, as in these opening lines from a lament for King by his brother Henry:

> No Death! I'le not examine Gods decree,
> Nor question providence, in chiding thee:
> Discreet Religion binds us to admire
> The wayes of providence, and not enquire,
> My grief is sober, and my faith knows thee
> To b'executioner to destinie;
> Brought in by sinne, which still maintains thee here,
> As famines, earthquakes, and diseases were. . . .[22]

King too here asserts that death is part of the order of things, is "something understood." But this is just the point: he asserts it; he does not assume it. The whole process of logical deduction—amounting, of course, to just such an "examination" as the speaker rules out at the start—is alien to the pastoral elegist's approach. The pastoralist consoles us, not by marshalling arguments, not by ingenious yokings, but by revealing to us that what we knew was true is still so. He shows us rather than tells us by placing his sorrow in a special setting. The pastoralist commemorates death; the metaphysical poet comments on it.[23]

Pastoral's simplifications begin to seem facile; they also begin to seem radically false. The pastoralist simplifies, as we all do, to get at some general, underlying truth. His large truth is the fundamental sympathy between his world and nature's. When he asks nature to weep for him, he is, of course, being hyperbolic. He does not really expect trees to shed tears or the world to turn upside-down. He can ask them to do these things in good faith because he knows (and he knows we know) that the sympathy is there, is real. But as the links in that "great chain of being," through which angels, men, beasts and trees are all bound together in love, are gradually dissolved, his hyperboles are no longer understood as hyperboles. As the pastoral elegist's way of seeing things becomes less and less our way of seeing things, we say: how silly to suppose that nature could weep for us! We take his commands literally because we have forgotten the assumptions that stand behind them. And understood literally, the various formulae of the convention seem mere absurdities.

The dissonance between the pastoral elegist's way of seeing things and a more naturalistic outlook is, I think, one of the things Ben Jonson is exploring in his unfinished pastoral drama *The Sad Shepherd*. This fragment, first published in the 1640 folio, is difficult to date, but what evidence there is places it at the very end of Jonson's career: if we take the opening lines of the prologue literally, in 1637, the year of "Lycidas." The jarring perspectives of the various pastoral personae in Jonson's drama have been noticed but have generally been considered to reflect some uncertainty in the poet's conception.[24] Here one finds Aeglamour, the sad shepherd and our pastoral elegist; Robin Hood, the sometime pastoral philosopher who discourses on the vanished "golden age"; Amie, love's innocent victim, drawn from the tradition of Greek romance; Lorel, the clownish lover, a derivative of the Theocritean Cyclops; the rustics, with their rude dialect and practical knowledge of the hunt; and finally, the whole world of English folklore, Robin Hood and the witches. We cannot, of course, know how Jonson might have resolved the various interactions between his different characters and groups of characters. But I suspect that the dissonances are deliberate, that Jonson (perhaps in the manner of Shakespeare in *As You Like It*) intended to play off one version of pastoral against another, thereby to evaluate the ideal (or ideals).

This, at any rate, is what begins to happen in the several encounters between the sad shepherd and the other characters. It is Aeglamour who, in the haunting opening lines of the play, impresses himself and his world upon us first. His is the sympathetic world of the pastoral elegist. Aeglamour surrounds his grief for his lost Earine with images of pastoral sweetness. His first words establish the "hereness" of that world, and Earine herself is, like Spenser's Dido, a maiden so closely linked to the May world as to be almost indistinguishable from it:

Here! she was wont to goe! and here! and here!
Just where those Daisies, Pinks, and Violets grow:
The world may find the Spring by following her;
For other print her aerie steps neere left.
Her treading would not bend a blade of grasse!
Or shake the downie Blow-ball *from his stalke!*
But like the soft West-wind, *she shot along,*
And where she went, the Flowers tooke thickest root,
As she had sow'd 'hem with her odorous foot.

$$(1.1.1–9)^{25}$$

Rarely has the sympathy between human life and nature's life been expressed so boldly or so beautifully. But at this point Aeglamour disappears and the rustic festivities commence.

Later, invited to share in the spring rites which the others are celebrating, Aeglamour replies that the springtime world has been turned upside-down for him by Earine's death:

A Spring, now she is dead: of what, of thornes?
Briars, and Brambles? Thistles? Burs, and Docks? . . .

Did not the whole Earth sicken, when she died?
As if there since did fall one drop of dew,
But what was wept for her! or any stalke
Did beare a Flower! or any branch a bloome. . . .

. . . Doe not I know,
How the Vale wither'd the same Day? How Dove,
Deane, Eye, *and* Erwash, Idell, Snite, *and* Soare,
Each broke his Vrne, and twenty waters more,
That swell'd proud Trent, *shrunke themselves dry. . . .*

$$(1.5.33–34, 37–40, 51–55)$$

And in our final glimpse of him, Aeglamour shares with his pastoral audience his vision of Earine enskied, ushering in on earth, like Vergil's Daphnis, a new "golden age":

. . . now her sweet soule hovers,
Here, in the Aire, aboue us. . . .

. . . tempring all
The jarring Spheeres, and giving to the World

Againe, his first and tunefull planetting!
O' what an age will here be of new concords!
Delightfull harmonie!

                        (3.2.24–25, 30–34)

But Aeglamour's audience is composed, not of sympathetic herdsmen and listening trees, but of more-or-less realistically conceived woodsmen. These react to his outpourings with such comments as,

Good Karolin, *sing,*
Help to divert this phant'sie
                  (1.5.63–64)

and

How sad and wild his thoughts are!
                  (3.2.22)

In their eyes Aeglamour is

. . . The lost man!
Whom, wee shall never see himselfe againe;
Or ours, I feare! He starts away from hand, so,
And all the touches, or soft strokes of reason,
Yee can applie! No Colt is so unbroken!
Or hawke yet halfe so haggard, or unmann'd!
He takes all toies that his wild phantsy proffers,
And flies away with them. He now conceives
That my lost Sister, his Earine,
Is lately turn'd a Sphere amid the seven . . .

                        (3.3.3–12)

The pastoral elegist, in short, is now viewed in terms of our modern notions of "reasonable" behavior; to the woodsmen his complaints appear as the ravings of a madman—for they insist on taking his words purely at face value.

As for Jonson's own attitude toward Aeglamour and his "wild phantsy," certainly it is not simply that of the parodist. His portrait of the sad shepherd is too exquisite, too sympathetic for that. What Jonson may be suggesting, though, is that in the light of everyday reality the imaginative truths of the pastoral elegist will always look like distortions. And perhaps he is also suggesting that only by admitting those other truths into his dramatic world can he still preserve the integrity of the pastoralist's vision. For Milton, too, in 1637, reaffirms the pastoral elegist's way of seeing things by exposing it to other, conflicting visions.

What all this forces upon us is the unlikeliness of a poet in the year 1637 bringing our convention to its climax. And indeed, Milton's "Lycidas" is the only pastoral elegy among the thirty-six poems in English, Latin and Greek in the volume issued in 1638 to commemorate the death of Edward King. Yet King is just the sort of subject who would have been a candidate for this form thirty years earlier—an academic, a poet, one who died before his prime. But by 1638 the pastoral elegy is decidedly out of fashion. New ways of looking at life and death, and new poetic forms, are already firmly established. Death is viewed more often in this volume as a problem which requires a solution from the elegist than as a sorrowful event to which he brings his melodious tear.[26] The truths he might discover in transporting his grief to an imaginary landscape of shepherd-singers seem less real than the truths of actual experience, however fragmentary these may be. The basic assumptions of our convention no longer hold: that a poet can express his deepest emotions through a form which others have used before him; that truth is not what is new and startling, but is in some important sense what it has always been; that there is indeed a special virtue in saying what has been said before. Insofar as history can "explain" anything, then, this very brief survey of the English funeral lament in the early seventeenth century suggests why, if in "Lycidas" we see the culmination of our convention, we also see its transformation.

7

''LYCIDAS''

Finding the Time and the Place

YET once more, O ye Laurels, and once more
Ye Myrtles brown, with Ivy never-sear,
I com to pluck your Berries harsh and crude,
And with forc'd fingers rude,
Shatter your leaves before the mellowing year.
Bitter constraint, and sad occasion dear,
Compels me to disturb your season due . . .[1]

"Yet once more," that tolling of the bell which opens "Lycidas," invokes former occasions, both personal and literary ones.[2] Probably to a larger extent than any previous pastoral elegist, Milton brings to the writing of his own poem all that has come before him.[3] In "yet once more" itself we hear the distant echo of Vergil's opening of his tenth, and last, eclogue: "extremum hunc, Arethusa, mihi concede laborem." In Milton's own beginning there is a consciousness, too, of being at the end, not only of his own sojourn in pastoral (though it is that), but also at the end of a long literary tradition. And, as the phrase is reiterated, we sense some weariness. Milton, we have seen, comes late to the pastoral elegy convention—perhaps too late.

But to this sense of belatedness is joined an equally strong sense of precocity. The delayed subject and verb in the third line suddenly transform the oft-rehearsed literary gesture into the act of a particular man at a particular moment. "I com"—and come, perhaps, not too late but too soon. For the berries on the lasting evergreens are not yet ripe; the speaker's act of plucking them is premature, a violation of nature's due season. And the "forc'd fingers rude" in the next line (an intrusion in a double sense, having been inserted as a revision into the body of the text)[4] heightens the sense of urgency. As to the act itself, the shattering of the leaves, this too suggests at once a repetition of a familiar, ritual act and a precipitous violation of decorum. To "shatter" the leaves here is to "scatter" them (the separate sense of "shatter" as a violent dissolution, or scattering, of the individual particles was not yet firmly established in 1637).[5] Thus in the "shattering of the leaves" Milton invokes the pastoral elegist's traditional tribute to the dead, the scattering of leaves on the ground. "Spargite humum foliis," says Vergil's Mopsus, and Milton's elegist echoes the command. But Milton uses "shatter" in its destructive sense elsewhere,[6] and I think he wants us to feel the *shattering* in this scattering of the leaves, wants us to feel, that is, both his participation in the ritual, commemorative act and the rending of the leaves which is, ultimately, a shattering of the conventional form itself. Here we see in its most concentrated form the characteristic mode of this pastoral elegy: the act of participation in the convention is at the same time a violation of its order.

Yet once more or for the very first time? Where others have gone before, or alone and unaided? Belatedly or prematurely? In the opening lines of "Lycidas" these several contrary impulses confront one another violently. They will only be reconciled in the course of the poetic journey itself. And it is only when we have reached the end of that journey that we realize the speaker comes neither too late nor too soon, but precisely at the right time.[7]

In their concern for that which is timely and that which is untimely, for the seasonable and the unseasonable, these lines rehearse, however obliquely, the familiar preoccupations of the pastoral elegy. The pastoral elegist always disturbs nature's due season with a lament for one who has died out of season. He always sets nature's cyclical course, from year to mellowing year, against the uncertain and irreversible course of his own life. And the sense we have here that the speaker pursues a predetermined course of action, strews leaves on the ground where others have strewn leaves before him, and yet, at the same time, freely and even precipitously initiates that action—this too is familiar to us. It recalls most vividly the way in which the very first pastoral elegist, the Theocritean Daphnis, met his fate.

The same—and yet not the same. A reader coming to "Lycidas" from earlier pastoral elegies has this sense repeatedly. We hear those echoes but we cannot get our bearings. For this poet exercises his grief on the surface of the poem itself. His assault breaks apart, "shatters" the familiar signposts. We see the elements of the pastoral landscape, the evergreen trees with their leaves and berries, the suggestion of a gravesite; but none of this is organized into a setting. A speaker "comes" but where is he standing? Sorrow is not placed in these opening lines.

One way of describing more precisely that sense of mingled familiarity and strangeness is to consider what Milton has done with the most formal and conspicuous of the devices by which the pastoral elegist places sorrow: the frame. Some Renaissance elegists (among them Sannazaro, Marot and Spenser) continue in the classical manner, framing the sorrowful lament within a dialogue between two happier, or at least more detached, herdsmen. Others (as Castiglione and Scève) expose their speakers' sufferings to our more immediate view by dispensing with the frame altogether. And still others (as Petrarch and Boccaccio) convey sorrow's gradual encroachment by placing it in a sweet, framing world at the outset but then permitting that world to merge with the world of the lament at the close. Milton is, to my knowledge, the only pastoral elegist to dispense with the opening frame while retaining the closing one.[8] And the effect of this maneuver is to reveal the elegist only gradually discovering through the course of the poem itself those assurances of order traditionally conferred by the frame: the poise, the detachment, the knowledge that our sorrows have a place in nature's world of death and regeneration. We can no longer assume these things at the start. The happy outcome of this elegist's journey toward his consolation must remain in doubt right up to the final stage of that journey. Milton's handling of the frame epitomizes his handling of the convention as a whole and his synthesis of the two main Renaissance approaches to the tradition. He brings the self-consciousness, the isolation of the Petrarchan elegist, or of Scève's Arion on his lonely shore, home to his own version of that consoling pastoral landscape rediscovered and revitalized by Sannazaro, Marot, Ronsard and Spenser. Milton brings the anguish and singularity of an individual mourner's grief into nature's round and into the consolations of an aesthetic order. But he brings them in gradually and not without a struggle.

The fortunate outcome of this elegist's journey is not assured at the start. But we do know where we are going when we embark. "Lycidas" pursues a wayward course but not an aimless one. The destination is what it has always been in the pastoral elegy:

> *He must not flote upon his watry bear*
> *Unwept, and welter to the parching wind,*
> *Without the meed of som melodious tear.*
>
> (12–14)

The end is to make a melody, to make order and sense out of disorder and grief. And, these lines suggest, a *pastoral* melody. The song will be a symbolic burial for the man drowned at sea, whose body even now welters to the parching wind. The song will release him from an uncertain sea grave and bring him home to the known land—bring him home, that is, to pastoral. But to bring Lycidas home this elegist will have to venture farther out onto those waters than any previous pastoral elegist before him.

More than any other pastoral elegy "Lycidas" conforms to the pattern of mourning itself. And it reveals that pattern as we experience it from within: as process. It is a process of ebb and flow, of resolutions won and lost again before the final victory. Twice the apocalyptic thunder gathers, the poem appears to draw itself toward some sort of climax, only to dissolve again in pastoral tears until that final culmination which precipitates yet another return, and, at last, the apotheosis. "Lycidas" thus reiterates the pastoral elegy's traditional progression from death to regeneration, sorrow to rejoicing, this world to the next, three times before it effects the decisive reversal.

The first critic to describe this three-part structure of "Lycidas" relates it, rightly I think, to the structure of the poem's argument:

> The first movement laments Lycidas the poet-shepherd; its problem, the possible frustration of disciplined poetic ambition by early death is resolved by the assurance, "Of so much fame in heaven expect thy meed." The second laments Lycidas as priest-shepherd; its problem, the frustration of a sincere shepherd in a corrupt church, is resolved by St. Peter's reference to the "two-handed engine" of divine retribution. The third concludes with the apotheosis . . . [which] not only provides the final reassurance but unites the themes of the preceding movements in the ultimate reward of the true poet-priest.[9]

All this is true. And yet Barker's vocabulary of "problem" and problem "resolved" cannot explain how this slow progression from tentative resolution to dissolution and back again moves us. More is involved in the three-part structure of "Lycidas" than the construction of a bulwark against mortality on several fronts. True, each new assurance of order does add something important to what was said before. But as important as what is added each time is what is said again—the fact of repetition itself. And if it is said again, this need not mean that the speaker has not understood what was said the first time.[10] Let us suppose that, emotionally and intellectually, he has understood these truths but needs to hear them again before he can fully absorb them. Phoebus' answer and St. Peter's answer are, in important ways, partial answers; but they are also premature ones. Thus we come back again to the themes of the prologue: too late and too soon. Death always comes too soon, comes when we have it least in mind. But the abruptness of those "forc'd fingers rude" has its counterpart in the elegist's insistence on taking his time. He must go backward as well as forward and retrace his steps more than once. Like the first pastoral elegist, this one too will arrive at the destined end in his own due season.

The wayward progress of this pastoral elegy is perfectly served by its unique prosody. "Lycidas," in the words of F. T. Prince, who has carefully studied the poem's versification and its possible analogues, "consists of eleven 'verse-paragraphs' of lengths varying from ten to thirty-three lines, closely but irregularly rhymed, and including ten lines, scattered throughout, which do not rhyme at all; the last verse-paragraph is of eight lines, rhymed like an ottava rima."[11] Comparisons, such as those which Professor Prince suggests with the Italian *canzone*, are apt. But, more importantly (as Prince acknowledges), "Lycidas" refuses to conform to those expectations of regularity which the poem itself generates, right up to that final coda which corresponds to the pastoral elegy's closing frame. Thus the effect of this irregular versification is as different from the highly-patterned verse forms favored by Sannazaro and Spenser as it is from the classical hexameter. If the former call attention to the order which the poet brings to his pastoral world, the latter takes that order for granted. But "Lycidas," in its prosody as in other ways, makes us feel the elegist's struggle to achieve order, an order which is not mysterious, which is indeed always in sight, half-realized yet still eluding us, right up to that final coda.

The abbreviated six-syllable lines, scattered at irregular intervals among the ten-syllable ones and usually rhyming with the lines immediately preceding them, create an effect of temporary stasis, of a pause which at the same time impels us onward. In

> *I com to pluck your Berries harsh and crude,*
> *And with forc'd fingers rude,*
> *Shatter your leaves before the mellowing year.*
> (3–5)

or,

> *Nor yet where* Deva *spreads her wisard stream:*
> *Ay me, I fondly dream!*
> *Had ye bin there . . . for what could that have don?*
> (55–57)

the rhyme on the second, short line creates a temporary pause; but the momentum established by the regular beat of the pentameters carries us onward, on our journey's way once more. So it is everywhere in "Lycidas," that moments of repose seem themselves to propel us out again, away from the safe harbor. Yet that harbor is not lost to view. In the unique prosody of "Lycidas" Milton has designed a verse-form perfectly adjusted to the way in which this elegy and this elegist proceed. We still pursue the destined course;

we see where we are headed, and we touch the shore several times before that last time only to veer away from it again. For we refuse to get there in the traditional way; we refuse, right up to the end, to follow a predictable line.

It is the waywardness of its progress toward that destined end, as "answers" are found only to be lost again, that sets "Lycidas" apart from all other poems in the convention: that is what makes this pastoral elegy uniquely true to the experience of mourning itself. It is a difference, not of ends, not of meaning in the largest sense, but a difference in procedure, in how to reach the end. Yet this difference, we feel, makes all the difference.

The speaker who comes upon us so precipitously in the opening lines of the poem is identified neither by name nor by a setting. Nor do we know the cause of his suffering. But gradually, as he reveals his subject to us—"For Lycidas is dead, dead ere his prime"—and then begins to explore his own loss, a context, a setting, is established; and then, quite suddenly, the pastoral landscape, Milton's pastoral, rises before us:

> Together both, ere the high Lawns appear'd
> Under the opening eye-lids of the morn,
> We drove a field, and both together heard
> What time the Gray-fly winds her sultry horn,
> Batt'ning our flocks with the fresh dews of night,
> Oft till the Star that rose, at Ev'ning, bright
> Toward Heav'ns descent had slop'd his westering wheel.
>
> (25–31)

Saturated with reminiscences of other pastoral landscapes, this is a characteristically Miltonic image of felicity. The tiny gray-fly winding its horn, at the very center of the passage and mid-way too in the day whose progress it charts, recalls the cicada and the detached, serial mode of observation in Theocritus. But Milton's noon moment opens up in geographical and temporal vistas broader than those in Theocritus or in any other pastoral poet. The minutely detailed insect at the center emphasizes by contrast the open fields, lightly sketched in with broad free strokes on either side. And from that moment of noon quiet (so quiet we can hear the insect's song) we are carried, through the momentum of a single sentence, back to dawn and forward to evening.[12] The change from "glimmering" to "opening" eye-lids is one of those revisions Milton made on his Trinity manuscript of the poem that permit us to see him making this pastoral elegy more and more *his* pastoral elegy. For it is the sense of openness (or of things "opening") that defines this landscape. Milton's pastoral is a world awaking to its own possibilities under the eye-lids of the morn. Everything here is in motion, in a state of becoming. We see the high lawns coming into view as the sun rises, before they actually *appear*. Even at the day's end there is more to come: for the evening star is not "west" but still "westering." The pastoral sense of preciousness is created, not by insulating the landscape from encroaching dangers without, but by investing it with an air of tender expectancy, of openness to what lies ahead. Milton's pastures are unenclosed. The vital freedom of Adam and Eve in Eden is already foreshadowed in the open-eyed innocence of this earlier Miltonic version of paradise.

This original landscape will, as time and the poem go on, be displaced by others. But it remains the primary setting of the poem. Not that, once lost, it can ever be regained in this world; but that the kindliness we first know here (between man and man, between man and nature) continues to sustain us in the larger world without. More importantly, if this original landscape cannot itself contain our sorrows, the state of openness it exalts anticipates the way in which an enlarged pastoral world will eventually contain them.

When Lycidas dies the crops do not fail, nor do streams turn back in their courses. Nature grieves for us—

> *Thee Shepherd, thee the Woods, and desert Caves,*
> *With wilde Thyme and the gadding Vine o'regrown,*
> *And all their echoes mourn.*

$$(39-41)$$

but she cannot really share our loss. Death does not undo Dame Nature's kindly course; it undoes us. We feel the shock more inwardly now: it is *our* order which has been turned upside-down, and the magnitude of the shock felt here dwarfs all other, secondary responses. Milton does not deny us the soothing effect of sorrow's diffusion through a wider world. But he keeps pulling us back; he will not let this human sorrow be displaced onto nature, will not let nature bear what must be borne by man alone. Thus, when the herdsman dies, we may at first suppose that here (as elsewhere in the convention) nature dies with him:

> *The Willows, and the Hazle Copses green,*
> *Shall now no more be seen,*
> *Fanning their joyous Leaves to thy soft layes.*
> (42–44)

But only at first: for, when we read these lines closely, do we not rather suspect that it is *we* who no longer have eyes for nature's joys?[13] Milton subtly "corrects" the conventional motif: he allows us the consoling images of nature's sympathetic grief but keeps reminding us that death in nature can only give us back the *similitude* of our own, human loss. So in the following lines,

> *As killing as the Canker to the Rose,*
> *Or Taint-worm to the weanling Herds that graze,*
> *Or Frost to Flowers, that their gay wardrop wear,*
> *When first the White-thorn blows;*
> *Such,* Lycidas, *thy loss to Shepherds ear.*
> (45–49)

Lycidas' death is a loss to *Shepherds ear.*

But, if nature is less able now to share our human sorrows, we look to her all the more eagerly for an affirmation of continuing life and vitality. And this we do find in nature's world. In some Christian pastoral elegies earthly fields fade, even disappear, as heavenly ones grow greener. This does not happen in "Lycidas." The pastoral landscape *is* here. More, perhaps, than any other poet, Milton has all the resources of this world, of the convention, at his command. The question he keeps coming back to is: can any landscape, any words, console?

It is not against nature that this elegist turns. It is against the human impulse to ask more from nature than she can ever give. When Lycidas died the nymphs were not there; but the nymphs, of course, never *are* there. Indeed their very absence is traditionally consoling, since it permits the speaker to pretend, as Theocritus pretended, that, had they been there, they might have saved his Daphnis. It is that fond hope Milton turns against now, not the nymphs. He forces us to acknowledge (as Theocritus did not) what we knew all along to be true: the fantasy is but a fantasy; the nymphs could not have changed anything:

> *Where were ye Nymphs when the remorseless deep*
> *Clos'd o're the head of your lov'd* Lycidas?
> *For neither were ye playing on the steep,*
> *Where your old* Bards, *the famous* Druids *ly,*
> *Nor on the shaggy top of* Mona *high,*
> *Nor yet where* Deva *spreads her wisard stream:*
> *Ay me, I fondly dream!*
> *Had ye bin there . . . for what could that have don?*
>   (57–64)

Yet even now, as the poet turns against his "fond dream," that dream is working its way in us—and in him. Even as he calls after those absent nymphs he is (as Theocritus was) bringing his sorrow home. A new pastoral landscape begins to be born, here, in the Welsh countryside bordering on the Irish Sea where Edward King was drowned. This is not simply the right place geographically; it is the right *kind* of setting—a rougher, wilder country than that earlier one of open pastures. Now nature's sweetness is associated with a certain unruliness and also with a primitive grandeur. Here monumental stones in the earth testify to the shaping powers of our poetic forefathers, the ancient Druids. Among these Welsh hills the pastoralist's song too takes on monumentality. This is no place for smooth, Arcadian laments. But might this rougher world, this British landscape, contain our own rougher sorrows?

Not yet. For still the poet asks, Can any worlds console him? And it is when he has just heard the tenderest, most consoling words possible that the question assails him with its greatest force:

> *. . . for what could that have don?*
> *What could the Muse her self that* Orpheus *bore,*
> *The Muse her self, for her inchanting son*
> *Whom Universal nature did lament,*
> *When by the rout that made the hideous roar,*
> *His goary visage down the stream was sent,*
> *Down the swift* Hebrus *to the* Lesbian *shore.*
>
> (57–63)

The assault gathers momentum as it progresses. Orpheus' name is associated in our convention with the elegist's transforming powers. He is the lyrist who moved woods and rocks to rapture with his song and enchanted even the stony gods of the under-world. To hear his name now is to think first of those earlier triumphs.[14] And we are lulled too by the pastoral iteration of "Muse her self that Orpheus bore, / The Muse her self, for her inchanting son . . . " The savage spectacle of the singer's dismem-berment then comes upon us with a terrifying suddenness. We are not prepared—nothing in any previous pastoral elegy could have prepared us—for this. The "gory visage" of the mutilated Orpheus epitomizes all that the pastoral elegist traditionally excludes from his presentation of death. Milton will not, or cannot, exclude it. Again, the pastoral sympathies are still there. They have not de-serted us. But that makes it all the worse, for they are there but are helpless to shield us from this sight. Art and nature have gathered round; yet still Orpheus dies a savage death. It is not the death itself that pastoral might have spared us; it is death seen this way, in its naked horror.

For the triumph of "rout that made the hideous roar" is, as the words declare, a triumph, not only of death over life, but of inarticulateness over speech. The death of Orpheus portends the death of song. So again in *Paradise Lost* this same "savage clamor" threatens "to drown both Harp and Voice."[15] In the epic poem, but perhaps even more so in the pastoral one, we need to find not so much right answers as right words. Words for the pain as well as words to ease the pain. For the most terrifying pain of all is the one which cannot be given a name. Orpheus is not only the victim of these wild revellers; he is, in a sense Milton understood, also their companion. For it is out of the hideous roar, out of the harsh, crude pain that knows no words, that the poet must fashion his melody. "Lycidas" is about that struggle, the elegist's struggle to articulate the agony and turn it to song.

But Milton keeps coming back to the possibility that this song, all song, is in the end but a desperate effort to cover over the sound of that roaring while men drown beneath the sea's smooth surface. "Inchanting" is a key term here. Orpheus is the Muse's "inchanting" son and, in one sense, all art is enchantment, a defense against the chaos of experience, hence a delusion. "Lycidas" shares in the suspicion with which its age looks on poetic enchantments; it asks whether the designs the artist imposes on reality might not have their source in his own need for design rather than in the nature of reality itself. And "Lycidas" shares in the seventeenth century's interest in those truths which lie outside enchantments, the truths of immediate experience. What's true is what "shatters" us; or, as one of Milton's contemporaries puts it in another quasi-pastoral poem, his love for his mistress must be a true love "because her truth kills me."[16]

Unlike Donne, however, Milton questions conventional truths in order to reaffirm their veracity. "Lycidas" reaffirms our faith in the pastoral elegist's enchantments, our faith that, as he creates a concrete setting for his sorrows, he is resolving them, and as he finds words for his grief, he is finding consolation. But Milton reaffirms that earlier way of seeing things by questioning it—and sometimes he reaffirms it even as he questions it. Thus the description of the triumph of speechlessness over speech is itself a triumph of speech. It gives expression in the fullest possible way to the very fears of helpless dissolution it describes. And the same current which drives Orpheus' head down the swift Hebrus also brings him to the Lesbian shore. We know what the poet does not tell us here: that when he reaches that shore Orpheus will be made whole again, taken up to heaven and turned into a constellation. Thus the journey through Hebrus to the Lesbian shore hints at Milton's strategy in the poem as a whole—that larger expressiveness which brings us home to pastoral by way of the open sea.

"I am that Daphnis that herded here his cows, and watered here his bulls and calves." So the first pastoral elegist tells us who he is and where he is as he takes his leave of his world. For Milton's elegist, the act of self-definition is both more gradual and more arduous. But this elegist too finds consolation for his grief as he finds his own voice. And he too places himself in his world (more than once) as he prepares to leave it.

As the elegist comes back to pastoral a second time, after the hideous roar of the Bacchantes and after Apollo's assurances of poetic fame hereafter, he comes back to the possibility of expressiveness in this world; he comes back to pastoral's vocal reeds:

> O Fountain Arethuse, and thou honour'd floud,
> Smooth-sliding Mincius, crown'd with vocall reeds,
> That strain I heard was of a higher mood:
> But now my Oate proceeds . . .
>
> (85–88)

The vocal reed is richly expressive of all the pastoral landscape offers the elegist: a place where he might, not lose, but speak his sorrows; a place where he might speak in his own voice, but through nature's instrument and supported by her love, in his own voice but on the pipe which others have played upon before him.

But the instrument must be refined still further. With these same vocal reeds others have fashioned landscapes that sorrow cannot penetrate, or penetrates only to be dissolved into airy sweetness. The temptation remains—

> To sport with Amaryllis in the shade,
> Or with the tangles of Neæra's hair . . .
>
> (68–69)

Pastoral has served as a refuge from grief before and might so serve again. Milton knows all too well the pain that drives men to such retreats. But his sense of reality is too strong for the Arcadian dream world to hold him for long. "Tangles" is a suggestive term linking this image to all those other images of dark mazes and tangled woods in Milton's poetry. For the Puritan elegist, losing oneself is getting lost.[17]

Milton's elegist has already found support of a different kind, and more congenial models than the Arcadian one, elsewhere. Even as he asks himself,

> . . . . What boots it with uncessant care
> To tend the homely slighted Shepherds trade,
> And strictly meditate the thankles Muse . . .
>   (64–66)

he is posing the question in a way that implies the answer. The lines themselves recall us to the pastoral ideal of humility: the careful devotion of the Spenserian herdsman-moralist to his flock, of the Vergilian herdsman-poet to his craft. And they recall for us something even more important to Milton: the freedom his humble position confers on the herdsman. The Spenserian passage upon which Milton drew for his own description of the "homely slighted Shepherds trade" is worth remembering here:

> Of Muses Hobbinol, I conne no skill:
> For they bene daughters of the hyghest Ioue,
> And holden scorne of homely shepherds quill.
> For sith I heard, that Pan with Phoebus stroue,
> Which him to much rebuke and Daunger droue:
> I neuer lyst presume to Parnasse hyll,
> But pyping lowe in shade of lowly groue,
> I play to please my selfe, all be it ill.
>
> Nought weigh I, who my song doth prayse or blame,
> Ne striue to winne renoune, or passe the rest . . .
>   ("June," 65–74)

The note of sincere modesty which sounds through this Spenserian passage is a note Milton could never hit. But Spenser's insistence on the herdsman-poet's privileged immunity from the world and its flattering ways does speak to him. The pastoralist is not "lowly and servysable"; he is lowly and hence free to please himself.

And so, as he comes back to the vocal reeds, Milton's elegist finds in the shepherds' world the freedom to launch his bold attack against the clergy. And he finds his own voice, his way out of his sorrows, in that attack, as the Theocritean Daphnis (in a lighter vein) found his voice in countering the thrusts of Aphrodite.

Speaking through the vocal reeds, all those earlier herdsmen's voices—Spenser's voice most clearly and, beyond that, the voice of Scripture—support the elegist now as he takes up the pastoral pipe once more, and St. Peter tunes it to a sterner note:

> How well could I have spar'd for thee young swain,
> Anow of such as for their bellies sake,
> Creep and intrude, and climb into the fold?
> Of other care they little reck'ning make,
> Then how to scramble at the shearers feast,
> And shove away the worthy bidden guest;
> Blind mouthes! that scarce themselves know how to hold
> A Sheep-hook, or have learn'd ought els the least
> That to the faithfull Herdsmans art belongs!
> What recks it them? What need they? They are sped;
> And when they list, their lean and flashy songs
> Grate on their scrannel Pipes of wretched straw,
> The hungry Sheep look up, and are not fed,
> But swoln with wind, and the rank mist they draw,
> Rot inwardly, and foul contagion spread:
> Besides what the grim Woolf with privy paw
> Daily devours apace . . .

(113–29)

The herdsman's world has changed. The dawn's promise is succeeded by this darker day—and the speaker seems to have aged with it. He speaks in generalities now; with St. Peter, he knows the ways of a crueler world. In this somber landscape the grim wolf carries off, one by one, the herdsman's tender sheep; and no one prevents it. Worse, those that remain "rot inwardly, and foul contagion spread." It is a fallen world. The corruption is within us as well as without. Little good to enclose these sheep within pastoral's protective fold! Nothing can protect them from exposure to this dread disease.

And yet, though this is a fallen world, it remains a pastoral world and it remains very much Milton's world. If there is no immunity from the disease, still the sheep *need* not succumb. Though exposed in all their frailty, they still remain open to healing words as well as to vain or vicious ones. Here there are still sheep to be fed and those who might feed them. Here a herdsman's sweet song might still nourish his flock. For (and this is perhaps what matters most of all) the sweet song and the virtuous, life-sustaining one, the faithful herdsman's art and the pastor's healing art, are still fundamentally one. The prelate's "lean and flashy songs" are but lean and flashy; they cannot please any more than they can nourish us. At the same time St. Peter's own words testify to the continuing power of the herdsman's art to do both. We are free, even here, to choose a better life.

The mounting rage which courses through St. Peter's speech has a positive basis, then, and it has a positive role in the elegist's movement from grief toward recovery. To a degree unprecedented in any other pastoral elegy, Milton admits into his pastoral world the rage as well as the grief we feel at death. He makes room for our anger at all the irrational things that happen in a world where virtuous men are suddenly cut down and people are poisoned by the ones who should be feeding them. In "Lycidas"' larger openness to turbulent feelings generally, this anger has an important place. St. Peter's speech is anything but a digression; for the righteous indignation it releases is vital to this elegist's progress. As he moves toward his destined end through the terrifying spectacle of the dismembered Orpheus, so he also moves toward it by acknowledging the rage as well as the fears such violations of life and art provoke in us. It is a healing anger, another way (and an important one for Milton) of placing sorrow.

But if this is a healing anger, it will eventually take us beyond any pastoral landscape, any pastoral expressiveness. As the sheer senselessness of it, of hungry sheep who still listen to those empty songs while the contagion spreads, becomes unbearable, the pressure mounts, and we are, finally, swept over the edge:

> . . . *and nothing sed,*
> *But that two-handed engine at the door,*
> *Stands ready to smite once, and smite no more.*
> (129–31)

The promise of a retribution, of a final day of reckoning when the virtuous will be vindicated and the tyrant brought low (in this world or, perhaps, hereafter), is a consolation, and, we may be sure, no small consolation to Milton. The engine that will "smite once, and smite no more" answers the repeated cries of the mourner who came, in the first lines of the poem, "yet once more . . . and once more." What is the precise nature of this answering blow? Perhaps we should not press the image of the two-handed engine too hard. Whatever engine Milton had in mind, the image works best, it seems to me, if we allow it a certain vagueness. If the pastoral world is one we cherish because it is a world we know, the world beyond that door where the two-handed engine waits is an unknown world. That judgment will be just; it will be final; and its ways are inscrutable. Here we must stop.

Milton takes us just to the threshold of his epic universe, but no farther. We contemplate the divine justice that awaits us from a human, earthly—which is to say a limited—perspective. The image captures wonderfully both our yearning for the final retribution and our recognition that it is, no matter how even-handed in its dealings with men, still a blow. "Engine" itself is a term Milton will use again in *Paradise Lost*, where it is most often applied to diabolical instruments of warfare. But angels too must sometimes resort to such engines of destruction to accomplish their virtuous ends.[18] How heaven's wrath can be justified to man is a problem the epic poet must grapple with as best he can. In the pastoral world of "Lycidas" we glimpse the problem, but we need not yet deal with it. The pastoral poet can afford to consider that engine more simply, to see its blows as blows. And, assured of final retribution, he can accept his own human need to come back to this world. Milton's phrase, "and nothing sed," refers, of course, to the silence of those who might have spoken out against the abuses in the church. Were Lycidas still alive, he would have said something. But "nothing sed" suggests further that, in one sense, there is nothing we can say to corruption, to sin and death, to "all complexities of mire and blood"—nothing save those dread words which follow; nothing save: it shall be answered.

But from our point of view, from the pastoral point of view

which is the poem's central perspective, that saying, however sufficient in itself, is not enough. The elegist needs that answer, needs that assurance, to continue on his journey's way, but it cannot mark his journey's end. The very suddenness with which we are brought up short here (this verse couplet coming after one of the longest verse-paragraphs in the poem, and concluding as it does with those heavy monosyllables in the last line) might suggest what we know in other ways: it is too abrupt, too overwhelming to mark the journey's end. The elegist needs, among other things, time for the journey itself. This is where Dr. Johnson's criticism of "Lycidas" is exactly wrong: it is just because we do have leisure for fictions here—for Arethuse and Mincius, for rough satyrs and fauns with cloven heels—that we also have time for grief, or time to express our grief.[19] St. Peter's answer is not false; but it is premature. And there will be another answer from heaven later, one which recognizes in a different way the human frailties St. Peter's speech has exposed, an answer which is the more conclusive for appearing less so.

St. Peter's speech has assured us that the two-handed engine stands ready; and, more than that, it has assured us of the indissoluble bond between poet and moralist in this world. And with that assurance we come back once more to pastoral. Or rather, it is the elegist who, with the self-consciousness typical of this exercise as a whole, invites the pastoral world to return to him:

> Return Alpheus, *the dread voice is past,*
> *That shrunk thy streams;* Return Sicilian *Muse . . .*
> (132–33)

It is a return, the most explicit in the poem, to the convention itself. And now, after the bitterness of the preceding paragraph, it is the Sicilian muse we summon—pastoral sweetness at its source. The Theocritean gesture of invitation ("here are oaks and galingale, here sweetly hum the bees about the hives . . . ") is extended now to the pastoral world itself; the elegist summons it "hither," to him:

> *And call the Vales, and bid them hither cast*
> *Their Bels, and Flourets of a thousand hues.*
> *Ye valleys low where the milde whispers use,*

> Of shades and wanton winds, and gushing brooks,
> On whose fresh lap the swart Star sparely looks,
> Throw hither all your quaint enameld eyes,
> That on the green terf suck the honied showres,
> And purple all the ground with vernal flowres.
>
> (134–41)

This landscape, with its "milde whispers," its "wanton winds" and cool, refreshing waters, brings like a balm a kind of sweetness familiar to us from other pastoral elegies but hitherto excluded from this one. It brings us a sweetness like that which Vergil's Menalcas felt when he compared the sweetness of his friend's song to that of "sleeping on the grass when one is tired, or quenching one's thirst in the heat of the day with sweet water from a running stream" (5.45–47). As there, the sense of refreshment depends on a prior experience of deprivation. Here the landscape itself, with its "quaint enameld eyes," seems conscious of the pleasures it brings. Its sweetness is not the unself-conscious sweetness of the earlier pastoral world, under the opening eyelids of the morn. We know, and these flowers know, how much we need them now.

And, in the lovely catalogue of flowers which follows, nature does come "hither," and she does console us:

> Bring the rathe Primrose that forsaken dies,
> The tufted Crow-toe, and pale Gessamine,
> The white Pink, and the Pansie freakt with jeat,
> The glowing Violet,
> The Musk-rose, and the well-attir'd Woodbine,
> With Cowslips wan that hang the pensive hed,
> And every flower that sad embroidery wears:
> Bid Amaranthus all his beauty shed,
> And Daffadillies fill their cups with tears,
> To strew the Laureat Herse where Lycid lies.

Here we feel once more, as we did most of all in Theocritus, nature's sympathy *and* her separateness. The flowers do not lose their own identity when they weep for us. The primrose does die an early death; cowslips do hang their heads. And Amaranthus, were he to shed all his beauty, would not be violating the natural order of things; rather, were he to forfeit his legendary immortality, he would be conforming to nature. Nature consoles us here by being herself.[20]

Certainly the catalogue of flowers does "interpose a little ease," and that ease is not to be despised. The naming of those sweet names refreshes the elegist after the "dread voice" he has just heard and strengthens him for what still lies ahead. For his journey is not yet over. And it is, I think, this sudden, painful realization that provokes the abrupt turn in the next line:

> For so to interpose a little ease,
> Let our frail thoughts dally with false surmise.
>
> (152–53)

What is the "false surmise"? On the literal level it is the elegist's fond illusion that he could scatter any flowers on Lycidas' grave, the illusion that his body is *here*, not weltering somewhere in the open sea. Readers of the poem have, however, generally felt that in this sudden turn Milton is expressing some deeper disillusionment with the consolations of the preceding passage. And so it seems to me too that he is—but only a disillusionment we and the elegist feel in retrospect, one that does not cancel those consolations or their healing effect. The elegist's summoning of the flowers *is* soothing; and on a first reading that is all we feel, and all we are meant to feel. But the flowers, though genuinely consoling, promise more than they can give: they promise a burial—not merely the literal one, but also that symbolic burial of his grief which the convention (and particularly its scattering of flowers at the grave-site) traditionally grants the elegist. This symbolic burial, as well as that literal one, is premature. For the recognition that Lycidas yet lies unburied, "washed far away," is also a recognition that the extremities of the elegist's grief have not yet been charted.

Now, and only now, having come to that recognition, does the elegist look back on the preceding passage as an interlude. Once he has been brought back to a harsher world (as Gallus was brought back and Castiglione's Iolas was brought back), then, and only then, does he feel there is something false about what the flowers bring. And now, as we too look back over the passage, we feel there is something too willed in its vision of peace. The bitter constraint which first compelled this elegist with "forc'd fingers rude" to disturb nature's due season, the anger which later drove him to force an answer prematurely down from heaven—these have left their mark upon the flowers too. Pastoral's peace is something given; it cannot be forced. And, in retrospect, we feel that, for all his exquisite mastery of the pastoralist's art, the elegist is still forcing things. He invokes this peace too fervently. Something of his desperation is reflected in the very intensity (atypical of the genre) with which he contemplates these delicate blooms. It is Eden seen through the exile's eyes,[21] or Arcadia as Gallus saw it when he said, "atque utinam ex vobis unus vestrique fuissem. . . ." "Utinam": would that it were so! The pastoral peace of the poem's last lines, its contours so much a part of our own consciousness that we hardly pause to enumerate them, is of a higher order than this willed peace. But that, I repeat, is something we feel only as the recognition that Lycidas is not here breaks over us. The flowers have, in the meantime, done their work. And the kind of sweetness they can bring counts for something in Milton's pastoral world—if not for everything. Perhaps the only lesson we can take away from this interlude of sweetness is that we cannot linger among these flowers too long. Though the elegist's "dallying" here does allow him to move forward, once he sees it as dallying, it is time to depart.

Yet, as he turns on pastoral's way of easing grief, the elegist's gesture is ambivalent, charged with sympathy for what it rejects. The revision from "sad thoughts" to "frail" ones is another decisive revision in a poem that is constantly revising itself, turning on its own progress. "Sad thoughts," whether somber or sorrowful ones, can be relieved by the change of mood which the flower passage brings. "Frail" ones are less easily assuaged, by flowers or other balms; for frailty (one of Milton's favorite terms for Adam and Eve)[22] is built into the human condition. If we were not frail we would not suffer, would not need those balms. Yet being frail, do we not also "use" words, rituals, these pastoral flowers for instance, to escape the pain? How are we to confront our human fate with open eyes and yet still be protected, comforted, in our frailty? In the next lines Milton confronts that fate most boldly, not by another retreat into the sweet interior, but by an unprecedented expansion of the pastoral frontier:

> Ay me! Whilst thee the shores, and sounding Seas
> Wash far away, where ere thy bones are hurld,
> Whether beyond the stormy Hebrides,
> Where thou perhaps under the whelming tide
> Visit'st the bottom of the monstrous world;
> Or whether thou to our moist vows deny'd,
> Sleep'st by the fable of Bellerus old,
> Where the great vision of the guarded Mount
> Looks toward Namancos and Bayona's hold . . .
> (154–162)

These lines immediately precede the poem's decisive reversal, with its homeward turn, and must be crucial to any reading of the poem. How does Milton win that reversal? In part, as I have suggested, by his very willingness to leave the safe shore, to follow Lycidas out into the sounding seas—the largest expression of the poem's openness, this elegist's willingness to take risks with his own form. Such marine excursions, we have seen, are not unprecedented in the pastoral elegy. But Milton goes farther, particularly in the way his lines express the terrifying randomness of the sea's movement, its power to displace all we know and cherish. Lycidas' body might be anywhere beneath its whelming tide.

Yet here we are penetrating the glassy surface, even to the bottom of this monstrous world. And what this voyage out into the open waters triumphantly reveals is that the poet can give a name, even to his deepest fears. For as his imagination follows Lycidas out into the sea, "where ere thy bones are hurled," landmarks are also being erected: the Hebrides Isles to the north, St. Michael's Mount at the southwestern tip of Lands End, looking toward Spain. The contours of that other paradise, that blessed isle, England herself, rise before us: we are bringing Lycidas home.

And, as we turn with St. Michael, from the sea back to the shore, from Spain back to the English coast, the great tide of nature's sympathy for human suffering, so long held in check, is released:

> Look homeward Angel now, and melt with ruth.
> And O ye Dolphins, waft the hapless youth.
>   (163–64)

Lycidas is borne home by the angel's pity and the dolphin's love (that same dolphin, surely, who bore home an earlier pastoral elegist).[23] Now the supernatural angel and the natural creature unite in their sympathy for frail man, who shares his uniquely human fate with neither of them. The pastoral term "melt" seems just right here. Now, just because there can be no more retreat from pain, we can feel all the pity of it, can "melt" with ruth. With this homeward turn "Lycidas" navigates its decisive turn, the pastoral elegy's traditional turn from sorrow to rejoicing. The voyage out becomes a voyage home; our sorrows are placed on an English shore—and all this, as in no other pastoral elegy, Christian or classical, *before* the translation of Lycidas into heaven. Here the pastoral sympathy alone effects the decisive reversal; but it is a sympathy based now more on the recognition of difference—of that human frailty which separates "hapless" man from both the angel and the dolphin who unite to rescue him—than likeness. Christ's sympathy, "the dear might of him that walk'd the waves," which then bears Lycidas up to heaven, confirms these earlier acts of love which have borne him home. Only after we have come home do we make the traditional ascent up to heaven and repeat the cycle out and back once more.

Milton's celebration of the Christian redemption is announced by the boldest of all his modifications of the pastoral elegy's convention. Traditionally, as we have seen, from the "Lament for Bion" on, the pastoral poet *contrasts* nature's cyclical course (the dying and reviving vegetation, then, later, the rising and setting sun) with our human mortality. Milton celebrates his poem's reversal with a triumphant reversal of that conventional motif:

> Weep no more, woful Shepherds weep no more,
> For Lycidas your sorrow is not dead,

> *Sunk though he be beneath the watry floar,*
> *So sinks the day-star in the Ocean bed,*
> *And yet anon repairs his drooping head,*
> *And tricks his beams, and with new spangled Ore,*
> *Flames in the forehead of the morning sky:*
> *So* Lycidas *sunk low, but mounted high,*
> *Through the dear might of him that walk'd the waves . . .*
>
> (165–73)

Up to this passage, Milton's revisions of conventional motifs tend to undercut the pastoral elegy's assumption of sympathy between man and nature: the nymphs (he reminds us) could not have saved Lycidas had they been there; nor can mere pastoral flowers, however beautiful, bring him home to us. But now, to celebrate our coming home, our reunion with the convention and its traditional sympathies, Milton invokes a parallel which the convention itself traditionally denies. Now man *does* follow nature's cyclical course: now he too is reborn.[24] Perhaps it is just because Milton has exposed, so much more fully than any pastoral elegist before him, the painful gap between man and nature, that he can now celebrate this fuller harmony.

Yet here too sympathy is not identity. Our rebirth is not, like the sun's, fixed and assured for all times. It depends upon a free act of mercy, and thus it remains in each instance open and undetermined, dependent on continuing acts of love for frail humanity. So again the larger pattern of the poem reveals itself: we rehearse the familiar cycle of death and regeneration but we fulfill the pattern in our own way, through a free act. Christ's redemption of our souls by that willing walk upon the waters corresponds in the divine sphere to the elegist's own venture out into the sounding seas in the human sphere. Both ventures are acts at once of daring and of love.

And only *after* these affirmations do we follow Lycidas into heaven and see him enjoying that other, more perfect pastoral peace:

> *Where other groves, and other streams along,*
> *With* Nectar *pure his oozy Locks he laves,*
> *And hears the unexpressive nuptiall Song,*

> *In the blest Kingdoms meek of joy and love.*
> *There entertain him all the Saints above,*
> *In solemn troops, and sweet Societies*
> *That sing, and singing in their glory move,*
> *And wipe the tears for ever from his eyes.*
>
> (174–81)

Milton makes no attempt to describe to us those other groves and other streams; nor does he describe the sound of that singing. If the vocal reeds speak eloquently of what can be said in this world, the other-worldly song is "unexpressive," that is, beyond our powers to express it.

What Milton does tell us about this other world is significant. For the Spenserian image of a protected world ("No daunger there the shepherd can astert"), Milton substitutes one of continuing consolation. Even Milton's heaven is in motion, is a place where angels sing "and singing in their glory move." And as they wipe the tear from Lycidas' eye, the angels promise us, as the poem promises, not immunity from sorrow, but sympathy. The note of *contemptus mundi* we hear in many other Christian pastoral elegies once the joyful ascent has been made is entirely absent here. "Lycidas" is, pre-eminently among Milton's poems as well as among other pastoral elegies, a song of human expressiveness. The joyfulness it releases is a joy in saying what seemed unspeakable, in sharing what seemed unable to be shared.

And so in this Christian poem it seems entirely right that having made that ascent, we should now come back, as Vergil came back, to the pastoral shore. And, as in that poem, the new saint is himself the agent of the final return:

> *Henceforth thou art the Genius of the shore,*
> *In thy large recompense, and shalt be good*
> *To all that wander in that perilous flood.*
>
> (183–85)

That Milton can so freely appropriate Vergil's "bonus Daphnis," the tutelary god of the herdsmen, is one measure of the distance which separates his age from Petrarch's. But his Lycidas is not only, like Daphnis, the god of the pastoral sanctuary; he is the guardian of a wider world, of that "perilous flood" in which Petrarch and Milton and all Christian men are wanderers.

The resolution which the poem and the poet have achieved is crystalized in the concluding eight-line coda, that closing frame which has no opening frame to balance it. Only now are we permitted the luxury of pastoral detachment: now allowed to see the lament as the performance of an uncouth swain; now allowed to give his song a name; and now, finally, allowed to place the song itself in its setting:

> Thus sang the uncouth Swain to th'Okes and rills,
> While the still morn went out with Sandals gray,
> He touch'd the tender stops of various Quills,
> With eager thought warbling his Dorick lay:
> And now the Sun had stretch'd out all the hills,
> And now was dropt into the Western bay;
> At last he rose, and twitch'd his Mantle blew:
> To morrow to fresh Woods, and Pastures new.
>
> (186–93)

It is a quieter close to a pastoral elegy than any we have seen, and a fitting conclusion to the most turbulent poem in the convention. The sense of renewed vitality is there in the "eager thought" and in the twitching of the herdsman's mantle. But these lively motions are, as it were, retarded by the just barely perceptible movements in the larger world around us: by the quiet footsteps on which the morning mist steals away and, later, by the slow gathering of the evening shadows. Many different things are converging in these last lines to create an effect of profound peace. There is the poet's full reunion now with his convention and our disengagement from the pressing sorrows of the lament. There is the shift, with that disengagement, from the irregular versification of the lament to the even rhymes of the coda. But most of all, I think, there is the sense that, after all the rude forcing (both of painful questions and of answers to those questions), now nothing is being forced. Milton creates an effect in these lines of things happening—in nature and in us—quite without our willing them and almost without our noticing them. So we see the sun casting the shadows of the hills onto the ground; we look again and realize the sun has set: it is evening. We take in these changes in nature's world, as day succeeds to night, without seeming to have to pause (so finely does Milton manage it) to record them. And so too in the herdsman's world there is no insistence upon the resolution which has now been won: the singer simply rises, "at last," with those gathering shadows. We want no explanation, for we know that now the timing is right: now he is neither rushing nor dallying. The elegist's departure with the evening shadows speaks for a new and a deeper sympathy between man and nature, deeper for being so entirely taken for granted. We feel it again in Milton's bold but utterly unself-conscious appropriation of his shepherd's sandals for the morning mist. This image too, like the action it describes, seems to slip by us as the sense of it sinks in. Here, in this landscape with its soft colors and imperceptible motions, with its air above all of being so unconcerned with its own effects, we are no longer celebrating that ideal harmony between man and nature—or, not celebrating it in quite the way we were on that earlier day "under the opening eye-lids of the morn," that day whose progress is in so many ways recapitulated here. Here we neither celebrate that harmony nor, as elsewhere so painfully in the poem, lament its passage: for now nature is simply there, understood to be a part of our lives as we are part of hers.

And yet, even as the pastoral sympathies gather about him at the close, Milton's herdsman remains, significantly, alone in his world. He sings his song "to th'Okes and rills," but to no listening human ears. Once more Milton's pastoral elegy—even now, as the poet affirms most strongly his reunion with his convention—declares its uniqueness. For elsewhere (e.g., in Sannazaro, Marot, and Spenser) we are brought back with a closing frame to the give and take of dialogue; while the solitary singer in other Renaissance pastoral elegies (in Castiglione or in Scève) is a figure we associate with the poet's renunciation of those consolations conferred both by the frame and by the dialogue form. Again Milton unites the two strands of the Renaissance convention: he allows us the detachment of the frame but not the comforts of a companion. And that is as it should be. For this speaker's journey from grief to recovery has been all along a peculiarly solitary one. He has had to find his own way to the destined end; while, to a greater degree than that of any other pastoral elegist, the rhythms of his song have been dictated by the ebb and flow of the elegist's own feelings. For in his lament there is less sense of what needs be told *to* someone, more sense of what the speaker needs to tell himself—and that more than once. So it is entirely right that this elegist's solitude now be confirmed at the close, that he be revealed to us without the customary interlocutor, or even the familiar sheep, by his side. Milton's elegist stands large in his pastoral landscape. He is not lonely, not bereft, as others before him have been at the song's close; but he embodies the essential condition of fallen man—that of aloneness.

And finally, Milton suggests, as Vergil had in his last pastoral poem, that the herdsman's homeward journey at dusk now coincides with (or shades into) a departure from the pastoral world altogether. Milton's final lines, like Vergil's, cherish what they relinquish. Perhaps even more so: for there is no hint of danger lurking in these shadows. As the consolations of pastoral are deeper now (deeper than for Vergil and deeper than for Milton himself earlier in this same poem), we can afford to linger awhile: Milton's herdsman will enjoy both evening's repose and progress onward—but that latter motion is postponed for the morrow. Indeed Milton's farewell is richly ambiguous, for the leave-taking itself is clothed in the language of pastoral: the herdsman moves on, but on to new "pastures."

Yet to woodlands also. And thus, if Milton allows us to hope for a continuation of the pastoral affections in the new world to which his herdsman will soon be moving, still his very mention of woods (in a pastoral landscape composed predominantly of groves and open fields) suggests that it is indeed a *new* world, one unlike the world the herdsman has known up to now. The pastoral poet will not accompany him there: that is tomorrow's journey, tomorrow's poem. But we know, I think, where Milton's herdsman will be going: into the world of labor, Dante's dark wood of experience. And there too the pastoral sympathies may help sustain him, for the woods contain the promise of fresh pastures to be cleared and new kinds of growth.

If "Lycidas" celebrates life's victory over death by being more open than any previous pastoral elegy to the destructive and painful elements in life itself, it also celebrates its convention by unifying divergent strands within the Renaissance tradition. In the neo-Latin lament he wrote two years later for his friend Charles Diodati, Milton takes up just one of those strands, the personal, introspective mode of Castiglione's "Alcon." That neo-Latin lament was in fact probably the one Milton had most in mind when he composed the "Epitaphium."[25] The theme of the "Epitaphium" is the theme of "Alcon"—that of solitude, a solitude occasioned by the loss of a perfect intimacy. The speaker asks, as Iolas asked, how can I go on in life without the presence of that one individual who knew my whole soul? Whether or not Diodati and Milton ever really enjoyed such a perfect intimacy is, of course, beside the point. It is an ideal relationship, and what it means to lose it, that Milton describes so movingly here. Like Castiglione, he feels his grief the more intensely because he was not there at the time of his friend's death (121–23); and he too spins fantasies of reunion, not realizing that his friend is already dead (145–46). The poem itself becomes, like "Alcon," an attempt to effect a symbolic burial, a symbolic farewell—and again, one feels, the effort fails. The elegist's absorption in his own private sorrows once more estranges him from pastoral and its consolations. Thyrsis' refrain here, "Ite domum impasti, domino jam non vacat, agni" ("Go home unfed, for your master has no time for you, my lambs"),[26] recognizes that men might succor nature, but not the reverse.

But Milton's revisions of the convention go further than Castiglione's. The "Epitaphium," in its vision of remembered pastoral felicity, is probably the most intellectual of pastoral elegies. Milton's Thyrsis longs, not for a loving embrace in pastoral's open fields, but for the perfect meeting of true minds within doors:

> At mihi quid tandem fiet modò? quis mihi fidus
> Haerebit lateri comes, ut tu saepe solebas
> Frigoribus duris, & per loca foeta pruinis,

Aut rapido sub sole, siti morientibus herbis?
Sive opus in magnos fuit eminùs ire leones
Aut avidos terrere lupos praesepibus altis;
Quis fando sopire diem, cantuque solebit?
  Ite domum impasti, domino jam non vacat, agni.
Pectora cui credam? quis me lenire docebit
Mordaces curas, quis longam fallere noctem
Dulcibus alloquiis, grato cùm sibilat igni
Molle pyrum, & nucibus strepitat focus, at malus auster
Miscet cuncta foris, & desuper intonat ulmo.

(37–49)

[But what now is to become of me? What faithful comrade will always be at my side, as you used to be when cold was biting and the fields were in the grip of frost, or when under the hot sun green things were dying of thirst, whether it was our task to face great lions or frighten hungry wolves from the high sheepfolds? Who now will lull the day to rest with conversation and song?

Go home unfed, my lambs, your master has no time for you now. Whom shall I confide in? Who will help me to soothe devouring cares, or to beguile the long night with delightful talk, while the ripe pear hisses by the cheerful fire, and nuts crack open on the hearth, and the wicked south wind makes hurly-burly outdoors and the elm-tops groan?]

Compared to the parallel reminiscences in "Lycidas"—of life beneath the opening eyelids of the morn, where "rural ditties were not mute" and Fauns and Satyrs came to hear the glad songs—these lines present a cloistered and rarified ideal, one which owes more to Horace than Vergil. The world of the two shepherd-friends in "Lycidas" is a world we all know. Everyone has (or thinks he has) lived for a time in such a state of perfect innocence, in perfect communion with his friend and nature. But in the "Epitaphium" Milton commemorates the sort of friendship which is defined by its rarity. There is no one else, the poet says, with whom he could ever converse as he once conversed with Diodati.

When the things that sustain us in our relations with men are so far removed (as they are here) from the things that might sustain us in nature, the traditional pastoral affirmations count for little. We do not envy the flowers their repeated blossoming. Mere longevity, or loveliness, or animal vitality is not to be desired. Thus the usual contrast between nature's renewal and the single span of human life on earth (the contrast Milton reverses so triumphantly in "Lycidas") could have little force in the "Epitaphium." And here Milton makes a telling, and very moving, revision of that traditional motif. He contrasts instead the ease with which nature's creatures can unite in pairs with the near-impossibility of true human unions:

> *Hei mihi quam similes ludunt per prata juvenci,*
> *Omnes unanimi secum sibi lege sodales,*
> *Nec magis hunc alio quisquam secernit amicum*
> *De grege, sic densi veniunt ad pabula thoes,*
> *Inque vicem hirsuti paribus junguntur onagri;*
> *Lex eadem pelagi, deserto in littore Proteus*
> *Agmina Phocarum numerat, vilisque volucrum*
> *Passer habet semper quicum sit, & omnia circum*
> *Farra libens volitet, serò sua tecta revisens,*
> *Quem si fors letho objecit, seu milvus adunco*
> *Fata tulit rostro, seu stravit arundine fossor,*
> *Protinus ille alium socio petit inde volatu.*
> *Nos durum genus, & diris exercita fatis*
> *Gens homines aliena animis, & pectore discors,*
> *Vix sibi quisque parem de millibus invenit unum,*
> *Aut si sors dederit tandem non aspera votis,*
> *Illum inopina dies, quâ non speraveris horâ*
> *Surripit, aeternum linquens in saecula damnum.*
>
> (94–111)

[Ah me, how like one another are the young steers sporting in the pastures, all companions, of one mind, linked by one law; and no one singles out a particular friend from the herd. So the wolves come in packs to feed, and the shaggy wild asses have mates in turn. The same law holds for the sea; on the deserted shore Proteus numbers his troops of seals. Even the lowest of birds, the sparrow, has always a mate with whom to flit about happily among all the heaps of grain, and returns late to his own nest. And if by chance his mate is carried off by death, whether it comes from the hawk's curved beak or the peasant's arrow, forthwith he seeks another companion for his flights. But we men are a hard race, driven by cruel fates, with minds alien to one another and hearts discordant. Scarcely can you find one friend among thousands; or if destiny, at length yielding to your prayers, has granted one, an unexpected day and hour snatch him away, leaving for ever an irreparable loss.]

(p. 164)

The contrast takes us all the way back to the first pastoral elegy. There Priapus taunts Daphnis with the suggestion that, while he holds himself proudly aloof, a maiden whom he might enjoy if he would is searching for him. Daphnis' humanity and his freedom, we said, consist in his refusal to accept this Priapian ethic. If Daphnis cannot have the maid he wants, he need not, like an animal, search out another mate. Daphnis can die as well as live for love. But we saw too that Priapus is at least half right about Daphnis: he *is* the victim of nature in him; he also belongs to the world of the goats and the goatherds. Theocritus, like later pastoral elegists, balances the sense of Daphnis' separateness from nature against the sense of his participation in her order. But in the "Epitaphium" the half-truth of the earlier poem has become the whole truth. The bonds which unite one man with another are not only finer than, they are contrary to the kinds of bonds which unite one creature with another.

As the poem progresses, the sense of our separateness from pastoral's consolations intensifies. Where in "Lycidas" doubts and affirmations are gradually drawn together in the course of the elegist's journey from grief to recovery, in the "Epitaphium" we move in exactly the opposite direction. Unlike the earlier lament, this one announces its place in the convention explicitly at the very outset:

HIMERIDES *nymphae (nam vos et Daphnin et Hylan,*
Et plorata diu memisistis fata Bionis)
Dicite Sicelicum Thamesina per oppida carmen.

[Nymphs of Himera, since you remember Daphnis and Hylas and the long-lamented fate of Bion, sing a Sicilian elegy through the cities of the Thames. . . .]

But the vision of Damon in heaven with which the poem concludes seems a willed consolation rather than an achieved one. The final assurance that Damon is indeed a member of the heavenly company, couched as it is in such negative terms ("where else," the poet asks, "would he be"), suggests denial rather than mastery of grief:

> *Tu quoque in his, nec me fallit spes lubrica, Damon,*
> *Tu quoque in his certê es; nam quò tua dulcis arbiret*
> *Sanctáque simplicitas, nam quò tua candida virtus?*
> *Nec te Lethaeo fas quaesivisse sub orco,*
> *Nec tibi conveniunt lacrimae, nec flebimus ultrà,*
> *Ite procul, lacrimae . . .*

(198–203)

[You also, Damon, are among these—for no vain hope deceives me—you also are assuredly one of them; for where else should go your sweet and pure simplicity, your shining virtues? It would be sin to look for you in the Lethean underworld. Nothing is here for tears, and I will weep no more. Away, my tears!]

There is little sense of celebration in this conclusion. The description of the heavenly joys which follows (considerably fuller than the description of those joys in "Lycidas"), where the virginal purity of Diodati is clothed in the garb of ecstatic Bacchante, seems both strained and overwrought. One feels this poem might more honestly have ended where Castiglione's ended, with continuing bitterness rather than consolation. We feel that in the "Epitaphium" Milton is commemorating the convention rather than participating in it, reaching out for a world and a way of seeing things that are no longer his.[27]

EPILOGUE

The Gathering Shadows

The pastoral elegist, we have seen, places sorrow in a daylight world. He brings to death what light can bring: illumination, intensification, simplification. The noon hour, at the very apex of the sun's journey through the sky, is his favorite hour. And if elegists from Vergil to Milton admit both the dawn and the dusk into their pastoral worlds, these have only a peripheral place: they mark boundaries, beginnings and endings; their shadows accentuate the brightness which radiates from the poem's center. When the mountain shadows spread across the plains, the pastoral elegist turns homeward; his song is finished. Whatever sorrows the darkness might in its turn sustain, they are not *his* sorrows.[1]

But almost without exception, the modern funeral lament (that is, the post-Renaissance one) is an evening or a night-time song; and this preference dictates, too, the setting of later pastoral elegies. We see it influencing Dryden, for instance, when he renders Vergil's "successimus antro" (in the fifth *Eclogue*) as "the gloomy grotto makes a doubtful day" (1697).[2] In Pope's pastoral elegy (the "Winter" of his four pastoral seasons, 1709), Dryden's "gloomy day" has become night.[3] This is not the place for a full discussion of these later "pastoral elegies" and their very different purposes and effects;[4] I would, however, in these last few pages like to suggest, by way of conclusion, at least one reason why I should prefer to call them something other than "pastoral elegies"—why, that is, the night-time setting makes such a large difference.

Thomas Gray's "Elegy in a Country Church-yard," written approximately one hundred years after "Lycidas" (between 1742 and 1750), offers a convenient model for comparison. Gray does not, of course, as Shelley and Arnold will, ask us to read his elegy as a pastoral elegy; but the poem's large pastoral setting and its numerous allusions to the convention do invite the comparison—a comparison which can only bring home to us the great distance between these two funeral laments (each the greatest of its respective age) and their very different ways of placing sorrow.

Gray begins his elegy (deliberately perhaps?) just at the point where Milton concluded his: at that time when the herdsmen and their flocks depart the fields. Only now does his elegist emerge; this is his chosen hour:

> The Curfew tolls the knell of parting day,
> The lowing herd wind slowly o'er the lea,
> The plowman homeward plods his weary way,
> And leaves the world to darkness and to me. [5]

It is an hour of quietude—

> Now fades the glimmering landscape on the sight,
> And all the air a solemn stillness holds,
> Save where the beetle wheels his droning flight,
> And drowsy tinklings lull the distant folds . . .
>
> (5–8)

and of mysteriousness:

> Save that from yonder ivy-mantled tow'r
> The moping owl does to the moon complain
> Of such, as wand'ring near her secret bow'r,
> Molest her ancient solitary reign.
>
> (9–12)

The elegist no longer wants to let the daylight "play upon" the scene of death and mourning: the subject is too solemn for that,[6] and also too indeterminate. Gray's elegist does not wish to dispel the obscurity that hovers in the twilight air here. For it is only at this uncertain hour, only as the glimmering landscape fades, that the essential obscurity of all things is revealed to him. What is most real and valuable to this elegist is what is hidden (and perhaps must remain hidden) in the shadows. Where the sunlight in "Lycidas" celebrates our triumph *over* obscurity, the shadows in Gray's "Elegy" celebrate obscurity itself. They speak eloquently for all that is tentative and unrealized, in life as in death. Milton's elegist feels all the cruelty of a life cut down before it could fulfill its great promise. Not to accomplish, not to be able to speak and share our sorrows—these are the threats perceived and countered in his elegy. But Gray's elegist cherishes, as he cherishes the shadows rather than the light, the very obscurity in which his simple farmers lived out their undistinguished lives. We do not grieve here for the might-have-been. Instead we celebrate it; for it points to the larger richness of the inner life, of what is hidden in the shadows. That is what matters now. And if among these farmers' graves may be one belonging to "some Cromwell guiltless of his country's blood," then here may also lie a "mute, inglorious Milton" (59–60). If a life of unrealized action may now be thought the more accomplished for being less so, then may not a poet too be the more eloquent for being less so? We cannot, at any rate, as we stand over these farmers' graves, allow ourselves to find words too easily; that is the danger now. And the elegist's own words must be as tentative as those which adorn these "frail" memorials, with their "uncouth rhimes and shapeless sculpture deck'd" (79). In the half-light of the country churchyard Gray's elegist honors the very shapelessness of things, a shapelessness which denies the familiar contours of the daylight world, forces us to look inward, to acknowledge the essential obscurity of life and, beyond this, the great, impenetrable mystery of death in which the obscure farmer and the melancholy elegist are one.

Shelley's use of light and shade in "Adonais" (1821) is considerably more complex. As his elegist will not be confined to any one perspective on death, he does not place his sorrow in any single landscape. Taking the whole universe as his field of vision, he discovers more than one kind of light—and more than one kind of darkness. He journeys from the reflected lights of this world ("Rome's azure sky," the "dying lamps" of earthly poetry) toward the "white radiance of Eternity," and from "the shadow of our night" into the unknown darkness of that other world. Here I want simply to emphasize that, while Shelley's journey is a journey toward eternal light, it is also a journey *away* from whatever illuminations an earthly light might bring. His is a profoundly anti-pastoral, and anti-conventional, quest.

The end and climax of "Adonais" comes as the elegist's bark is driven away from this world, away from the pastoral shore. And, as he is borne "darkly, fearfully, afar," we realize (if we did not before) that the journey toward eternal light is also a journey into the eye of the storm, into the dark mystery of death:

> The breath whose might I have invoked in song
> Descends on me; my spirit's bark is driven,
> Far from the shore, far from the trembling throng
> Whose sails were never to the tempest given;
> The massy earth and spherèd skies are riven!
> I am borne darkly, fearfully, afar;
> Whilst, burning through the inmost veil of Heaven,
> The soul of Adonais, like a star,
> Beacons from the abode where the Eternal are. [7]

Milton's elegist too ventured out into these dark, tempestuous waters; but he did so in order to bring us, and Lycidas, home again. Here, we know, there will be no return. No guardian angel watches over the wanderer now to protect him and rescue him (if he could) from the perilous sea. The dark, mysterious underwater world, which in Milton's poem symbolized the extremity of the elegist's despair, is now his end and destination. Shelley's elegist wills the very uncertainties that Milton's would rescue us from. [8] And if he invokes intermittently along his own course the journeys of earlier pastoralists, those elegists cannot lend him much support now, not at that part of his journey that matters most: its climactic finale. They can only be placed among that "trembling throng" who remain behind on the shore, as Shelley's elegist is borne afar—far at once from the things of this world and from the convention.

To take one final example, consider the prominence of the shadows in Arnold's "Thyrsis" (1866), another latter-day pastoral elegy. "Thyrsis" is a lesser poem than either Gray's "Elegy" or Shelley's "Adonais," but it is an interesting one for my present purposes. Now the darkened landscape speaks, not only for the obscurity in which the elegist wishes to place the fact of death itself, but for the obscurity, the ambivalence, of his own response to it. Arnold is not quite sure what to make of Clough's death, and he allows his uncertainties free play in the poem. Arnold knows we can feel more than one thing, and even not be altogether sure what we feel, when we have suffered a profound loss. So his elegy works, not by clarifying and simplifying the elegist's feelings, but by letting them wander, as the poet wanders, under the shade of night.

As he strays alone through the once-familiar fields of Oxford in the soft dusk of a winter's evening, Arnold's elegist recalls the former days when he walked here with his friend, days when life seemed simple, the way to Truth, as she shone "in life's morning sun so bright and bare,"[9] open and easy. And as he searches for the old landmarks in a changed landscape, under a darkened sky, the elegist knows that nothing will ever be clear and simple for him again:

> Yes, thou art gone! and round me too the night
> In ever-nearing circle weaves her shade.
> I see her veil draw soft across the day . . .
> (131–33)

Like Gray's elegist, Arnold's welcomes the darkness as a truer companion to him now than the light. And he explores in that consoling darkness the complexity of his own emotions. He mourns for Thyrsis' death; he feels bereft here without his friend; but that death also represents an obscure betrayal of both the singer and his world:

> He went; his piping took a troubled sound
> Of storms that rage outside our happy ground;
> He could not wait their passing, he is dead.
> (48–50)

Arnold comes back to this theme at the very end of the poem, though now it is Thyrsis' voice that calls out to his friend: "Why *faintest thou? I wander'd till I died"* (236–37). The elegist's genuine grief at his friend's death is mingled throughout the poem with some resentment, perhaps also with a certain uneasiness: for who is the betrayer here? who the betrayed? We cannot, anymore than the singer himself, be altogether sure. We must rather accept, as Arnold's elegist accepts, along with the other complications of the shadows, the complex tangle of emotions in which the death of a dear friend (perhaps, especially of a dear friend) involves us.

Ambiguous rather than clear, complex rather than simple, mysterious and diffuse rather than concrete and palpable: these are the kinds of emotions the modern elegist brings to his experience of grief, as they are the aspect in which he contemplates death itself. And because this mourner wishes not to dispel such feelings but to elaborate and explore them, he generally makes his complaint in the shadows rather than the sunlight. To him the pastoral elegy can only appear an obsolete form. Knowing as he does that mourning is never simple, never pure, never so easily resolved into sweetness as the pastoralist supposes, the noon-day light could only falsify his truths. And if such a modern elegist invokes our convention, we can only suppose he does so (like Arnold) for the sake of nostalgia, to show how little it now applies.

But that the pastoral elegist's way of seeing things might still have some meaning for us, that his simplifications are not necessarily over-simplifications, that there is, in short, some permanent truth in this way of placing sorrow as in other ways—this is the note on which I should like to conclude this study. It is, I think, a note eloquently sounded in a recently published posthumous story by John Berryman. And a brief discussion of Berryman's "Wash Far Away" may make a fitting end to our story of the pastoral elegy's convention: for the agent of consolation in this story is "Lycidas" itself. And Berryman commemorates our convention by recalling, not only its greatest achievement, but also (more subtly) its way of placing sorrow.

Berryman's hero, a disillusioned young college professor, is very much a man of his times—the late 1940s or early '50s.[10] Some years previously the Professor's closest friend and colleague has died, but all he can bring himself to feel is an aching sense of numbness. It seems indeed to have taken over his whole life: "He thought: I enjoy myself, I quarrel, but I am really dead" (p. 2).[11] He is dead, to feeling. What he does feel, however, in connection with this loss is jealousy and rage—rage at that more successful "rival" who died too soon to make a similar mess out of his own life. There is nothing he can "do" with such feelings; they are simply there, dully but persistently present in the background (sometimes in the foreground). The Professor knows all about the ambiguities of loss, and he cannot mourn.

Yet Berryman places all this, not in the shadows, but in the bright sunlight of a spring morning. The Professor is on his way to the classroom:

> He stepped down into the brilliant light, blinked, sweating, and set out. My god, away. The small leaves of the maple on the corner shook smartly as he passed. Alice's fierce voice echoed. Sunlight plunged to the pavement and ran everywhere like water, vivid, palpable. I am a Professor, he reflected, moving rapidly, or a sort of professor; there is a breeze, a wild sun. As he leveled his palm sailing along the even hedge, it tingled. He felt his toes in his shoes. The hedge danced faintly.
>
> My life is in ruins, he thought. She begins the quarrels, but they are my fault. Here is this weather and we are desperate . . .
>
> (pp. 1–2)

Here *is* the weather blooming, brilliant . . . a bitter reminder to the Professor that his own life is in a state of decay. But in this clear light ("vivid, palpable") the Professor's vague sense of desperation is even now being placed as it is being intensified. And this "pastoral" flowering anticipates the renewal of human life at the story's close.

The Professor has assigned "Lycidas" to his class of undergraduates. It is his favorite poem, and if he knows himself to be a less adventurous teacher than when he first began, he still looks forward to the teaching of this poem. He rehearses in his mind the poem's "lesson," the lesson he himself has found in "Lycidas" and which he will impart, if he can, to his students. It is this: " 'Whatever we do and think we are doing, however objective or selfless our design, our souls each instant are enacting *our own* destinies' "

(12). The Professor, as I said, knows all about the ambivalences of what we call mourning, and he reads this exercise in grief with the critical insights of his own generation. Milton may think he is mourning King's death, but it is really *his own* fate (both personal and poetic) that absorbs him. What the Professor's "lesson" requires of us is not merely an act of substitution; we are not, that is, simply to read Milton's name everywhere we see King's (or Lycidas'). Rather, the "lesson" points an ironic finger at the mourner. The poem's meaning is in the fact of the displacement itself, in the way we think we are being objective and selfless just when we are least so.[12] Needless to say, the "lesson" has a special application to the Professor's own case and one that is not unperceived by him. He can well appreciate what Milton, at twenty-eight, obscure, untenured and passionately ambitious, must have felt for the successful Fellow three years his junior.

It takes the "pastoral" naiveté of a student in the Professor's class to teach him that "Lycidas" is both a simpler and a more profound poem than he knew, and, in teaching him that, to teach him, finally, to mourn his own friend's death. The student, artless, blundering, annoyingly persistent, will have nothing of the Professor's ironies. When his teacher analyses the poem's "digressions" for the class and reveals Milton turning away from King's situation to his own, the student balks: "It might be his own situation," he concedes. "It *is* King's though, isn't it? . . . It's King's life that got slit, and then Apollo consoles Milton by saying that his lost friend, after all, will be judged in Heaven, not here. So will Milton, but that doesn't keep it from being about King"(22, 23). As the Professor keeps trying to turn the discussion to Milton, to his *self*-preoccupations, the student keeps coming back to King, to the *other*, to the fact of loss. So when the Professor asks why the elegist should move at the end to "new pastures," if not to pursue those private goals which all along have most deeply concerned him, the student naively replies that the elegist departs because "he doesn't want to be any more where his friend was with him, and all the things he sees will remind him of his loss" (16).

The Professor feels confused. The class isn't going where he'd intended it to go. It's not that he insists on directing his students' responses, but that (for obscure reasons) much depends for him on preserving his "lesson," his reading of the poem, intact. He can't sustain it, however; and suddenly the Professor finds himself reading those crucial lines with a new emphasis, as the full realization of loss, the awesome loss of another, washes over him:

> "whilst THEE the shores, and sounding seas
> Wash far away, where'er thy bones are hurled,
> Whether beyond the stormy Hebrides,
> Where THOU perhaps under the whelming tide
> Visit'st the bottom of the monstrous world—"
>
> (26)

It is *thee*, he suddenly understands, it is *thee* the shores wash away; it is Edward King; it is the Professor's own friend as well. This is the most painful truth, as it is the one the Professor has so successfully hidden from himself. It is the fact of loss we must acknowledge. For is the Professor's relentless need to refer all emotions back to some persistent self-preoccupation, to see even in the death of another only the echo of some imagined loss to that self—is it all really that bold "facing up" to reality he thought it was? Might it not be just the opposite—the easier, not the harder way? An attempt to protect himself from what is more painful than this shallow irony: the fact of loss itself? For Lycidas is lost to us in a way we can never be lost to ourselves: he is "washed far away."

And it is through the sudden, acute experience of these two losses, his own and Milton's, that Berryman's hero is (like the earlier elegist) brought back to life again. It is a pastoral return:

> The Professor sat a long time in his office, not thinking of anything and perhaps not unhappy, before he went home. Once he read over the transfiguration of Lycidas, and was troubled by the trembling of light on the page; his eyes had filled with tears. He heard the portrait's voice [his friend's voice, which he has not, up to this point, in seeing his image, been able to recall]. At last he rose, closed the window and took his hat. Shutting the door, as he left, in the still-bright hall he looked at the name engraved on his card on the door. He felt older than he had in the morning, but he had moved into the exacting conviction that he was . . . something . . . not dead.
>
> (26)

The Professor's deeper "lesson" (a lesson both in loss and in renewal) comes to him, like the pastoral elegist's, passively. He does not formulate his revised reading of the poem any more than he formulates what he is now able to feel for his dead friend; he simply discovers that his eyes have filled with tears. It is, to be sure, a twentieth-century affirmation—tentative, understated. Berryman's hero is "perhaps not unhappy," only "something . . . not dead." We do not claim too much.

Yet it is an affirmation, nonetheless, and one which recalls at several points (most explicitly, of course, in the echo of Milton's "at last he rose") the poem which brought it into being. Fainter echoes sound throughout the passage: again the elegist's departure coincides with the fading of the light and again there is a promise of a fresh beginning in that leave-taking. The sunlight that still trembles on the Professor's page and glimmers in the still-bright hall places this elegist's grief (and now, finally, it *is* grief he feels) in a simpler, clearer world than the one he knew before, places it, we might be tempted to say, in a pastoral world.

Berryman's story is not, of course, a pastoral elegy. Impossible now to rewrite Milton's lines or resurrect a dead convention. But by presenting his hero's encounter with "Lycidas" simply as an encounter (a "reading"), Berryman is able to recapture something vital to the experience of writing within a poetic convention: the appropriation of another writer's words and feelings in such a way as to make them our own. This we do have here. And we also have (and have more persuasively, I think, than in the anachronistic revivals of the form by Shelley and Arnold: their laments succeed for different reasons) a fully contemporary reinterpretation of the pastoral elegist's way of seeing things. Perhaps it is just because he comes at the convention indirectly, writing about it rather than in it, that Berryman can do it, can show us that the pastoral elegist still might teach us how to mourn.

NOTES

INTRODUCTION

1. "But man is a Noble Animal, splended in ashes, and pompous in the grave, solemnizing Nativities and Deaths with equall lustre, nor omitting Ceremonies of bravery, in the infamy of his nature." "Hydriotaphia or Urne Buriall," *The Prose of Sir Thomas Browne*, ed. Norman J. Endicott (Garden City, N.Y., 1967), p. 284.

2. Ibid., p. 251.

3. "Notes on Convention," in *Perspectives of Criticism*, ed. Levin, HSCL 20 (1950): 55–83.

4. *Theocritus*, ed. A. S. F. Gow, 2nd ed., 2 vols. (Cambridge, Eng., 1952), 1:43, *Idyll* 5.45–47 (italics mine—Gow is the translator).

5. *P. Vergili Maronis Opera*, ed. R. A. B. Mynors (Oxford, 1969), p. 27, *Eclogue* 10.42–43 (italics mine).

6. *Works*, ed. Hereford and Simpson, 11 vols. (Oxford, 1961), 7:11 (italics mine).

7. *The Poetical Works of John Milton*, ed. Helen Darbishire, 2 vols. (Oxford, 1955), 2:194 (italics mine).

8. Text based on Gow, *Theocritus* 1:5, *Idyll* 1.1–3.

9. Pastoral poetry, Parry suggests, occupies a place midway in the evolution of attitudes toward nature between the earlier poetry (as that, e.g., of Homer), in which we look to nature for confirmation of what we *are*, and the later poetry (as that of the Romantics), in which we look to nature to tell us what we are not but *yearn* to be. "Landscape in Greek Poetry," YCS 15 (1957): 3–29. I do not take issue with this metaphorical view of the pastoral landscape (indeed pastoral would be a barren ground if it did not have the kinds of significance Parry suggests) but with the allegorical view which would deny it that primary literal significance—supposing that because the shepherd is not a "real" shepherd, the landscape cannot be a real landscape. Pastoral is a country of the mind, but it is a landscape too. I would take issue, then, in a general way with all those interpretations of the pastoral landscape which suggest it is less sustaining as well as less real insofar as it is removed from our ordinary world. For recent criticism of pastoral poems along these lines, see: on Theocritus, Gilbert Lawall, *Theocritus' Coan Pastorals, A Poetry Book* (pub. Center for Hellenistic Studies, Washington, D.C.; distrib. Harvard University Press, Cambridge, Mass., 1967); on Vergil, Michael Putnam, *Virgil's Pastoral Art: Studies in the "Eclogues"* (Princeton, 1970); and on Milton, Jon S. Lawry, "Eager Thought: Dialectic in *Lycidas*," PMLA 77 (1962): 27–32.

10. William Empson, for instance, defines pastoral as poetry which is about the people, but not by or for them, in *Some Versions of Pastoral* (Norfolk, Conn., 1960). This is stimulating criticism and Empson seems to me essentially right about the relations between the various groups concerned. I would, however, restrict "the people" to a particular segment thereof—those who live on the land.

11. For the pastoral elegy as an exposé of pastoral felicity see, for instance,

Jacques Perret: "the pastoral world is that of eternity in an instant, the world of perfect moments. . . . Death . . . has no meaning there and no place. . . . No one should die in Arcadia; and if one does, then Arcadia is an illusion." "The Georgics," in *Virgil, a Collection of Critical Essays*, ed. Steele Commager (Englewood Cliffs, N.J., 1966), p. 30.

12. The motto, "Et in Arcadia Ego"—which frequently appears in seventeenth-century pictorial representations of a pastoral, golden age—and its shifting innuendoes are the subject of Erwin Panofsky's essay, "Et in Arcadia Ego: Poussin and the Elegiac Tradition," in *Meaning in the Visual Arts* (Garden City, N.Y., 1955), pp. 295–320. Panofsky suggests that in the early Renaissance representations death enters Arcadia as an intruder, a harsh (even gruesome) reminder that even here we are not immune from mortality. But Poussin, significantly, mistranslates "Even in Arcadia there am I" as "I too was born, or lived in Arcadia"; and in his later paintings the melancholy presence of the deceased only enhances the sweetness of the Arcadian world.

13. Compare Wordsworth's feelings upon hearing the song of the Solitary Reaper, a "melancholy strain . . . [of] some natural sorrow, loss or pain" which, as the poet says, brings more cheer to the weary traveler than do the glad notes of the nightingale. The Wordsworthian narrator feels a sense of awe before this child of nature which reflects the ultimate mysteriousness of the ideal she embodies. The pastoral poet may long for what he cannot have, but what he longs for is always something definable, palpable. Yet he and the Wordsworthian "traveler" are alike in their perception of the pleasurable feelings which the expression of a "natural" sorrow confers on the urbanite, whose emotions are always more complex.

14. "Theme, Pattern, and Imagery in *Lycidas*," in *Milton's "Lycidas," the Tradition and the Poem*, ed. C. A. Patrides (New York, 1961), p. 172.

15. *Theocritus* 1:37, *Idyll* 4.43.

16. *Poems of Ben Jonson*, ed. George Burke Johnston (Cambridge, Mass., 1955), p. 130.

17. Renato Poggioli, in one of the most stimulating modern interpretations of the genre, suggests that pastoral and Christian ideals are inimical. And so they must be if we see Christianity as entirely concerned with the life beyond and the psychological root of pastoral as (in Poggioli's words) "a double longing after innocence and happiness to be recovered not through a conversion or a regeneration but merely through a retreat." "The Oaten Flute," *HLB* 11 (1957): 147. I do not want to minimize other-worldly impulses in Christianity or regressive ones in pastoral. Poggioli's antithesis between the two ideals covers roughly the same ground as my distinction between pastoral "hereness" and Christian "thereness." I would, however, suggest that, while distinct, these two ideals need not be antipathetic. There may, that is, be room for both the here and the there, for both retreat and regeneration within a single poem or poetic vision. Let us remember that impulses toward regeneration and those toward retreat are often less easy to disentangle from one another than Poggioli's definition suggests. In pastoral we are always going backward, losing our way, only to discover that the mistaken path was the right way all along. And the Christian sojourner too must often go backward (retreat in certain ways) before he can advance.

18. Even among eighteenth-century poets, with their passion for classification, we find a variety of names for the form I am calling the pastoral elegy. Thus Dryden writes a "pastoral elegy" but Congreve a "pastoral lamenting the death of . . . " and Walsh a "pastoral eclogue." Pope's "Winter" is simply subtitled "the fourth pastoral, or Daphne." Among nineteenth-century English pastoral elegists, Shelley's "Adonais" is described as an "elegy," Arnold's "Thyrsis" as a "monody"; Yeats' "Shepherd and Goatherd" (1919), the most recent example of the form with

which I am familiar, bears no further title than that. Thus our term "pastoral elegy" would appear to owe its prominence to the twentieth-century critic's need for some single, unifying name for this convention. It is a useful term, no more.

19. Renaissance pastoral theory owes its lack of theoretical precision to the absence of any classical foundation on which it might rest. Looking to Aristotle and Horace for a definition of this genre comparable to those they found for epic, comedy, tragedy, etc., the Renaissance theorists found no mention of a separate pastoral genre. Indeed they found no mention of pastoral poems at all. Renaissance pastoral poetry—by the sixteenth century a genre *de facto*, and a highly popular one—looked back to the ancient commentators on Theocritus and Vergil for its theoretical justification. Here the poets found that mixed definition which—emphasizing the humble (*humile*) style and subject matter appropriate to pastoral poetry, while allowing more serious matters to be brought in allegorically—forms the basis of Renaissance pastoral theory. For the Theocritean scholia see *Scholia in Theocritum Vetera*, ed. Carolus Wendel (Leipzig, 1914). The most important of the ancient commentators on the *Eclogues* is Servius (late fourth century A.D.), whose commentary absorbs (and revises) earlier work by Donatus (mid fourth century A.D.): *Servii Grammatici . . . Commentarii*, eds. G. Thilo and H. Hagen, 3 vols. (Leipzig, 1881–1902), 3. Alice Hulubei, in the first chapter of her study of French pastoral poetry, *L'Eglogue en France au XVIe siècle, époque des Valois* (Paris, 1938), traces the evolution of pastoral theory as it is formulated by these early commentators and transmitted thence through Renaissance editions of Theocritus and Vergil into such Renaissance *artes poeticae* as those of Julius Caesar Scaliger in Italy and Thomas Sébillet in France. Pp. 1–25.

If we turn to these Renaissance theorists for some discussion of the pastoral elegy, if we ask them how, or why, the intrinsically serious and seemingly "high" subject of death should be admitted into the simple world of the herdsmen, the best they can tell us is simply that it is so. Thus Sébillet recommends the following subjects to the pastoral poet: "mortz de Princes, calamitéz de temps, mutations de Republiques . . . et téles choses ou pareilles . . ."—and all these to be treated "soubz propos et termes pastoraus." *L'Art poétique françoys* (1548), ed. Félix Gaiffe (Paris, 1932), p. 159. But how are death and the other high subjects Sébillet recommends to be brought into this pastoral landscape without violating that humility which is the very essence of the genre? Sébillet and the other theorists do not answer this question. The pastoral theory they know (inherited from the ancient commentators) is essentially descriptive rather than analytic; it has no answers to such questions as why the funeral lament should be introduced into the herdsman's world. The answer those commentators, and the Renaissance theorists after them, give to this question is a historical one. The explanation (which Renaissance poets would find in their editions of Vergil and Theocritus) runs roughly like this: Theocritus mourned the death of the Sicilian neatherd, Daphnis, in his first pastoral poem because this same Daphnis was the inventor of pastoral poetry. So the death of the genre's founder is commemorated in the genre itself. Later Moschus, a follower of Theocritus, appropriated the pastoral elegy form to mourn another neatherd's death; but now the "neatherd" is really a poet, Bion, who enters the herdsman's world only by proxy, as the *author* of poems about herdsmen. And finally, in his fifth *Eclogue*, Vergil mourned the great Julius Caesar, neither a herdsman nor a poet of the countryside but the "custos" (or "guardian") of the fair flock. This composite picture is drawn from the following major sources of Renaissance pastoral theory: Josse Ascensius Badius' preface to the *Eclogues* in his edition of Vergil's *Opera*, first published in 1500–01 and frequently reprinted in the sixteenth century; Juan Luis Vives' commentary on the *Eclogues*, *The Allegory of the Eclogues*, first published in 1544 and often included in Renaissance editions of Vergil (see, e.g., *P. Vergilii Maronis . . . universvm poema . . .* [Venice, 1562], which includes the commentaries of Badius and Vives); Julius Caesar Scaliger's *Poetices Libri Septem* (Paris, 1561, 2d ed. 1586), 1.3 and 1.4 (1.4—which includes the ritualistic theories on the origins of the genre inherited from the ancient commentators—is translated in F. M. Padelford's *Select Translations from Scaliger's Poetics* [New York, 1905], pp. 21–32); Thomas Sébillet's *L'Art poétique françoys*, pp. 159–61; E. K.'s epistle to Harvey prefaced to Spenser's *Shepheardes Calendar* (1579), in *Elizabethan Critical Essays*, ed. G. Gregory Smith, 2 vols. (Oxford, 1904), 1:127–134; William Webbe's *Discourse of English Poetrie* (1589), in *Elizabethan Critical Essays*, 2:39–40; and George Puttenham's *Art of English Poesie*, in *Elizabethan Critical Essays*, 2:39–40.

Thus the way is open for a Renaissance poet to introduce almost anyone he wishes into the pastoral world and, more importantly, to consider almost any subject, however serious, in the humble setting. How the poet is to accommodate the seriousness of his theme—should he choose to introduce even death itself—to the sweetness of that setting, is a problem he must resolve himself. The commentators cannot help him; they do not even acknowledge the difficulty. Since this is a problem—the crucial problem indeed to which my study addresses itself—that the poets (at times ineptly, at times brilliantly), and not the theorists deal with, I have not dealt more thoroughly with Renaissance pastoral theory in these pages. That subject has, I think, been adequately treated elsewhere. See, in addition to Hulubei, the first chapter of J. A. Congleton's *Theory of Pastoral Poetry in England, 1648–1798* (Gainesville, Fla., 1952).

20. Compare, for instance, the love lament or the singing match, both of which traditional pastoral forms grant the poet considerably more freedom. The success of the latter indeed depends precisely on the poet's ability (or that of his herdsman-singer) to improvise.

21. See Levin, "Notes on Convention," p. 64.

22. There are in fact two names, but neither is generic. "Lycidas" suffices when the poem is published among its companion pieces in honor of King's death. When this tribute stands on its own, "monody"—which tells us that this speaker himself stands alone, rather than in the somewhat more customary position as one of a pair—and biographical information, helpful in this new context, are added. All these ways of placing the poem are important; the term "monody" in particular is highly important. But it places the poem *within* the possibilities of the Renaissance convention; it does not place it as a pastoral elegy. (A poem might be a monody without being a pastoral elegy.)

23. We have not yet had an extended historical study of this convention, though there have been numerous studies of influences at work in particular poems. In 1911 George Norlin isolated and described the various internal conventions of the genre, citing passages from a large number of poems as illustration. "The Conventions of the Pastoral Elegy," *AJP* 32 (1911): 294–312. In his study of *Neo-Latin Poetry and the Pastoral* (Chapel Hill, 1965), W. Leonard Grant provides a very useful catalogue of the most prolific branch of the convention, the neo-Latin Renaissance pastoral elegy, or "epicedium" (pp. 306–330). The best single survey of the convention from a historical point of view is still to be found in *The Pastoral Elegy: An Anthology*, with Introduction, Commentary and Notes by Thomas Perrin Harrison, Jr., and English translation by Harry Joshua Leon (Austin, 1939)—though this is in need of some critical updating.

24. *Some Versions of Pastoral*, p. 6. See above, Intro., n. 10. On what can, and cannot, be deduced about Theocritus' life from the evidence of the poems see Gow, *Theocritus* I, pp. xvii–xxii.

25. For discussion of the cultural climate of the Alexandrian age, see P. M. Fraser, *Ptolemaic Alexandria*, 3 vols. (Oxford, 1952): 1. For affinities between the

Theocritean aesthetic and Epicureanism see Thomas G. Rosenmeyer, *The Green Cabinet: Theocritus and the European Pastoral Lyric* (Berkeley and Los Angeles, 1969), pp. 42–44.

26. "Landscape in Greek Poetry," 10–14.

27. W. W. Greg's portrait of Theocritus (*Pastoral Poetry and Pastoral Drama* [London, 1906]) is representative:

> It was for his own solace, forgetful for a moment of the intrigues of court life and the uncertain sunshine of princes, that he wrote his Sicilian idylls. For him, as at a magic touch, the walls of the heated city melted like a mirage into the sands of the salt lagoon, and he wandered once more amid the green pastures of Trinacria. . . . There once more he saw the shepherds tend their flocks . . . or else there sounded in his ears the love-song or the dirge. . . . All these memories he recorded with a loving faithfulness of detail that it is even now possible to verify from the folk-songs of the south (pp. 9–10).

28. See Rosenmeyer, *The Green Cabinet* (1969), and Lawall, *Theocritus' Coan Pastorals, A Poetry Book* (1967).

29. *The Green Cabinet*, p. 114; quoted from M. Jacobs, *The Content and Style of an Oral Literature: Clackmas Chinook Myths and Tales* (Chicago, 1959), p. 204.

30. "Years Vanish like the Morning Dew," trans. Arthur Waley, in *Man Answers Death: an Anthology of Poetry*, ed. Corliss Lamont (New York, 1936), p. 204. This poem shares with the pastoral elegy not only the notion that nature shares our sorrows but also the complementary one that we participate in her eternal cycle of death and renewal. The lines immediately preceding the ones quoted here are:

> The old graves are plowed up into fields,
> The pines and cypresses are hewn for timber.

31. "On the Pathetic Fallacy," *Modern Painters* 3.12.

32. Gow, *Theocritus* 1:61.

33. *The New Golden Bough*, ed. Theodor Gaster (New York, 1959), pp. 284–85. As Frazer's modern editor points out, the original theory needs some revision: "It is now no longer accepted that the 'dying and reviving' gods of ancient religions, i.e., such figures as Tammuz, Adonis, Attis, and Osiris, merely personify vegetation. . . . Rather are they to be considered as embodiments of 'providence' in general—that is, of the divine force which permeates a community or region and gives it life and increase. The myths and rituals associated with them are thus no mere allegories of sowing and reaping, but are designed rather to account for the rhythm of nature by furnishing reasons (e.g., umbrage or discomfiture) why that providence is periodically withdrawn or absent (Ibid., p. xvii).

34. Ibid., p. 285.

35. *The Pastoral Elegy*, p. 1. In the second sentence Harrison is quoting from W. Y. Sellar, *The Roman Poets of the Augustan Age* (Oxford, 1883), p. 155.

36. *English Pastoral Poetry from the Beginnings to Marvell* (London, 1952), p. 21.

37. "Levels of Meaning in Literature," *KR* 12 (1950): 258.

38. See below, pp. 24–25.

39. Claudius Aelianus, *His Various History*, trans. Thomas Stanley (London, 1666), p. 203.

40. *The Library of History*, trans. C. H. Oldfather, Loeb Library, 10 vols. (London and New York, 1933), 3:85.

41. The ritualistic accounts of the origins of pastoral recorded by the scholiasts also link in suggestive ways the origins of the genre as a whole with the special concerns of the pastoral elegy. One version, for instance. locates the origins of pastoral during the period of the Persian wars (5th century B.C.). It is said that the

Spartan maids, neglecting on one occasion their customary worship of Artemis, hid themselves out of fear of the invading army. In their place farmers from the surrounding countryside entered the city and substituted their own rites for those of the frightened maidens. This practice became an annual custom, and each year the farmers would return to the city and engage in singing contests among themselves. In a second version of the same story, the farmers bring rustic gifts, such as bread molded into the shape of animals, with them to the city. Out of such rites, the scholiasts say, pastoral poetry is born ("Prolegamena," *Scholia in Theocritum Vetera,* ed. Wendel, pp. 2–3). The theory, like that of the mythological origins of the genre, is highly dubious from a historical point of view. The intimacy of the pastoral exchange would seem to militate against a theory of popular, cult origins. Yet the situations described in these accounts is tantalizingly close to the underlying situation of all pastoral poetry: a tired civilization, one threatened by war and death, is refreshed by renewing its ties with the representatives of nature. This pattern, moreover, is most evident in the pastoral elegy. The most likely explanation is not that the scholiasts have some information about the origins of pastoral which we are lacking; probably they do not. But there is no reason to suppose that they are any less well equipped than we to understand the dynamic of pastoral poetry. Thus I suppose that these ritualistic explanations represent some very good intuitions about the *meaning* of the poetry which are then referred back to fill the gap in our knowledge of its sources. But for a modern defense of the theory of ritualistic origins see Richmond Y. Hathorn, "The Ritual Origins of Pastoral," *TAPA* 92 (1961): 228–238.

CHAPTER 1

1. In all the other bucolic idylls (with the exception of the highly discursive fourth) we also see songs framed by narration or dialogue. Two herdsmen converse, then sing, and the poem ends with praise, rewards, or some comment upon the song. This is the general pattern to which the bucolic idylls conform. But in most of them the song is an *extension* of the speech which precedes it, with varying degrees of separation between the herdsman-as-speaker and the herdsman-as-singer. In the fifth *Idyll* the two roles are scarcely distinguished; in the third, the herdsman's spoken words betray a somewhat different attitude (a more "realistic" one) toward his beloved from that which informs the song. The first song in the seventh *Idyll*, like Thyrsis' in the first, has the appearance of a traditional set-piece, but the situation there might, at the same time, be the speaker's own. In the sixth *Idyll* (as in the first) the song transplants us to the world of myth; but the comedy in that song revolves around the way the herdsman transforms that mythical world into one scarcely distinguishable from his own. The three separate episodes in the first *Idyll*, however, are distinguished from one another not only by their different casts of characters, but by the fact that these characters *cannot*, aesthetically speaking, all inhabit the same world.

Gilbert Lawall (*Theocritus' Coan Pastorals, A Poetry Book* [pub. Center for Hellenistic Studies, Washington, D.C.; distrib. Harvard University Press, Cambridge, Mass., 1967]) compares the structure of the first *Idyll* to that of the non-bucolic second *Idyll*. But there too we have a more fluid relationship between the speaker and the song: the situation presented in the frame (a woman's frustrated passion) leads directly into the matter of the song (her vain efforts to retrieve her lover).

2. My text of the first *Idyll* is based on A. S. F. Gow's literal translation (*Theocritus*, 2nd ed., 2 vols. [Cambridge Eng., 1952], 1:5 ff.), but I have made some changes in diction and word-order.

3. This detached posture is characteristic of the way herdsmen register their feelings. A passage in the seventh *Idyll* (130 ff.) offers an interesting exception.

There the herdsmen submit themselves to the pleasures of the harvest; they are "drinking in" the loveliness of their world as they drink in the rich harvest wine. That more subjective stance is appropriate to the sense of pleasure beyond all measure which the harvest brings. Generally, however, the herdsmen in the bucolic idylls are more detached than this—the recorders of isolated pleasures.

4. See Thomas Rosenmeyer's discussion of what he calls "paratactic naiveté" in Theocritus (*The Green Cabinet: Theocritus and the European Pastoral Lyric* [Berkeley and Los Angeles, 1969], pp. 45–64, esp. p. 46 ff. and 63). According to Rosenmeyer, Theocritus typifies the poetic sensibility (the opposite of the lyric one) which seeks to reduce experience to a series of disjunctive units. Theocritus tends to avoid progression in his bucolic idylls and thereby disappoints our expectations of dramatic development. "Paratactic naiveté" thus supports an authorial stance of disengagement; where there is no development there is no "message." I think Rosenmeyer is essentially right about Theocritus' preferences. His own discussion of the first *Idyll*, however, in which he speaks of a dissonance between Daphnis and his world which must be resolved by the poem's progress (p. 119), suggests that in this respect as in others the first *Idyll* is not entirely typical of its author. "Paratactic naiveté" is an element here, particularly in the frame. But in the interior world of the lament it must contend against that spirit of insistent purposefulness embodied in Daphnis himself.

5. Professor John Finley suggests to me that these conversions, or qualifications, in the scenes on the cup move in an opposite direction from the one I describe here and prepare us for an opposite kind of qualification in the song to follow: i.e., the men love, but are thwarted; the old man fishes, but has lost his youth; the boy is happy, but he is about to be robbed; and Daphnis himself is loved by the nymphs, but he must die. I think that Professor Finley and I are responding to the same tensions in the poem, but I feel that these tensions are resolved in a positive rather than a negative way: i.e. Daphnis dies, but life and art continue on.

6. The seventh *Idyll* is the only one in which the geography is firmly established and plays an important role in the narrative. There we not only know that we are on Cos, but we know too the relations between one place and another on the island—where the herdsmen are coming from, where they are going, and how long it takes them to get there. None of the other idylls is bound to its setting in this way, though place names are mentioned in other poems (*Idylls* four and five, for instance, seem to be set in southern Italy). However, such allusions to place names as we see at 9.15 or at 11.47 should probably not be interpreted as definite keys to the locations of the poems in question. Rather, as Gow suggests, "geographical names are used, like those of persons, to give an air of precision and verisimilitude to the scene, but . . . the setting is no more strictly local than the dialect" (1:xx). Thus, Gow continues, "the debate whether, for example, *Id*. I is staged in Sicily or in the East is misconceived." Certainly we are not *in* Cos in the frame or *in* Sicily in Thyrsis' song in the same sense that we are in Cos (and a particular part of the island) in the seventh *Idyll*. Yet the suggestion of a shift from the one location to the other is, I think, important. What is involved is not simply a shift from the one place to the other, but a shift in the *way* in which characters are allowed to exist in a given setting. For Calydna see Gow, *Theocritus* 2:14–15.

7. But contrast the presentation of Daphnis' death at 7:71–77; see above, p. xxvii.

8. This interpretation, first proposed by G. A. Gebauer in 1856 (*De Poetarum Graecorum Bucolicorum* . . . [diss., Leipzig], pp. 74–83) is endorsed by our editor, Gow, *Theocritus* 2:1–2. "Duseros" at line 85, as Gow says, is "applicable to anybody whose love is in any way perverse" (p. 19). He supposes Daphnis' perversity, or as he translates it, "cursedness," to reside in the fact that, bound to his oath, he is "*gauche* or *backward* in pressing a suit which, if pressed, will not be contested."

9. See above, p. xxxii.

10. The "second Hippolytus" theory tends to make Daphnis into a hero of withdrawal and the poem itself a celebration of withdrawal from life rather than a celebration of life. See especially Gilbert Lawall: "It becomes clear that Theocritus' preferences . . . are heavily weighted toward the country, toward release from passion and an ideal tranquility attainable more readily in the inner landscape of dreams and imagination than in the real world of external reality" (*Theocritus' Coan Pastorals*, p. 116). But if Theocritus is quite ready to show us the pains of love, he does not suggest that we should therefore disavow it—or that we could do so if we wished to.

11. See R. M. Ogilvie, "The Song of Thyrsis," *JHS* 82 (1962): 106–110.

12. See F. J. Williams, "Theocritus, Idyll I 81–91," *JHS* 89 (1969): 121–123. Williams thinks that Daphnis' "perversity" at line 85 is not due to his being, as Gow suggests, a "laggard in love" and cites other passages to support the reading "obsessed with desire [for that which is unattainable]."

13. There is a nice example of the Theocritean presentation of love in the seventh *Idyll*. A certain Simichidas "loves Myrto as dearly as goats love the spring. But Aratus . . . guards deep at heart desire of a boy" (96–99). The animalistic desires of the one, the romantic love of the other—these are given. Simichidas sees the folly of his friend's attachment. But he doesn't try to reason with him; that would be a waste of time. Instead he says, "No more, Aratus, let us mount guard by his porch, nor wear our feet away; but let the morning cock with his crowing deliver up another to the numbing pain." These words acknowledge the permanence of romantic love—and romantic suffering—as a state of mind and acknowledge too the helplessness of the lover before his own emotions. "We all take our turn at that altar," suggests Simichidas. "Tomorrow, I hope it may be someone else instead of you who is led to the sacrifice."

14. I discount the facetiously presented suicide contemplated by the amorous Cyclops at 3.25 ff.

15. E. R. Curtius has traced the rhetorical figure which he calls the *topos* of "the world upside-down" to Archilochus in the seventh century B.C.:

> The eclipse of the sun of April 6, 648 B.C., would seem to have given him the idea that nothing was any longer impossible now that Zeus had darkened the sun; no one need be surprised if the beasts of the field changed their food for that of dolphins.—*European Literature in the Latin Middle Ages*, trans. Willard R. Trask, Bollingen Series 36 (New York, 1953), p. 95.

This is an example of nature imitating nature, of course, not, as in the Theocritean passage, of nature imitating man. The figure, used in both these ways, becomes an extremely popular one, not only in pastoral poetry. See Gow's citations of instances in Latin poetry (2:28).

16. Daphnis is not the only Theocritean herdsman to suggest that nature might reverse her own order out of sympathy with reversals in the human world. In the eighth *Idyll* (41 ff.) the shepherd Menalcas testifies to the attractions of his beloved on whose presence all nature attends:

> There does the sheep, there do the goats bear twins; and there the bees fill the hives with honey and the oaks grow taller, where the fair Milon steps. But if he depart, parched is the shepherd there and parched the pasture.

To whom his companion replies, in praise of his own beloved:

> Everywhere is spring, and pastures everywhere, and everywhere udders gush with milk and younglings are fattened, where the fair Nais ranges. But if she depart, wasted the neatherd and his cattle wasted.

But there is, of course, a difference between according one's lover the power to turn the world upside-down and claiming such powers for oneself. Daphnis is a more assertive figure than any of the other Theocritean herdsmen, none of whom makes a comparable demand on nature.

17. The first collected edition of the Greek bucolic poets was evidently made by Artemidorus of Tarsus sometime before the end of the first century B.C. An epigram in the Greek Anthology, attributed to Artemidorus, says that now the bucolic poets, formerly separated, have been brought together. On the Greek texts, particularly on which poems would have been available to Vergil, see Ulrich von Wilamowitz-Moellendorf, *Die Textgeschichte der Grieschischen Bukoliker, Philologische Untersuch-ungen*, vol. 18 (Berlin, 1906), pp. 110–11, 124.

The "Lament for Adonis" and the "Lament for Bion" were first published in the Aldine edition of the Greek bucolic poets in Venice in 1495.

18. Evidence that Vergil is indebted to the "Lament for Adonis" in his fifth *Eclogue* reduces itself to his description at lines 22–23 of Daphnis' mother embracing the body of her dead son. But while the romantic tone of the Vergilian passage may owe something to Bion's description of Aphrodite's grief at the death of Adonis, the cruel but still sorrowful love goddess of the Theocritean poem would be a sufficient source. Bion's Aphrodite, moreover, nowhere calls the stars cruel (which is the one thing Daphnis' mother does in the fifth *Eclogue*); in the "Lament for Adonis" there can be neither cruelty nor protest on our part—only grief, for it could not have been otherwise.

As for Vergil's possible indebtedness to the "Lament for Bion" in the fifth *Eclogue*, while he may have derived the general ideal of turning the neatherd's lament into an elegy for a contemporary from that poem, only one specific motif in the fifth *Eclogue* can be directly traced to the intermediate poem. In the "Lament for Bion" we are told that since Bion died "the cows that wander by the bulls lament and will not graze." *Greek Bucolic Poets*, ed. and trans. A. S. F. Gow (Cambridge, Eng., 1953), p. 134. In the fifth *Eclogue* cattle again refuse to graze when the neatherd dies (24–26). But Theocritus also tells of cattle refusing to eat (in the fourth *Idyll*—though they mourn an absent, not a dead master). Most likely Vergil follows "Moschus" when he shifts this motif from its original, casual setting in Theocritus to the funeral lament. But, if so, it is noteworthy that Vergil only follows the intermediate poet when that poet is himself being "Theocritean."

19. *The Greek Bucolic Poets*, p. 145.

20. Ibid., p. 133.

CHAPTER 2

1. J. M. André tells us that "otium" was originally a Roman military term for soldiers' leave of duty. "Recherches sur l'otium romain," *Annales littéraires de l'Université de Besançon* 52 (1962): 8. "Otium," then, as Thomas G. Rosenmeyer suggests, might mean to Vergil and his world "a vacation, freedom, escape from pressing business, particularly a business with overtones of death." *The Green Cabinet: Theocritus and the European Pastoral Lyric* (Berkeley and Los Angeles, 1969), pp. 42–44.

2. See 1.79–83; 2.66–67; 6.84–86; 7.44; 10.77.

3. The first *Eclogue* begins with a suggestion of the noonday rest and closes with evening. The second opens with an explicit reference to the noon hour and closes with the oxen pulling the ploughs home at dusk. The third is the most Theocritean of the *Eclogues*; neither time nor setting is established. The fourth and fifth transcend the events of particular days. The sixth opens with an allusion to the effects of last night's drinking—presumably it is morning; and again we close with the approach of night. The seventh, like the third, is Theocritean in mood and hints at both the noon rest (1) and the evening return home (44). Damon's song in the

eighth is set at dawn, itself, as Vergil describes it here—"frigida uix caelo noctis decesserat umbra" (14)—a moment of transition. In the ninth the speakers dally with the pastoral convention of the noon rest, only to pass it by. This whole poem is, indeed, about the passage of time. The tenth opens in daylight while the goats are at pasture, and it is at the end of this last eclogue that the evening shades are most prominent.

4. See 1.49; 3.30; 4.21–22; 6.4–5; 7.3; 9.30–31; 10.77; the perversion of the ideal at 3.5–6 and its antithesis (the beasts who will not feed) at 5.25–26.

5. The Vergilian pastoral world is generally considered to be an imaginary world because it is removed from that harsher, urban world which most of us inhabit. Thus, for instance, Steele Commager: "The *Eclogues*, despite their contemporary political and social allusions, are essentially an attempt to substitute a world of imagination for that of fact." *Virgil: A Collection of Critical Essays* (Englewood Cliffs, N.J., 1966), p. 2. See also Michael Putnam's *Virgil's Pastoral Art: Studies in the "Eclogues"* (Princeton, N.J., 1970). Putnam assumes the same basic duality but suggests that the pastoral world of fantasy is redeemed insofar as it is gradually reconciled to the world of fact.

6. Not characteristic, at any rate, of Theocritus, Vergil, or English pastoral. It is characteristic, however, of Italian pastoral—particularly that of Sannazaro, whose Arcadia is very much an escape world; see below, pp. 88–98.

7. That the *Eclogues* are organized by an elaborate system of internal mathematical correspondences—according to which *Eclogues* 1 and 9, 2 and 8, 3 and 7, etc. are paired—was first proposed by Paul Maury in "Le secret de Virgile et l'architecture des *Bucoliques*," in *Lettres d'humanité* 3 (1944): 71–147. The case has perhaps been overstated. In any event, we should bear in mind that mathematical correspondences do not in themselves confer aesthetic merit. The scheme seems to be useful insofar as it confirms our general sense of a movement toward the interior and out again.

8. In a brief but illuminating article Viktor Pöschl identifies harmony through opposition as the governing moral and aesthetic principle of Vergil's art. "The Poetic Achievement of Virgil," *CJ* 56 (April 1961): 290–99.

9. Text for the fifth and tenth *Eclogues*: R. A. B. Mynors, ed., *P. Vergili Maronis Opera* (Oxford, 1969).

10. Compare, for instance, the amoebean contest in the seventh *Eclogue* to its closest Theocritean counterpart in the eighth *Idyll*.

11. Servius (*Ad. Ecl.*, 5.20) mentions the identification of Daphnis with Julius Caesar without endorsing or rejecting it. The various candidates and arguments for and against each are examined by H. J. Rose in *The Eclogues of Vergil* (Berkeley and Los Angeles, 1942), pp. 124–38. If Daphnis is Caesar, then the "mater" who mourns him at 23 might be Aphrodite, the mother of the Julian line; and so again Vergil would be recalling his Theocritean source (in which Aphrodite first taunts Daphnis with his death, then laments it), while, at the same time, re-interpreting it: here Aphrodite has only tears for Daphnis' death.

12. Cf. Catullus, 62.49 ff.; there it is the vine which depends entirely upon the support of the elm. But later variations on the same motif (e.g., Horace, *Carm.* 4.5–30: "vitem viduas ducit ad arbores") suggest that the tree may have something to gain from the marriage as well. If the vine in Vergil's simile does indeed stand in the same relation to the tree as the grape to the vine, the bull to the herd and the corn to the field, then Vergil, like Horace, implies a mutual dependency.

13. In the *Georgics* Vergil repeats (with slight variation) line 37 (1.154). But there nature's resurgent wildness acts as a spur to the farmer's industry instead of suggesting, as here, that, no matter what the farmer does, without the "deus," all is lost.

14. See *Aeneid*, 1.379.

15. Here Vergil conflates two Theocritean scenes, not from the first *Idyll* but the seventh. There Theocritus describes two festivals separated from one another by an intervening song. In the first song Lycidas describes a winter feast in honor of a lover's homecoming. After the second song we have the description of the Coan harvest festival. Thus Theocritus does not enforce the contrast between two seasons, two sorts of recreation. Nor do fireside and shade within each scene create (as in Vergil) an inner circle which shelters the herdsmen from the weather without. In Lycidas' song, for instance, the stars and the allusion to the halcyons tell us that it is winter, but Theocritus does not "make anything" of this when he comes to his fireside feast.

16. Compare, for instance, this typical Theocritean series from the eighth *Idyll*:

Dread plague to trees is tempest, drought to the waters, the springe to birds, and nets to game; and to man desire for a tender maiden. (57–59)

Here the common element is the "plague"—physical injury inflicted on nature, psychological injury inflicted on man. By associating the latter with the former, Theocritus simplifies a complex emotional situation and suggests that it too conforms to the general laws of nature.

In the first *Eclogue* we have an even clearer example of how Vergil revises this sort of Theocritean series in order to shift the emphasis to the idea of duration. Lines 59–63 are based on Daphnis' demand in the first *Idyll* that nature suffer a series of reversals to match the reversal that he must suffer in his own death (132–136). Vergil recalls these images of a world upside-down when he asserts that Tityrus' feelings for his patron will remain unchanged *as long as* nature herself keeps to her same course. Vergil is not simply inverting the Theocritean motif—substituting changelessness for change; he recomposes the series so that we ask, not changed or unchanged, but how long?

The question is one Vergil keeps asking. In the *Aeneid*, when Aeneas is first formally introduced to Dido, he commends the queen for her enduring reputation in lines which echo Menalcas' commendation of Daphnis' fame:

In freta dum fluvii current, dum montibus umbrae
lustrabunt convexa, polus dum sidera pascet,
semper honos nomenque tuum laudesque manebunt . . .
(1.607–609)

[*While rivers run into the sea and shadows*
still sweep the mountain slopes and stars still pasture
upon the sky, your name and praise and honor
shall last. . . .

The Aeneid of Virgil, trans. Allen
Mandelbaum (New York, 1972), p. 22.]

Aeneas' comparisons are drawn from the epic sphere of cosmic order: rivers rushing to the sea, shadows falling across a mountain's shoulder, stars grazing in the heavens. Menalcas' are drawn from the lesser sphere of natural affinity, or custom: the boar's fondness for the mountain, that of the bee for honey and the cricket for dew. But the identical last line of the two passages underlines Vergil's preoccupation with the idea of continuity. And in both these passages continuity is not assumed, but is rather urged into being. Indeed Aeneas, the very one who assures Dido here that her name and praises will endure, will shortly be the instrument of her death.

17. Compare the beautiful prologue to the eighth *Eclogue* where Vergil, addressing himself (it is generally supposed) to Pollio, interposes an image of his hero

on some military mission—skirting dangerous rocks in unknown seas—in the middle of the description of the herdsmen at their songs. Again the effect is to enhance the "islanded" security of pastoral by placing this world in proximity to the sea with its associations of unboundedness and potential danger.

18. Theocritus also plays with this motif in the first *Idyll*, when Daphnis teases Aphrodite by reminding her of the site of her tryst with Anchises: "There are oaks and galingale, and sweetly hum the bees about the hives" (106–107). In Theocritus see also the Cyclops' invitation to Galatea at 11.45 ff. and in Vergil see 1.53–58 and 7.49, as well as the passage in the tenth *Eclogue*.

19. In the *Georgics* the farmer's greatest fear is that of losing control over his own actions. Of this threat the image with which the first book of the *Georgics* concludes—comparing the world to a chariot run wild, its driver helplessly swept on by his maddened horses—is a potent symbol. But the pastoral herdsman-farmer does not expect to have control over his life. If he need not work to sustain his peace, he cannot ensure it either.

CHAPTER 3

1. "Ut superiore Ecloga de ortu Servatoris cecinit ex versibus Sibyllinis, quos Salonino applicavit male cohærentes: ita hîc de nece atque ascensu ejusdem Domini et Dei ex aliis Sibyllæ carminibus, quæ C. Julio Cæsari attribuit, temetsi sub Daphnidis nomine. Sunt qui ajant defleri a Poëta fratris sui mortem, sed vaticinia sunt Sibyllæ versibus:

    Extinctum Nymphae.

Et post,

    Candidus insuetum miratur limen Olympi.

Admiscet Poëta de suo nonnulla, ex ignorantia veri sensus, ut quadraret vaticinium, quo applicabatur."

"Bucolicorum Vergilii Allegoriae," *Joannis Ludovici Vivis Valentini Opera Omnia* II (Valencia, 1782; reprinted London, 1964), p. 39.

2. See, e.g., *P. Virgilii Maronis, Poetae Mantvani vniversvm poema cum absolvta servii honorati mavri, grammatici, & Badij Ascensi interpretatione: Probi, & Ioannis Viuis in Eclogas allegoris* . . . (Venice, 1562). This edition gives the reader a variety of choices when he comes to the fifth *Eclogue*. Servius mentions the association of Daphnis with Caesar without endorsing it; Badius (the Renaissance editor of Vergil) does endorse that interpretation; and Vives identifies Daphnis with Christ. This latter interpretation, however, never became established in the way that the "messianic" interpretation of the fourth *Eclogue* did—perhaps because, while no one historical candidate for the role of the babe in the fourth *Eclogue* presents itself as the inevitable choice, Caesar does seem the likeliest candidate for Daphnis in the fifth—if we are looking for a historical candidate. And, for the most part, the Renaissance follows tradition and accepts, with Badius, the established reading. Vives' interpretation confers on that poem, and the convention in general, a further dimension of significance. It does not displace the Renaissance reader's primary association of Daphnis with Julius Caesar.

3. See Giovanni Del Virgilio's epistolary eclogue to the poet Mussato in which he refers to his previous poetic correspondence with Dante in 1319 as the first appearance of the pastoral muse since Vergil:

    ludunt namque deae quas fistula monte Pachyno
    per silvas Amarilli tuas Benacia duxit,
    fistula non posthac nostris inflata poetis
    donec ea mecum certaret Tityrus olim . . .

[For now the goddesses are once more at sport, who were formerly led by the flute of Benacus [a lake near Verona, hence Vergil] down from Mount Pachunus [a mountain in Sicily, hence Theocritus], through the woods of Amarillis; by poets of our country until Tityrus [Dante] lately contended with me upon it.]

Quoted in P. H. Wickstead and E. H. Gardner, *Dante and Del Virgilio* (London, 1902), p. 176. This book also contains an English translation of the "pastoral" verses exchanged between Del Virgilio and Dante on the subject of the latter's "Paradiso" and the appropriateness of the vernacular tongue. Boccaccio, evidently dismissing this brief exchange, reserves for Petrarch the honor of being the first poet, of any importance at least, to revive the classical form: "Post hunc [Vergil] antem scripserunt et alii, sed ignobiles, de quibus nil curandum est." *Le Lettere*, ed. Corazzini (Florence, 1877), p. 267; from a letter to Martino da Signa.

4. For a brief summary of the medieval eclogue see W. W. Greg, *Pastoral Poetry and Pastoral Drama* (London, 1906), pp. 17–22. I omit discussion here of these medieval pastorals as well as of the late Roman ones by Calpurnius and Nemesian. Nemesian's first *Eclogue*, "Meliboeus," is an imitation of Vergil's fifth and has some influence on Renaissance pastoral elegies. For further comment on this poem, see below, Chapter 4, p.94 and note 6. For thematic affinities between medieval laments and pastoral elegies, see below, note 21.

The medieval "pastoral elegist" *converts* the pastoral landscape into a spiritual one, of this world only incidentally or by default. A lament by the Carolingian scholar and monk Paschas Radbert illustrates this other-worldly approach: "Egloga duarum Sanctimoniarum" (c. 826), in *The Pastoral Elegy: An Anthology*, with Introduction, Commentary, and Notes by Thomas Perrin Harrison, Jr. and English translation by Harry Joshua Leon (Austin, 1939), pp. 55–64; hereafter referred to as Harrison-Leon. Harrison's text is from *Monumenta Germaniae Historica, Poetae Latini Aevi Carolini*, ed. L. Traube, 4 vols. (Berlin, 1896), 3:45–51. One passage is particularly revealing. The mourner, a nun, is rehearsing the accomplishments of her subject, the abbot Adelhard—among them, his founding of a new monastery in Westphalia. The speaker describes Adelhard clearing away all the trees about the grove that he may plant in its place a sacred monastery filled with monks. The man who "plants" God's mansion in this world is, at least for Radbert, necessarily the same man who uproots the pastoral grove. In this context it means little to call Adelhard (as the poet does) "a second Daphnis."

5. "You would hardly credit in how few days I completed it, so strong was the stimulus which the scenery of Vaucluse supplied to my power." *Epist. Fam.* 10.4, *Francesco Petrarca, his Life and Correspondence*, trans. Edward H. R. Tatham, 2 vols. (London, 1925 and 1926), 2:387. The letter was written in 1349, some years after the poems themselves. We should not, in any case, take this reconstruction literally as a description of the kinds of feelings which lie behind Petrarch's composition of this series.

6. Petrarch read his eclogues to Boccaccio in 1357 as he prepared the definitive version of the *Bucolicum Carmen*; see note 3, above.

7. Tatham (*Francesco Petrarca*, 2:387–92) criticizes Petrarch for his allegorizing in the *Bucolicum Carmen* and places the series within the tradition of medieval rather than classical pastoral. See also Harrison-Leon, p. 271, for the same criticism. Thomas G. Bergin in a recent study (*Petrarch* [New York, 1970], pp. 140–43) finds more to interest him in the *Bucolicum Carmen*—but of a personal rather than a pastoral nature.

8. Petrarch's *Bucolicum Carmen*, and particularly the lament for Robert, should be read in conjunction with his other writings of these years (the 1340s) which trace the same progression we see here from an immersion *in* nature, in the "sweet"

world, to a solitary withdrawal. So in Petrarch's famous account of his ascent of Mt. Ventoux (*Epist. Fam.* 4.1)—probably composed, or at least revised, some years after the event it describes, which took place in 1336—the speaker moves from the contemplation of nature to the contemplation of the spiritual life within, withdrawing as he does so both from his surroundings and his fellow travelers.

The delightful verse epistles Petrarch wrote to his friends describing the pleasures of his "pastoral" life at Vaucluse also belong to this period of his life. One of these (*Epist. Metricae* 14) makes a particularly attractive companion piece to the lament for Robert of Naples. The letter is Petrarch's imaginative account of a visit paid by Robert and his royal entourage to Vaucluse. The poet describes the courtiers disporting themselves in the rustic setting. But Robert responds to the beauties of nature in a more kingly (or more Petrarchan) fashion. He goes apart from the others, sits down beside a little stream and meditates upon the problem of mortality. This letter is translated along with others by E. H. Wilkins in *Petrarch at Vaucluse* (Chicago, 1958), pp. 15–18.

The year in which the lament for Robert was written, 1346, is also the year in which Petrarch wrote the first draft of *De vita solitaria*, which goes considerably beyond the usual Christian celebration of the contemplative life in the degree to which it associates the benefits of contemplation with a congenial locale. Here too it is nature that best places us in touch with ourselves.

9. The first eclogue in the series, for instance, is a suggestive reworking of Vergil's first. This is a dialogue between two speakers, Silvius (who, as in the second, represents Petrarch) and Monicus (his brother Gherardo, a monk). Now the opposition is between the monastic peace which Gherardo enjoys and the exile which Petrarch, as an artist, feels bound to. Gherardo invites his brother to linger with him in his "pastoral" sanctuary. But Petrarch, though tempted, declines in the end: the exile's existence, and not that of the retired man, is now associated with imaginative fertility. The poem ends with a parting of the ways. The text of the first *Eclogue* is included in Petrarch's *Rime, Trionfi e poesie latine*, ed. F. Neri *et al.* (Milan and Naples, 1951), pp. 803 ff.

10. See above, n. 2.

11. Text and translation: Harrison-Leon, pp. 65–71. The Latin text, with the commentaries supplied by Petrarch's friends, may also be found in *Il Bucolicum Carmen e i suoi Commenti Inediti*, ed. Antonio Avena (Padua, 1906). Harrison's text is prepared from a collation of this edition with that of D. Rossetti, *Poemata Minora*, 3 vols. (Milan, 1829–1834), 1.

12. The *Bucolicum Carmen* was first published in the *editio princeps* of Petrarch's works at Cologne in 1473. This edition included the elaborate keys to the allegory of the eclogues written during the poet's old age by his acquaintances Benvenuto Rambaldi da Imola and Donato Albanzani. The commentary was apparently made without the poet's authorization, since its interpretations do not always accord with those set forth by Petrarch himself in his letters for three of the twelve eclogues. The commentators are consistently more abstruse than Petrarch, and have contributed to the general impression that the eclogues are more obscure than they really are—though they are not, and particularly the political poems are not, free from difficulties. The relevant glosses from the commentary on the second eclogue are included in Harrison's notes, pp. 270–72. A complete edition is that of Antonio Avena, cited above, n. 11.

Petrarch's own key to the lament for Robert may be found in a letter he sent to his friends Barbato and Barili (who figure in the lament) in Naples, along with a copy of the poem. This letter was not revised by the poet for publication and did not come to light until it was printed by Fracassetti in 1863. *Var.* 49 in *Francesci Petrarcae de Rebus Familiaribus et Variae*, 3 vols. (Florence), 3:439. The poet's own explanatory remarks are the following:

In order that the sense of this Eclogue may be plainer you should learn that, according to the "argument" I mention, by the shepherd full of eyes is meant our most watchful lord king, who had been the far-sighted shepherd of his people; by 'Idaeus' I mean our 'Jupiter' that is, Barili (for Jove was brought up in Ida and Crete); by 'Pythias' I mean our Barbata from his signal renown for friendship; and since I may not assume this for myself, I have chosen to be not Damon, but 'Silvius'—both from my ingrained love of the woods, and because this form of poetry occurred to me (as I said) in my woodland solitude. The rest is clear. (Trans. Tatham, 2:393–94)

Clearly Petrarch is having fun with his pseudonyms here. But I think that on the whole we can take him at his word: the rest *is* clear enough. The elaborate glosses of Imola, who sees allusions to Christ and the Virgin as well as to politics in the pastoral narrative (see Harrison's notes, p. 271), and those of other commentators add little to our understanding or appreciation of the poem.

13. I am confirmed in my impression that the storm functions on a literal as well as an allegorical level—as a response to the disaster as well as an image of it—by the fact that the description here conforms quite closely to Petrarch's description of a real storm which he witnessed in Naples shortly after the King's death. Robert died in January of 1343 and when Petrarch visited Naples late in the same year he was profoundly shaken by the combined earthquake and tidal wave which devastated the city. In a letter from Naples (*Fam.* 5.5) Petrarch describes the various stages of the storm vividly and, further, considers these disorders in the natural world as responses to disorders in the political sphere. This letter is translated in full by Tatham, 2:326–330.

14. Like Petrarch, Boccaccio wrote brief keys to the personae of his eclogues. The key to this poem comes from a letter to his friend, Martino da Signa (c. 1374): "The fourteenth eclogue is called Olympia from the Greek 'Olympos,' which means 'splendidum' or 'lucidum' in Latin, and thence the sky is called Olympus. The reason for assigning the name Olympia to this eclogue is that there is considerable talk therein about the character of the celestial region." Boccaccio goes on to explain that he takes the name "Silvius" for himself for the same reason Petrarch does: "because I had the first idea of this eclogue in a certain forest" (trans. Harrison-Leon, p. 77; for the Latin text of this letter see *Opere Latine Minori del Boccaccio*, ed. A. F. Massèra [Bari, 1928], p. 220.).

15. Text and translation: Harrison-Leon, pp. 77–91. Harrison's Latin text is from Massèra, pp. 66–74. Boccaccio's *Bucolicum Carmen* circulated in MS during the fifteenth century and was first published in Florence by Guinta in 1504.

16. See, e.g., Harrison-Leon, p. 9. Harrison feels that the pagan imagery in "Olympia" is an intrusion in what is essentially a Christian lament. (See his note on lines 284–85, p. 274.)

17. See lines 176, 195, 202–03, 243 and 269.

18. Harry Levin, in *The Myth of the Golden Age in the Renaissance* (Bloomington and London, 1969), p. 11, characterizes this type of ideal landscape as all that the contemporary world is *not*; he cites Howard Patch's term "negative formula," by which Patch identifies that device favored by medieval writers in descriptions of the other world (*The Other World according to Descriptions in Medieval Literature* [Cambridge, Mass., 1950], p. 12 and passim).

19. E. R. Curtius (*European Literature and the Latin Middle Ages*, trans. Willard R. Trask, Bollingen Series 36 [New York, 1953], pp. 195–200) traces the history of the *locus amoenus* as a rhetorical topic from the classical period through late antiquity. He sees the source of the term itself in *Aeneid* 6.638, when Aeneas first glimpses the Elysian Fields: "Devenere locus laetos et amoena virecta." Curtius quotes Servius' comment on this line: "lovely places are such as only give pleasure, that is, are not

cultivated for useful purposes." This exemption of the *locus amoenus* from cultiva-
tion is, I should say, one of the things that distinguish it from the pastoral land-
scape. Pastoral *is* a cultivated world, though we do not see it being cultivated.

20. Some of the more prominent literary antecedents of Olympia's world are:
first in importance, Dante's Earthly Paradise (*Purgatorio* 27:91–144), whence the
mountain-top setting and the swirling winds; Vergil's Elysian Fields (*Aeneid* 6.637
ff.), recalled specifically in Olympia's initial description of her new home (lines
102–103) and again at line 162 where Olympia tells us that Vergil there anticipated
something, but not all, of the splendors of the true paradise; and, finally, Vergil's
account of the return of the Golden Age in the fourth *Eclogue* (where the setting as
well as the style of pastoral is left behind), whence the animals bathed in gold. All
of these landscapes fall into what I have called the *locus amoenus* tradition as
opposed to the pastoral one. They are all removed, in different ways, from the
world of ordinary experience. Numerous other paradisial landscapes lie behind
Olympia's. The influence of the medieval tradition, for instance, can be felt in the
exhaustive, cataloguing style of the account. See A. Bartlett Giamatti, *The Earthly
Paradise and the Renaissance Epic* (Princeton, 1966), for a detailed survey of the literary
genealogy of the ideal landscape. Giamatti considers the pastoral landscape a sub-
species of the *locus amoenus* rather than a distinct type. (See pp. 33 ff.)

21. In this respect Boccaccio's "Olympia" offers an instructive contrast with the
roughly contemporary Middle English *Pearl* (c. 1360–1395)—another dialogue be-
tween a bereaved father and the spirit of his young daughter, newly received in
heaven—to which Boccaccio's poem has frequently been compared. In *Pearl* there is
the same bewilderment, the same refusal to comprehend, on the part of the father
and the same Christian exegesis on the part of the child. But the father in *Pearl* is, in
the end, able to return to this world, for he *is* sustained by the vision of the other
world which his daughter has granted him. The Middle English poem, for all of its
painful questioning of life and death, is finally a more serene, a more internally
consistent work, than Boccaccio's lament. E. V. Gordon, however, in his edition of
Pearl (Oxford, 1953), sees Boccaccio's classicism as an element which undercuts the
seriousness of Christian lament rather than (as I should say) one which complicates
it: "Boccaccio's treatment of the theme is quite different. His poem is cast in the
more artificial form of an eclogue, serene and graceful: there is no rebellious grief,
no fever of doubt, no theological argument" (p. xxxv). The eclogue and the dream-
vision are both artificial forms. What deprives Boccaccio's lament, finally, of serenity
is not his adherence to one or the other of these forms but his juxtaposition of the
two.

22. Quoted here from Julia Cartwright, *Baldassare Castiglione*, 2 vols. (New
York, 1908), 1:141. For the Italian text of this letter see P. A. Serassi, *Delle lettere del
Conte Baldassare Castiglione*, 2 vols. (Padua, 1769–71), 1:24. The letter continues:

> When I think how unexpectedly he has been taken from me in the flower of
> his age, without a word of farewell, which will, I know, have grieved him
> more than death itself—I am sure and certain that this is a loss from which I
> can never recover. . . . Fortune has not suffered me to reward him with
> aught but my tears, which I would at least have liked to shed over his
> grave. . . .

In both this letter and in the lament for Falcone the poet expresses his feeling
that it is not only the friendship between the two men but his own act of mourning
which has been prematurely cut off and remains incomplete. Castiglione's regret
that he was not present at the time of his friend's death, was not there "to shed
tears over his grave"—circumstances stressed in both this letter and the poem—is
clearly related to the sense of inconclusiveness which haunts us in the lament. He is

still, as it were, reaching out for Alcon; the rites of death remain, so far as he is concerned, unconsummated.

23. Text and translation: Harrison-Leon, pp. 112–19. Harrison's Latin text of "Alcon" is that of *Selecta Poemata Italorum*, ed. A. Pope, 2 vols. (London, 1740), 2.

24. As in the fifth *Eclogue*, the stars are held responsible for the hero's death. See lines 7, 67, 131 and 152 as well as the passage (54–64) discussed below.

25. The "Lament for Bion" was first published in the Aldine edition of the *Greek Bucolic Poets* (Venice, 1495). Sannazaro's eleventh Arcadian eclogue (1502–04) is the first Renaissance pastoral elegy I know which reveals the influence of that Greek lament (see below, p. 91). Castiglione would certainly have been familiar with Sannazaro's *Arcadia*, published in its completed version in 1504, just two years before he wrote "Alcon." It may have been from the eleventh Arcadian eclogue that Castiglione borrowed, not only the contrast of human life with the annually reviving vegetation, but also of our life with the diurnal course of the sun. The contrast is softer there, however. In Sannazaro's lament the emphasis falls on the fact that we men do not return, like the vegetation and the sun, *to this world*; nothing is said about an everlasting sleep enshrouding us in darkness; the possibility that we may be reborn elsewhere is therefore not excluded:

> Ay, ay, the brambles wither and when a little
>   they have gone about to recover their former strength,
>   each one returns and springs up in its own place:
> but we, when once the Heavens take our strength,
>   wind, nor sun, nor rain, nor spring suffices
>   to bring us back upon the face of the earth.
> And the sun also fleeing from morn to eve
>   bears with him the days, and along with them our life:
>   and he returns even as he was before.
>
> Arcadia and Piscatorial Eclogues, trans.
Ralph Nash (Detroit, 1966), p. 130.

And when Luigi Alamanni in his second eclogue (1532–33) takes over this same motif, he rounds it out with an explicit assurance of that rebirth elsewhere: " . . . an eternal slumber, revered Cosmo, thou must sleep beneath the earth, while elsewhere thou receivest the victory and the palm of thy good deeds" (*Eclogue* 2. 125–27, "Cosmo," *Opere Toscane*; quoted here from Harrison-Leon, p. 132). "Moschus"' original contrast is frequently invoked by Renaissance elegists. But Castiglione's emphasis is unusual among them.

26. *The Book of the Courtier*, trans. Charles S. Singleton (Garden City, N.Y., 1959), p. 90. "Alcon" was written about a year after Falcone's death, possibly during Castiglione's sojourn in England in 1506, during which period of his absence from the court at Urbino the imaginary dialogues among its courtiers out of which Castiglione fashioned his treatise are supposed to have occurred. Thus the lament for Falcone and the *Book of the Courtier*, itself an elegy for a whole world of lost innocence, are closely linked thematically and temporally.

27. The earliest example of this second type of Renaissance pastoral elegy I know is the neo-Latin "Meliseus" (c. 1490) by Sannazaro's friend and fellow humanist in Naples, Giovanni Pontano. Pontano's lament for his wife is also the first pastoral elegy for a woman, another aspect of the domestication of the form. In "Meliseus" the poet re-creates the landscape in which his wife lived: the gardens she tended, the trees from which she picked the fruit, the little girls she fed from her own hand, the wool she spun on the distaff. Thus when nature turns upside down for Ariadna here, more than a poetic conceit is involved; without Ariadna's cultivation, nature's world, the world of this particular estate, falls into decay.

Pontano's is a sincere if somewhat long-winded tribute to his wife. "Meliseus" is included in *Poeti Latini del Quattrocento*, ed. Arnoldi, Sosa and Sabia, 2 vols. (Milan and Naples, 1964), 2:372–86. Sannazaro imitates parts of this eclogue and recalls Pontano's Ariadna in his twelfth *Arcadian Eclogue*; see below, p. 91 and n. 3.

28. The first eighteen *Idylls* were printed in Milan at the press of Bonus Accursius c. 1481. In 1495 Aldus at Venice printed *Idylls* 1–28 along with the bucolic poems of Bion and "Moschus." This edition includes a brief life of Theocritus and the standard accounts of the origins of the genre. Sannazaro might have read Theocritus in these Greek texts, but the *Idylls* were more widely disseminated through the Latin translations which became available in the early sixteenth century. In 1503 and 1510 Badius' press in Paris issued seven Idylls in the version of the Venetian Martin Phileticus.

29. This distinction emerges in Donatus (middle 4th cent. A.D.) and is elaborated by Servius (late 4th cent. A.D.), whose commentary on Vergil provides the basis for Renaissance pastoral theory. Servius says that "ille [Theocritus] enim ubique simplex est" while "hic [Vergil] necessitate compulsus aliquibus locis miscet figuras." *Servii Grammatici . . . Commentarii*, eds. G. Thilo and H. Hagen, 3 vols. (Leipzig, 1881–1902), 3:2. For him Vergil is not allegorical throughout but only, as it were, under compulsion, as when he wishes to allude covertly to the confiscation of his farm. But the Renaissance theorists discover an aesthetic justification for Vergil's allegorizing: through it he elevates the genre, which now only appears to deal with humble themes. As Vives puts it, in William Lisle's English translation, "did these Aeglogues contain in them no farther hidden matter, than the very bark of the works make show of, I cannot think that the Author had need to have taken three years time to have brought them to perfection." *Virgil's Eclogues translated into English* (London, 1628), p. 10. And Scaliger, having derived Theocritean pastoral from primitive folk cults, demonstrates how in passage after passage Vergil distills from the ruder terms and sentiments of the Theocritean herdsmen his own *cantus mellifluus*. *Poetices* 1.3 (1586), pp. 379–80. See my comments above (Intro., n. 19) on the "double conception" of pastoral inherited by the Renaissance. Pastoral simplicity is associated with the Theocritean model; the duplicity which adds a higher level of meaning is associated with the Vergilian model.

30. Text and translation: *Arcadia and Piscatorial Eclogues*, ed. and trans. Ralph Nash (Detroit, 1966), pp. 156–65. Nash's text of "Phyllis" is based on W. P. Mustard's edition of the *Piscatory Eclogues* (Baltimore, 1914). See Mustard for sources, analogues and imitations. "Phyllis" is also included in Harrison-Leon, pp. 105–11.

31. Sannazaro combines the Cyclops of the eleventh *Idyll*—who wishes he had been born with gills so that he might have followed his sea Nymph beneath the waters or at least learned to swim "that I [might] know what pleasure it is to you to dwell in the depths," (*Theocritus*, ed. A. S. F. Gow, 2nd ed., 2 vols. [Cambridge, Eng., 1952], 1:91)—with the love-sick herdsman of the second *Idyll* who contemplates a watery suicide: "I will strip off my cloak and leap into the waves from the cliff whence Olpis, the fisherman, watches for the tunny; and if I kill myself, at least thy pleasure will have been done" (Ibid., p. 33). Like Theocritus, Sannazaro can afford to smile at his hero. A passage from "Phyllis," in which Lycidas' fisherman companion, Mycon, consoles his friend with the suggestion that his Phyllis is better off dead than—who knows—the bride of another! is particularly reminiscent of the *Idylls*, and especially reminiscent of the teasing Daphnis endures from his more cynical companions. Here is Sannazaro's Mycon:

> O Lycida, Lycida, nonne hoc felicius illi
> Evenisse putas quam si fumosa Lycotae
> Antra vel hirsuti tegetem subiisset Amyntae,

Et nunc heu viles hamo sibi quaereret escas
Aut tenui laceras sarciret vimine nassas?
(24–28)

[O Lycidas, Lycidas, do you not consider that this has turned out more happily for her than if she had gone into the smoky cave of Lycotas or the poor cot of hairy Amyntas, and even now [alas!] were gathering bait for his fish hooks, or patching his torn nets with the pliant osier?]

The joke is gentler here, however. We miss the hard edge of Priapus' taunts. Mycon's portrait of "a fate worse than death" is merely titillating, whereas Priapus' suggestions do really imply a fate worse than death because they are dehumanizing. But in "Phyllis" such passages prevent us from taking Phyllis or her fate very seriously.

32. Basle, 1546.

33. *Neo-Latin Literature and the Pastoral* (Chapel Hill, 1965), pp. 306–30. Grant's survey appears to be complete, though he evidently does not include in his definition of the form those *epicedia* (such as Sannazaro's "Phyllis") which honor fictional rather than contemporary figures.

34. Zanchi's "Meliseus" (c. 1503) honors the memory of Pontano; text in *De Horto Sophiae Libri Duo . . . Eiusdem uaria Poemata . . .* (Rome, 1540). As so often in the Renaissance pastoral elegy, the contrast between the mourner's sorrowful aspect and the happy, natural world around him is established in the opening frame:

Vix primum roseo spargebat lumine terras
Aurora Oceani exurgens natalibus undis,
Quum tristis consueta greges in pascua Amilcon
Propulit; e scopulo, summique cacumine montis
Quà pelagi horrentes late despectat in undas,
Et Baccho felix, felix viridantibus umbris,
Et cantu, & calamis Neptunia Mergilline.
Dumque illi exultim persultant pabula laeta,
Et tondent uario gemmantia prata colore,
Ille animo extinctum repetens Meliseon, & alto
Corde trahens gemitum, scopulo consedit acuto.
(1–11)

[Scarcely had Aurora, rising from the birth-giving waves of the ocean, begun to sprinkle the lands with rosy light, when sorrowful Amilcon drove forth his sheep into their accustomed pastures. There from the crag and summit of the highest mountain he looks down far and wide on the rough waves of the sea, where Mergillina-by-the-shore is happy in its vines, happy in its green shades, in song and in reed-pipes. And while his sheep gamble friskily through the joyful grasses and through meadows budding with their varied colors, he, recalling in his mind the dead Meliseus and drawing forth a groan from deep in his heart, sits down on the rugged crag.]

35. See the popular translation of the *Idylls* by the German humanist, Elius Eobanus of Hesse, *Theocriti Syracusani Idyllia Triginta sex, Latino Carmina reddita*, 2 vols. (Hagenau, 1530–31). In his version of the first *Idyll* we find, for instance, such Vergilian locutions as "carmen avena," "Quae nemora aut qui vos saltus habuere puellae / Naiades, indigno cum Daphnis amore periret," "formosus dum pascit Adonis" and "dum perit extinctus crudeli funere Daphnis" (1)—which suggest we are still looking at Theocritus through Vergil.

36. Text: Marco Publio Fontana, *Poemata Omnia* (Bergamo, 1752), pp. 252–55.

CHAPTER 4

1. Miguel de Cervantes Saavedra, *Don Quixote*, trans. Samuel Putnam, 3d ed. (New York, 1958), p. 949. Cervantes had himself discovered the pleasures of such sweet lamentations as his hero describes here. He recalls Sannazaro's Arcadian laments in Book 6 of his own pastoral romance, *Galatea*.

2. It is fitting that the best short appreciation of Sannazaro's *Arcadia* comes from one of our most sensitive critics of the visual arts in the context of a discussion of the latter: Erwin Panofsky, "Et in Arcadia Ego: Poussin and the Elegiac Tradition," *Meaning in the Visual Arts* (Garden City, N.Y., 1955), pp. 303–04. For a fuller description of the Arcadian atmosphere, and for Sannazaro's relation both to the Petrarchan lyric tradition and to later transformations of Arcadia, particularly Sidney's, see David Kalstone, *Sidney's Poetry: Contexts and Interpretations* (Cambridge, Mass., 1965), pp. 9–39.

3. The twelfth *Eclogue* places sorrow in a familiar landscape (the same Neapolitan landscape that we see again in the *Piscatories*) and finds solace in that familiarity:

> But yet it must be that I often return to you,
> ye places once soothing and pleasing to my heart,
>   since I find no place to conceal my weeping self.
> O Cumae, O Baiae, O warm and pleasant springs.
>
> Arcadia and Piscatorial Eclogues, trans.
Ralph Nash (Detroit, 1966), p. 130.

This unites the lyricism of the Arcadian laments with the concreteness of the *Piscatory Eclogues*. The twelfth Arcadian *Eclogue* should also be compared with its immediate model, the neo-Latin "Meliseus" (c. 1490) by Sannazaro's friend and fellow humanist in Naples, Giovanni Pontano; see chap. 3, n. 27.

4. Text for *Arcadia: Opere volgari*, ed. Alfredo Mauro (Bari, 1961). Because versification is such an important element in the Arcadian eclogues I depart from my usual procedure and, instead of supplying literal prose translations to the passages quoted, I follow the verse translation by Ralph Nash, *Arcadia and Piscatorial Eclogues*. Passages quoted from the prose sections of the *Arcadia* are also rendered here in Nash's English translations.

5. In the "Lament for Bion," which Sannazaro is following here, nature is already on its way to being humanized by myth. The elegist who invites the nightingales and swallows to weep with him in that poem knows, and invites us to recall, that these birds are also maidens with sorrows of their own (Gow, *Greek Bucolic Poets* [Cambridge, Eng., 1953] p. 134). But "Moschus" does not insist, as Sannazaro does, upon the human dimension; his birds can stand simply as birds. Nor does he, like Sannazaro, describe a transferral of emotion from one object (their own woes) to another (his). At one point he says simply that the nightingale and swallow weep *with* him for Bion's death; at another he *compares* his present suffering to that of various metamorphosed birds for their own lost mates.

6. Here is the corresponding passage in Nemesian's lament:

> Apollo of the country-side plucks the laurel and offers you gifts of fragrant foliage. The Fauns offer, each according to his power, grape-clusters from the vine, harvest-stalks from the field, and fruits from every tree. Time-honored Pales offers bowls foaming with milk; the Nymphs bring honey; Flora offers chaplets of varied hue. Such is the last tribute to the departed.
>
> Minor Latin Poets, eds. J. W. Duff and A. M. Duff
(London and Cambridge, Mass., 1934), p. 463.

"Meliboeus" is also included in *The Pastoral Elegy: An Anthology*, with Introduction, Commentary, and Notes by Thomas Perrin Harrison, Jr., and English translation by

Harry Joshua Leon (Austin, 1939), pp. 50–54. The eclogues of Calpurnius and Nemesian were often published in Renaissance anthologies under the common authorship of "Calpurnius Siculus" and thus found their way into the body of tradition upon which the Renaissance poets drew. "Meliboeus" (c. 290 A.D.) is only on the periphery of our convention. A tribute to an elderly man rather than (as usual) a youth prematurely cut down, it sits somewhat uneasily on the border between pastoral and encomium. With an elderly subject more room needs be given over to what has been accomplished; there is less room for pathos. And the more we know (of a specific nature) about the subject of the lament, the more difficult it becomes to place his death in a pastoral setting. Sannazaro's fifth Arcadian *Eclogue* also commemorates an old man (possibly the poet's father), but in the Arcadian landscape the subject's individuating features are blurred and the encomiastic strain is, accordingly, considerably muted here.

7. Perhaps in this fulsome gesture Sannazaro is also recalling the most famous of literary floral tributes to the dead, that which Anchises offers the young Marcellus in the sixth *Aeneid*:

> . . . *Manibus date lilia plenis,*
> *purpureos spargam flores, animamque nepotis*
> *his saltem accumulem donis, et fungar inani*
> *munere.*
>
> (884–87)

> [*With full hands, give me lilies; let me scatter*
> *these purple flowers, with these gifts, at least,*
> *be generous to my descendant's spirit,*
> *complete this service, although it be useless.*
>
> The Aeneid of Virgil, trans. Allen
> Mandelbaum (New York, 1972), p. 162]

But to cite this passage is to recognize once again how differently death is experienced in the epic world and in the pastoral one. The epic poet acknowledges, even as he makes it and insists upon making it, that his gesture is a useless one. But in pastoral, and nowhere more so than in Sannazaro's pastoral, the gestures do console.

8. See "Mourning and Melancholia" (1917), reprinted in *A General Selection from the Works of Sigmund Freud*, ed. John Rickman, M.D. (Garden City, N.Y., 1957), pp. 124–140. For Freud the "work" of mourning involves the mourner's gradual disengagement of libido from the beloved object in accordance with the reality principle. Freud emphasizes (what is borne out in our laments) that this "work" takes time, is painful, and that its inhibition leads to such illnesses as melancholia. The pain of grief is an essentially healthy response; the denial of suffering suggests to the clinician something is amiss.

9. *Tutte le opere di Giovan Giorgio Trissino* (Verona, 1729), Part 2, p. 137.

10. Text: Ibid., Part 1, pp. 173–74.

11. Trissino's "Dafne" should be compared to Luigi Alamanni's first *Eclogue* (c. 1519), on the death of Cosimo Rucellai, which also places a dying hero's proud taunts at his cruel Fate within a softer, Italianate pastoral world; in Harrison-Leon, pp. 120–27. Alamanni mourned his "Cosmo"'s death in four different pastoral elegies, each one based on a different classical model; in *Versi e prose di Luigi Alamanni*, ed. Pietro Raffaelli, 2 vols. (Florence, 1859), 1.

12. Text: *Opere di Torquato Tasso*, ed. Bortolo Tommaso Sozzi, 2 vols. (Turin, 1955–56), 2:439–69.

13. The morality that underlies this pastoral work is the same morality advanced explicitly in Tasso's pastoral drama *Aminta* (1573); this world, like that one,

is, just beneath its Vergilian cover, a place where "'s' ei piace, ei lice" ("if it's pleasing, it's permitted"). In *Aminta* Tasso conveys most persuasively the seductiveness of the dream world. In the pastoral cantos of the *Gerusalemme liberata* (7.1–22) we feel again its absence of vitality. To the hero of the epic poem the pastoral retreat does, of course, always present itself as a digression, a temporary respite from the ardors of the quest. Still, it is remarkable how little fruit, how little true repose, Tasso's epic heroes and heroines discover in their pastoral retreats.

CHAPTER 5

1. The title of Alice Hulubei's exhaustive survey of French pastoral poetry in the Renaissance, *L'Eglogue en France au XVIe siècle, époque des Valois* (Paris, 1938), points to the most salient feature of the material under discussion: namely, its close association with the Valois court.

2. Nicolas Couteau, in the preface to his translation of Vergil's *Eclogues* into French (1529), feels compelled to explain why Vergil concerned himself with the humble subjects depicted therein, and he does so by associating the herdsman's life with the dignified recreations of ancient kings and queens:

> N'en soyez esbahys, car au temps passé tel pastoral sejour estoit en grande dignité, tellement que les plus grans comme roys et autres, leurs dyademes bas mis et posez, se tenoient aux champs herbus et floris. . . .
>
> [Do not be amazed, for in bygone days such pastoral sojourns were held in great esteem; so much so that even the very greatest, kings and others, having doffed their diadems and laid them aside, betook themselves to fields of herbs and flowers. . . .
>
> *Les OEuvres de Virgille translatees de latin en francoys* (Paris), quoted here from Hulubei, *L'Eglogue en France*, p. 6.]

Much French Renaissance pastoral poetry has the rather stilted air of such a courtly "picnic" as Couteau describes here.

3. See, e.g., Remy Belleau's "Chant pastoral sur la mort de Joachim Du Bellay" (1560). This lament (later to be incorporated into Belleau's long pastoral poem, the *Bergerie*) begins with a conversation between two herdsmen (Baïf and Belleau) who complain that while they are languishing in the countryside, neglected by fortune, two other shepherds of the famous "seven" are enjoying the favors of the court and the "great god Pan." This exchange looks back to that between Tityrus and Meliboeus in Vergil's first, but its thrust is quite different. Tityrus knows that his good fortune depends upon the "deus" from Rome, the God who makes it possible for him to stay *here*. But Belleau's herdsmen are not sure that they would not rather be in Paris. It is not surprising, then, that the pastoral elegy for Du Bellay which follows, as a nymph enters with news of his sudden death, is not very securely rooted in its pastoral setting. *Oeuvres complètes de Remy Belleau*, ed. A. Gouverneur, 3 vols. (Paris, 1867), 2:151–52.

4. "Chante moy d'une musette bien resonante et d'une fluste bien jointe ces plaisantes eglogues rustiques à l'exemple de Théocrite et de Virgile: marines à l'exemple de Sannazar, gentilhomme Néapolitain" (2.4). *La défense et illustration de la langue française*, ed. Henri Chamard (Paris, 1948), pp. 122–24.

5. Text of Marot's "Eglogue sur le Trespas de ma Dame Loyse de Savoye . . ." *Oeuvres lyriques*, ed. C. A. Mayer (London, 1964), pp. 321–37. Translation: *The Pastoral Elegy: An Anthology*, with Introduction, Commentary, and Notes by Thomas Perrin Harrison, Jr., and English translation by Harry Joshua Leon (Austin, 1939), pp. 50–54.

6. Compare Marot's allusion in his "Sermon du bon Pasteur et du Mauvais" (c. 1530) to the parable in John X which opposes Christ the "good shepherd" to the same ravening wolf who threatens the sheep in the lament for Louise. In the "Sermon" the association of the good shepherd with nourishment is more prominent. Marot's "bon pasteur" feeds his flock on scripture, while the false pastor feeds his with coarse brown bread "d'ergos, d'utrum, de quare." The more the sheep feed on that poor diet the hungrier they become, until they starve by feeding; *Oeuvres complètes*, ed. M. Pierre Jannet, 4 vols. (Paris, 1868), 1:85. This image strikingly anticipates the "hungry sheep" in "Lycidas" which are swollen with wind and rank mist.

7. Marot most likely read Theocritus in one of the Latin translations through which the *Idylls* were generally transmitted to the Renaissance (though his knowledge of Latin was not much more extensive than his knowledge of Greek). Possibly, too, he would have seen the imitation of the first Theocritean *Idyll* by Luigi Alamanni, then the most prominent of the Italian poets at the court of Francis I. There are, as I have suggested, indications in the lament for Louise that Marot's knowledge of the classical pastoralists came through the Italian poets. Alamanni's eclogues, dedicated to Francis I, were published in Paris in 1532–33.

8. Compare this passage to the similar catalogue (at lines 157–68) of all the French rivers weeping for the death of their queen.

9. "Arion" is the leading piece in a volume issued by a group of Lyonnais poets to commemorate the death of the young prince: *Recueil de vers latins et vulgaires de plusieurs Poëtes Francoys, composés sus le trespas de feu Monsieur le Daulphin* (Lyon, 1536). Scève's contributions, which include five Latin epigrams and two short French poems besides "Arion," make up the bulk of the volume.

10. *Fasti* 2.83–92.

11. This allegorical identification, strained as it may seem, is not original with Scève. In 1533, when the dauphin visited Lyon, he was presented with a medal on which was engraved the figure of a dolphin bearing a man on his back. Beneath the figure was the motto: "Diligens cunctator Dii te fortunent." Scève's poem also shows the influence of a short poem by Marot, which honored the dauphin's birth by describing in piscatory terms the calming of the seas at his arrival: "De la naissance de feu Monseigneur le Daulphin Françoys" (1517).

12. Text: *Oeuvres poétiques complètes de Maurice Scève*, ed. Bertrand Guégan (Paris, 1927), pp. 157–63.

13. "Arion" should be read in conjunction with Scève's other pastoral poem, *Saulsaye: églogue de la vie solitaire* (1547). Here too the pastoral retreat from passion leads to self-absorption and, ultimately, to death.

14. "A elle-mesme, ode pastoral 11," *Oeuvres complètes de Ronsard*, ed. Gustave Cohen, Pléiade ed., 2 vols. (Paris, 1950), 1:605, lines 7–16.

15. *Elégie* (contre les bûcherons de la forêst de Gastine). In a later lament by Ronsard, the epitaph for Claude D'Aubespine (1571), the shepherd is more clearly identified as the intruder. Ronsard borrows the Vergilian image of the nightingale lamenting her lost brood (*Georgics*, 1.507 ff.), to whom he compares the present mourners. But Ronsard focuses the attention on the act of violation itself:

> *Nous ressemblons à ces rossingnolets*
> *Qui retournant trouvent leurs nids seulets,*
> *Estant allez chercher quelque bechée*
> *Loin du taillis pour nourrir leur nichée,*
> *Que le pasteur de ses ongles courbez*
> *Cruellement sans plume a desrobez.*
> (*Oeuvres*, 2:522)

[We are like those little nightingales, who returning find their nests empty, having gone to search for some billful far from the brushwood to feed their young, whom the shepherd meanwhile with his curved nails has stolen away still unfeathered.]

Now the shepherd is the disturber of the peace that resides in nature, not the one for whom that peace exists.

16. Text and translation: Harrison-Leon, pp. 153–57; Harrison's text is from *Oeuvres complètes de Pierre de Ronsard*, ed. P. Laumonier, 2d ed., 5 vols. (Paris, 1914–19), 3:370–72.

17. See Elizabeth Armstrong's interesting study of the changing significance of the "golden age" ideal throughout Ronsard's poetry, *Ronsard and the Age of Gold* (Cambridge, England, 1968).

CHAPTER 6

1. Text: *Spenser's Minor Poems*, ed. Ernest De Sélincourt (Oxford, 1960), pp. 105–11.

2. Ibid., "Argument," p. 105.

3. This "May" is the Germanic "may," or "maiden." But when Spenser describes Dido as the "fairest May . . . that ever went" (and capitalizes the word) he is surely thinking also of the May month to which he referred some thirty lines earlier. Here the two kinds of "may" are one and the same; gradually, as the song continues, we see some of the differences between the maiden and the may.

4. Marot has: "Tous animaulx Loyse regretterent, / Excepté loups de mauvaise nature" (119–20).

5. These mixed emotions anticipate particularly the mood of the concluding scene in Book 1 of the *Faerie Queene*, when the Red Cross Knight comes down from the mountain and back to his dragon and his princess, after having had a vision of the New Jerusalem. There, too, nature's energies—kindly, malevolent, capricious—reassert themselves at the close.

6. The "Mutabilitie Cantos" are, of course, unfinished; we cannot know how, or with what apocalyptic vision, Spenser might have thought to conclude them. But there is a rightness, at least to my mind, in the ending as it is, just as there is a rightness in the more affirmative, more conclusive note on which the pastoral poem ends. Spenser's epic journey, like Vergil's, ends on an inconclusive note; the epic quest is perhaps never really finished. But when the pastoral songs are sung, what we have set ourselves to accomplish is accomplished.

7. See William A. Ringler, Jr., ed., *The Poems of Sir Philip Sidney* (Oxford, 1962), pp. xxxi–xxxiv, 365.

8. See David Kalstone's excellent discussion of Sidney's relation to the Italian tradition of Petrarch and Sannazaro in *Sidney's Poetry: Contexts and Interpretations* (Cambridge, Mass., 1965).

9. Text: *The Poems of Sir Philip Sidney*, ed. Ringler, pp. 125–29.

10. Sidney achieves a similar effect in the famous double-sestina (*Old Arcadia* 76), which belongs to this same final group of eclogues and has important affinities with the pastoral elegy. There the speaker, by the persistent pressure of his emotions, eventually shatters the Arcadian tranquillity and turns nature into a world upside-down.

11. For Spenser, too, keeps coming back to the pastoral elegy. The "November" eclogue is his only work in the mainstream of the Renaissance tradition. But "Daphnaida" (1590) invokes the convention at numerous points and this lament is better understood, I think, as a Renaissance pastoral elegy, in the tradition of Castiglione's "Alcon" or Scève's "Arion," than (as it usually is) as an inferior

medieval lament on the model of Chaucer's *Book of the Duchess*. Here we find a refrain linking the sorrowful elegist to a sympathetic pastoral world, the evocation of an original state of pastoral innocence before death (99–106); the association between human death and death in nature (232–45); the demand that nature's order be turned upside-down (320–43); and the wish that the elegist himself might be pitied in death by the other shepherds (530). One passage in "Daphnaida" particularly recalls the mood of Spenser's "November." Here again we feel nature gathering up the spirit of the young woman into her kindly order even as we protest against the violation of "kinde" that her death involves:

> *O that so faire a flower so soone should fade,*
> *And through vntimely tempest fall away.*
>
> *She fell away in her first ages spring,*
> *Whil'st yet her leafe was greene, and fresh her rinde,*
> *And whil'st her braunch faire blossomes foorth did bring,*
> *She fell away against all course of kinde:*
> *For age to dye is right, but youth is wrong;*
> *She fel away like fruit blowne downe with winde:*
> *Weepe Shepheard weepe to make my vndersong.*
> (*Minor Poems*, pp. 295–96)

But "Daphnaida," like a number of Renaissance pastoral elegies, ends with displacement rather than consolation. The final lines of Spenser's lament have nothing to do with Chaucer's poem or its mood; they are a reworking of the Vergilian exchange at the close of the first *Eclogue*. Again, as night approaches, the interlocutor invites his friend home with him. But this mourner will not tarry the one night in pastoral. Having told his sad story, he departs at once on his exile's way; and, the narrator concludes, "What of him became I cannot weene" (567). This is not, in the end, the way of "November," but it is the way of many other Renaissance pastoral elegies.

Spenser's "Astrophel" (1595), too, his tribute to Sidney, has important affinities with the pastoral elegy. It is interesting to observe how Spenser, as he revises the Adonis story, transfers us from the erotic landscape of Bion's lament (and Ronsard's) to his own pastoral one. The call to battle thrusts Astrophel-Sidney from a pastoral world of shepherd-singers and shearing feasts into forests "wide and waste." When he dies far from home, it is the comforting presence of the shepherds, not that of Venus, Astrophel misses. A characteristically Spenserian moment is the one in which the hero lies wounded and alone in a foreign land, when suddenly a band of shepherds emerges from the forest and, with a few words, transports us back into that kindly, healing world of Spenserian pastoral:

> *They stopt his wound (too late to stop it was)*
> *And in their armes then softly did him reare . . .*
> (*Minor Poems*, p. 341)

Again, in "The Ruins of Time" (1590), Spenser alludes intermittently to the pastoral elegy convention. (See, aside from the passage cited below, lines 323–43 and the echoes of "November" in lines 190–23.) This lament for the great Elizabethans, Sidney, Leicester and Walsingham, is technically at the opposite end of the spectrum from pastoral since the poem, modelled on Du Bellay's *Antiquités*, laments the decay of civilization rather than the death of innocence. But lament for what once was shades easily into scorn for what remains in the corrupt world of the court, and in "The Ruins of Time" we have come at least half way on the journey toward the "Mother Hubberds Tale" and "Colin Clouts Come Home Again." Speaking of the lament which he might have written for Leicester, but hasn't,

Spenser instinctively puts on his shepherd's mantle and with it the pastoral elegist's traditional powers:

> Ne doth his Colin, carelesse Colin Cloute,
> Care now his idle bagpipe vp to raise,
> Ne tell his sorrow to the listning rout
> Of shepherd groomes, which wont his songs to praise . . .
> (Minor Poems, p. 134)

And finally, in the *Epithalamion*, referring to the various poems that he has composed on sorrowful themes, Spenser introduces the consoling world of pastoral as the natural setting for a lament:

> And when ye list your owne mishaps to mourne,
> Which death, or loue, or fortunes wrech did rayse,
> Your string could soone to sadder tenor turne,
> And teach the woods and waters to lament
> Your dolefull dreriment.
>
> (Minor Poems, p. 422)

12. The "Lay of Corinda," as well as "Astrophel" (as C. S. Osgood suggests in a close study of its diction, *MLN* 35 [1920]:90–96) is probably Spenser's. The third pastoral elegy in the volume, Lodowick Bryskett's "Pastoral Aeglogue upon the death of Sir Phillip Sidney," provides an interesting example of the meeting of the English Spenserian and the Italianate pastoral traditions in a single poem. Bryskett, Spenser's friend and neighbor in Ireland, was a much closer acquaintance than was Spenser of Sidney, whom he accompanied on his European tour in 1602. Bryskett himself was an accomplished Italian scholar of Italian descent. His lament for Sidney is for the most part a paraphrase of Bernardo Tasso's first Eclogue "Alcippo" (as W. P. Mustard points out, citing the relevant passages, in "Lodowick Bryskett and Bernardo Tasso," *AJP* 35 [1914]: 192–199). But the Italianate idiom is intermittently displaced by the Spenserian one. The effect, as in these opening lines, is rather strange:

> Colin, well fits thy sad cheare this sad stownd,
> This wofull stownd, wherein all things complaine
> This great mishap, this greeuous losse of owres.
> Hear'st thou the Orown? how with hollow sownd
> He slides away, and murmuring doth plaine,
> And seemes to say vnto the fading flowres,
> Along his bankes, vnto the bared trees;
> Phillisides is dead. Vp iolly swaine,
> Thou that with skill canst tune a dolefull lay,
> Help him to mourn. My hart with grief doth freese,
> Hoarse is my voice with crying, else a part
> Sure would I beare, though rude. . . .
>
> (Spenser's Minor Poems, p. 352).

Here we move from Spenser (1–3) to Bernardo Tasso (4–8) and back to Spenser again (8–12) in the space of twelve lines. These alternations continue throughout the lament but are interrupted by a passage (84–92) in which the poet, speaking in his own voice, fondly recalls the visit of the two Englishmen to Italy.

Bryskett's "Mourning Muse of Thestylis" and Matthew Roydon's "Elegie, or Friends Passion" also contain elements of the convention.

13. See, aside from the poems mentioned here: "An eclogue made long since upon the death of Phillip Sidney," 1602, by the mysterious A. W. of Davison's

Poetical Rhapsody, ed. H. E. Rollins, 2 vols. (Cambridge, Mass., 1931), 1:36–44; Nicholas Breton's "Amoris Lachrimae, for the death of Sir Philip Sidney," 1586, esp. lines 266–312, *The Works in Verse and Prose of Nicholas Breton*, ed. Alexander B. Grossart, 2 vols. (Edinburgh, 1879, and New York, 1966), 1; Richard Barnfield's stanzas on Sidney's death in "The Shepherds Content or The Happiness of a harmless life," 1544, *Poems*, ed. Edward Arber (Westminster, 1896) p. 26; George Peele's "Eclogue Gratulatorie," 1589, which makes a passing reference to Sidney's death on line 71 in the language of the pastoral elegy, *The Dramatic and Poetical Works of Robert Greene and George Peele*, ed. Alexander Dyce (London, 1861), p. 562; and Thomas Watson's "Eclogue upon the death of the Right Honourable Sir Francis Walsingham," published simultaneously in Latin as "Meliboeus" in 1590, *Poems*, ed. Edward Arber (London, 1870), pp. 139–75.

14. *The Works of Thomas Nashe*, ed. R. B. McKerrow, 5 vols. (London, 1910), 3:236–37. These verses recall particularly "November" 126–27:

> The flouds do gaspe, for dryed is theyr sourse,
> And flouds of teares flowe in theyr stead perforse.

15. The fourth *Eclogue, Idea The Shepheards Garland*, in *The Works of Michael Drayton*, ed. J. W. Hebel, 5 vols. (Oxford, 1941), 1:61.

16. This is the sixth *Eclogue* in the 1606 edition, *Works* 2:54.

17 Not a very conventional one however. Basse uses Sidney's death to teach the poet in search of a patron a lesson in constancy. His eclogue series, "Clio . . . in nine eclogues" (*The Pastorals and other works of William Basse never before imprinted*) was not published until 1653, at which time the poet offers it to the reader as the unripe fruit of his youth.

18. "Great Brittaines Sunnes-Set," *The Poetical Works of William Basse*, ed. R. Warwick Bond (London, 1893), pp. 91–92.

19. One lament for Prince Henry, by the Scottish poet, William Drummond, successfully grafts the pastoral convention onto a more formal, public style of funeral lament. Drummond sacrifices the intimacy of pastoral—his mourning rivers have a new consciousness of their own dignity—but he brings back the sense of a whole countryside mourning the death of its "custos":

> When Forth thy Nurse, Forth where thou first didst passe
> Thy tender Dayes (who smyl'd oft on her Glasse
> To see thee gaze) Meandring with her Streames,
> Heard thou hadst left this Round, from Phoebus beames
> Shee sought to flie, but forced to returne
> By neighbor Brookes, Shee gaue her selfe to mourne . . .
>
> The lesser Brookes as they did bubbling goe,
> Did keepe a Consort vnto publicke Woe . . .
> (71–76, 87–88)

"Tears on the Death of Moeliades" (1613), *The Poetical Works of William Drummond of Hawthorndon*, ed. L. E. Kaster, 2 vols. (Manchester, 1913), 1:77–78; also in *The Pastoral Elegy: An Anthology*, with an Introduction, Commentary, and Notes by Thomas Perrin Harrison, Jr., and English translation by Harry Joshua Leon (Austin, 1939), pp. 193–202. Drummond's other-pastoral, at the threshold of which Henry stands wondering, is a political paradise; it is that other-England, perennial dream of poets and statesmen, where an ideal monarch presides over a purified realm:

> All worldly Pompe and Pride thou seest arise
> Like Smoake, that scattreth in the emptie Skies.
> Other Hilles and Forrests, other sumtuous Towres,

> Amaz'd thou findst, excelling our poore Bowres,
> Courts voyde of Flatterie, of Malice Mindes . . .
>   (169–73)

And see also Giles Fletcher's elegy, "Upon the most lamented departure of the right hopefull, and blessed Prince Henry Prince of Wales" (1613) in *The Poetical Works of Giles and Phineas Fletcher*, ed. Frederick S. Boas, 2 vols. (Cambridge, Eng., 1908), 1:266–68. Like Drummond, Fletcher identifies the pastoral world with England which was, before Henry's death, "The Garden of the world, whear nothing wanted, / Another Paradise, that God had planted." But since that death England has become a world upside-down. Both these laments anticipate Milton's extension of the pastoral world to the borders of the British isles in "Lycidas."

20. *The Whole Works of William Browne*, ed. W. Carew Hazlitt, 2 vols. (London, 1869), 2:211–12.

21. But, significantly, when Browne comes at the pastoral elegy indirectly, when he is not trying to write a poem in the convention, he is more successful. A lyric in his *Britannias Pastorals* (1616) has few of the usual hallmarks of the pastoral elegy, but it records far more feelingly than the "Spenserian" eclogue the elegist's impulse to place his sorrows in a sympathetic landscape. The song, which the shepherdess Marina finds engraved on a rock by the sea, also expresses the pastoral elegist's recurrent fear of dissolution by water. The last three stanzas of the poem, with their appeal to the saving dolphins, should be compared to the parallel passages in "Lycidas":

> Cease, cease, yee murdring winds
>   To moue a waue;
> But if with troubled minds
>   You seeke his grave;
> Know 'tis as various as your selues,
> Now in the deepe, then on the shelues,
> His coffin toss'd by fish and surges fell,
> Whilst Willy weepes and bids all ioy Farewell,
>
> Had he Arion like
>   Beene iudg'd to drowne,
> Hee on his Lute could strike
>   So rare a sowne;
> A thousand Dolphins would haue come
> And ioyntly striue to bring him home.
> But he on Ship-board dide, by sickness fell,
> Since when his Willy bade all ioy Farewell.
>
> Great Neptune heare a Swaine!
>   His Coffin take,
> And with a golden chaine
>   (For pittie) make
> It fast vnto a rocke neere land!
> Where eu'ry calmy morne Ile stand
> And ere one sheepe out of my fold I tell,
> Sad Willy's Pipe shall bid his friend Farewell.
>   (Works 1:173–74, Bk. 2, Song 1).

22. *Justa Edovardo King, Reproduced from the original edition of 1638*, ed. E. C. Mossner (New York, 1939), Part 2, p. 1.

23. On the anomalousness of "Lycidas" among the other tributes to Edward

King in the 1638 volume, see G. Williamson, "The Obsequies for Edward King," *Seventeenth Century Contexts* (London and Chicago, 1960–61), pp. 132–47, and J. B. Leishman, *Milton's Minor Poems*, ed. G. Tillotson (London, 1969), pp. 248–55. The style of "Lycidas" should also be contrasted with the roughly contemporary laments on the death of Prince Henry by Donne and Tourneur in the metaphysical style. These are reprinted in *Milton's "Lycidas": Edited to Serve as an Introduction to Criticism by Scott Elledge* (New York and London, 1966), pp. 121–29. See also, on the changing fashions in funeral poetry in the early seventeenth century, Ruth Wallerstein, "The Laureat Hearse," *Studies in Seventeenth Century Poetic* (Madison, Wisc., 1950), pp. 3–148.

24. Swinburne was the first to make this criticism and it has been repeated since; see Greg's discussion in *Pastoral Poetry and Pastoral Drama*, (London, 1906), pp. 301–16.

25. Ben Jonson, *Works*, ed. Herford and Simpson, 11 vols. (Oxford, 1961), 7:11.

26. See, for instance, the opening of John Cleveland's lament for Edward King:

> I like not tears in tune; nor will I prise
> His artificial grief, that scannes his eyes:
> Mine weep down pious beads: but why should I
> Confine them to the Muses Rosarie?
> I am no Poet here; my penne's the spout
> Where the rain-water of my eyes runs out . . .
> (*Justa Edovardo King*, pt. 2, p. 9)

Such passages as this one are sometimes cited as analogues to the opening of "Lycidas," which also introduces its elegist in a state of disarray. And "Lycidas" does share in the mannerist tendencies of its age. But the elaborate (and tuneful) profession of discomposure which we see here is at the opposite extreme from the painfully and gradually achieved composure of "Lycidas."

CHAPTER 7

1. Text: *The Poetical Works of John Milton*, ed. Helen Darbishire, 2 vols. (Oxford, 1955), 2:165–70; hereafter referred to as Darbishire. Miss Darbishire's text of "Lycidas" is based on that printed in the 1645 edition of Milton's *Poems*.

2. Milton brings to the writing of "Lycidas" not only his familiarity with other pastoral elegies, but also a considerable apprenticeship in the funeral lament. Such tributes as those Milton composed to prominent University men and Churchmen are, of course, the stock-in-trade of academic poets in any age. But these early exercises are important ones for the young Milton. In the various laments written before 1637 Milton sounds, faintly at first, then more loudly and with increasing assurance, the themes of his great elegy. In the two Latin elegies for the Bishop of Winchester (1626) and the Bishop of Ely (1627), Milton begins to shape the lament as a structure of successive moods reflecting the speaker's progression from grief to recovery or resignation. (That such a progression is not inevitable in seventeenth-century funeral laments is revealed by a survey of the Latin poems in *Justo Edovardo King, Reproduced from the original edition of 1638*, ed. E. C. Massner (New York, 1939). In the lovely lament "On the Death of a Fair Infant Dying of a Cough" (1628), we see, not only the conventional comparison between nature's annual cycle and the human cycle, but, more significantly, the plea that the deceased be a "genius of the shore" and protect those still wandering in this world. As yet, however, this office is performed (as in "Comus") by the passive, innocent child:

> But oh why didst thou not stay here below
> To bless us with thy heav'n-loved innocence,

> *To slake his wrath whom sin hath made our foe,*
> *To turn Swift-rushing black perdition hence,*
> *Or drive away the slaughtering pestilence,*
> > *To stand 'twixt us and our deserved smart?*
> *But thou canst best perform that office where thou art.*
>
> (Darbishire, p. 126, lines 63–70)

Finally, it is fascinating to observe Milton in the "Epitaph for the Marchioness of Winchester" (c. 1631) transforming the Jonsonian, epigrammatic mode into a vehicle for his own, now quite different, concerns. Gradually he extricates Lady Jane from her social milieu and transports her to a simpler, grander realm of biblical shepherds and shepherdesses. Lady Jane's death and retreat to heaven become, finally, through a comparison with her biblical ancestor, Rachael, a triumph of "pastoral" fertility:

> *Whilst thou bright Saint high sit'st in glory,*
> *Next her much like thee in story,*
> *That fair Syrian Shepherdess,*
> *Who after yeers of barrennes,*
> *The highly favour'd Joseph bore*
> *To him that serv'd for her before,*
> *And at her next birth, much like thee,*
> *Through pangs fled to felicity,*
> *Far within the boosom bright*
> *Of blazing Majesty and Light. . . .*
>
> (Darbishire, p. 135, lines 61–70)

3. Many of these reminiscences are recorded in the notes to the useful edition of the poem prepared by Scott Elledge, *Milton's "Lycidas": Edited to Serve as an Introduction to Criticism* (New York and London, 1966), pp. 251–316.

4. Milton first wrote:

> *I come to pluck yor berries harsh and crude*
> *before the mellowing yeare*
> *and crop you^r young*

then crossed out the last two lines and substituted,

> *and wth forc't fingers rude*
> *shatter yor leaves before ye mellowing yeare.*

See the Textual Commentary in Darbishire, pp. 330–31. Milton's so-called Trinity Manuscript (written sometime between November 1637 and April 1638), on which these and other important revisions of the poem are recorded, is also reproduced in facsimile by William Wright, *Facsimile of the Manuscript of Milton's Minor Poems* (Cambridge, England, 1899). As B. Rajan points out, in "*Lycidas*: The Shattering of the Leaves," *SP* 64 (1967): 53, the "new" fourth line might possibly not be a new line at all, but one which was omitted as Milton, in the first passage here, transcribed from memory an earlier draft. Rajan's essay, which approaches the poem through Milton's revisions of the Trinity Manuscript—revisions which intensify the oppositions in the poem—seems to me to present one of the best of recent readings of the poem. Of all the essays on "Lycidas" which add, and keep adding, to our understanding of the poem, I am particularly indebted to three: this essay by Professor Rajan; Rosemond Tuve's, "Theme, Pattern, and Imagery in *Lycidas*," from *Images and Themes in Five Poems by Milton* (Cambridge, Mass., 1957), reprinted in *Milton's "Lycidas,": The Tradition and the Poem*, ed. C. A. Patrides (New York, 1961), pp.

167–200, and hereafter referred to as Patrides; and Isabel G. MacCaffrey's "*Lycidas:* The Poet in a Landscape," in *The Lyric and Dramatic Milton*, Selected Papers from the English Institute, ed. Joseph H. Summers (New York and London, 1965), pp. 62–92. All three, I think, attend particularly closely to the *experience* both of creating and of reading the poem. Rajan's emphasis on the dialectical nature of this experience seems to me particularly valuable.

5. See *O.E.D. shatter*, 1: "To scatter, disperse, throw about in all directions; to cause (seed, leaves etc.) to fall or be shed," which cites this line from "Lycidas." And the editors of the new Variorum edition, *A Variorum Commentary on the Poems of John Milton*, vol. 2, *The Minor English Poems*, ed. A. S. P. Woodhouse and Douglas Bush (New York, 1972), Part 2, p. 641, also prefer the sense of "scattering" here.

6. As the Variorum editors also point out; see, e.g., *Comus*, 799: "Till all thy magick structures rear'd so high / Were shatter'd onto heaps o're thy false head." There is another "shattering of the leaves" in *Paradise Lost*, when, after the Fall, "the Winds / Blow moist and keen, shattering the graceful locks of these fair spreading Trees . . . " (10.1065–66.)

7. That the opening lines of "Lycidas," with their concern for "inward ripeness," rehearse feelings expressed five years earlier in the seventh sonnet, "How Soon Hath Time . . . ," has often been noted. The comparison is even more exact. There too (though the exposition is much more straightforward in the earlier poem) precocious haste and belatedness seem to jar against each other in the octet as, "My hasting days fly on with full career, / But my late spring no bud or blossom show'th." Then in the sestet these contrary possibilities are reconciled, as both are allowed for within time's even beats: "Yet be it less or more, or soon or slow, / It shall be still in strictest measure ev'n."

8. The headnote, which reads, "In this Monody the Author bewails a learned Friend, unfortunately drown'd in his Passage from *Chester* on the *Irish* Seas, 1637. And by occasion foretells the ruine of our corrupted Clergie then in their height," was first published in the 1645 edition of the *Poems*. An earlier version is written in on the Trinity Manuscript, but evidently at a later date (see Darbishire, pp. 330, 333). The headnote does not appear in *Justa Edovardo King* and, in the later edition, has rather the role of an explanatory note or key (such as those which other pastoral poets provide) than of an integral part of the poem. It does give us some orientation; it tells us what the poem will be about. But it does not replace the opening frame, for it does not perform the function of the frame—that of establishing the setting in which the lament will be placed.

9. Arthur Barker, "The Pattern of Milton's Nativity Ode," *UTQ* 10 (1941):17.

10. William G. Riggs, in "The Plant of Fame in *Lycidas*," *Milton Studies* 4, ed. James D. Simmonds (London, 1972), suggests, by way of explaining these apparent repetitions, that Phoebus is telling us how, as Christians, we should live in this world, while the final consolation points toward our future life in heaven, pp. 151–61. This is arguable: it is difficult for me to see the primary thrust of Phoebus' speech as anything but a directive to turn away from the earthly plant to that heavenly one, or to its heavenly source. But, more importantly, I think, we do not need to find different emphases (though there may be some) in the several consolations. Riggs acknowledges that Phoebus' consolation is close to the final one but suggests that the elegist himself does not realize just how close. This is possible too; but it is also possible that the elegist does realize, does take it in, and still turns away, for a time, from that truth. See also, for a much more radical effort to separate what the pagan elegist can know from what the Christian reader knows, William G. Madsen, "The Voice of Michael in *Lycidas*," *SEL: Recent Studies in the English Renaissance* 3 (1963), pp. 1–7. Madsen is so uncomfortable with the idea of the elegist

knowing the truth and yet not knowing it that he assigns the consolation (from line 165) to the Angel Michael.

11. "The Italian Element in *Lycidas*," from *The Italian Element in Milton's Verse* (Oxford, 1954), reprinted in Patrides, p. 154.

12. This passage should be compared to the beautiful one in *Paradise Lost* in which the still-innocent Adam describes his happiness with Eve in Eden from the sun's rising to the glittering starlight of the night (4.639–56).

13. As Isabel G. MacCaffrey suggests in "Poet in a Landscape," p. 74. I would not go so far as to say, with Mrs. MacCaffrey, that nature's continuing life apart from us implies "a desolating unconcern with man," for that continuing vitality is consoling as well as depressing to us, and Milton invokes both these responses.

14. See above, p. 97.

15. 7.36–37.

16. John Donne in "Twickenham Garden."

17. A "tangled" object or place in Milton's poetry is generally one whose seductive exterior masks a destructive interior. We enter in and discover we are lost or betrayed. Thus Belial in *Paradise Regained* suggests that Christ be lured by women who "in retiring draw / Hearts after them tangled in amorous nets" (2.162). And Satan, with Eve in tow, "swiftly rolled / in tangles, and made intricate seem straight" (*P.L.* 9.632). The lady in *Comus* finds herself lost "in the blind mazes of this tangled woods" (181). And, in a nice inversion of this motif, the tempter looks longingly at the wall of shrubs and "tangling bushes" which encloses Adam and Eve in Eden (*P.L.* 4.176).

18. Engines elsewhere in Milton's poetry (and perhaps we should say here as well) are instruments of warfare—the most memorable of these being the cannon invented by Satan and his cohorts in their war against the heavenly powers (*P.L.* 6.484, 518, 586, 650, 653)—and they are almost always diabolical. Moloch, speaking from Pandemonium, urges a second war against heaven, "when we meet the noise of his Almighty Engine he shall hear / Infernal Thunder . . . (*P.L.* 2.64–66); but this Almighty "Engine" and its "noise" are the projections of the diabolical imagination onto the divine one.

19. "[*Lycidas*] is not to be considered as the effusion of real passion; for passion runs not after remote allusions and obscure opinions. Passion plucks no berries from the myrtle and ivy, nor calls upon Arethuse and Mincius, nor tells of rough *satyrs* and *fauns with cloven heel*. Where there is leisure for fiction there is little grief." From the *Life of Milton* (1779), reprinted in *Milton's "Lycidas,"* ed. Elledge, p. 229.

20. In the earlier version of this passage, which Milton revised on the trial sheet of the Trinity manuscript, the sense of a sympathetic sorrow on nature's part is much stronger. The feeling is reminiscent of that in Sannazaro's Arcadian laments, where we are soothed by seeing our own melancholy reflected in nature and in the world of myth:

> Bring the rathe primrose that unwedded dies
> colouring the pale cheeke of uninjoyd love
> and that sad floure that strove
> to write his owne woes on the vermeil graine
> next adde Narcissus y^t still weeps in vaine
> the woodbine and ye pancie freak'd wth jet
> the glowing violet
> the cowslip wan that hangs his pensive head
> and every bud that sorrows liverie weares
> let Daffadillies fill thire cups with teares

> bid Amaranthus all his beautie shed
> to strew the laureat herse &c.
>
> (Darbishire, p. 335)

As Milton revised he cut away much of the mythological melancholy by giving more prominence to the flowers themselves—and particularly to those which do not wear sorrow's livery at all: the *"well-attir'd* Woodbine," for instance, is a new addition.

21. So Satan in *Paradise Lost* sees "in narrow room Nature's whole wealth" (4.207), sweetness piled on sweetness,

> And higher than that Wall a circling row
> Of goodliest Trees loaden with fairest Fruit,
> Blossoms and Fruits at once of golden hue
> Appear'd, with gay enamell'd colors mixt.
>
> (4.146–49)

These trees and fruit surely are good and fair, but we see them as Satan sees them—from the outside, and the description is informed by his desire and despair. Milton's elegist's despair is of a different order, but he too is an exile from bliss at this moment, and his description of enameled flowers has something of the ring of this one. Contrast Adam's description, already cited, later in this book (639 ff.) of a day spent in Eden with Eve, where the landscape is not, as here, separable from our own life in it.

22. God calls man's fallen condition "frail" at 3.180, as does Christ at 3.404. Beelzebub vows later generations of men will curse their "frail original" at 2.375. Satan comes to tempt "innocent frail man" at 4.11 and journeys to the "utmost orb / Of this frail world" at 2.1030. The wounded angels, unlike "frail man," bleed not at 6.345. And Eve declares her happiness in Eden "frail" if circumscribed in any way. The drama of *Paradise Lost* centers around this human frailty perceived so differently by God, Satan and Eve. We might describe the action of that poem in terms of the protagonists' gradual discovery of the true nature of that "frailty."

23. See above, p. 113 ff. and 148n.

24. As Mrs. MacCaffrey observes in "Poet in a Landscape," pp. 86–87, these lines constitute a denial of that "most poignant disparity between man and the nonhuman world . . . which is lamented everywhere in elegiac poetry."

25. T. P. Harrison discusses the parallels between the two laments in "The Latin Pastorals of Milton and Castiglione," *PMLA* 50 (1935):480–93.

26. Text: Darbishire, pp. 163–68. Translation: Douglas Bush, *The Complete Poetical Works of John Milton* (Boston, 1965), pp. 162–67.

27. Milton has been criticized for a lack of feeling in this poem, either for the pastoral tradition (see, e.g., Douglas Bush, *The Complete Poetical Works of John Milton*, p. 162, and Ralph W. Condee, "The Structure of Milton's *Epitaphium Damonis*," *SP* 62 [1965]: 577–94), or for Diodati himself (see E. M. Tillyard, *Milton* [London, 1930], p. 100). I think that there is indeed feeling here, both for the form and for the subject; but the two are not always integrated.

EPILOGUE

1. Boccaccio's "Olympia," on the borderline between our convention and the medieval dream-vision, is the only Renaissance poem discussed here which has a night-time setting. And Boccaccio uses that setting as a foil to show us how the spirit of his little daughter can, with her own radiance, transform night's darkness into pastoral's sunlit day.

Other pastoral elegies reveal their peripheral place in the convention, their partial estrangement from the pastoral world and its consolations, when their elegists mourn *both night and day.* This is the case in Castiglione's "Alcon" and in Milton's "Epitaphium." The sorrows of these two elegists belong to the darkness as well as the light. But, at the same time, both see the night-time grieving as an *extension* of the traditional daylight grieving. Thus Castiglione's Iolas *forgets* to yield to the late night ("serae oblitus decedere nocti," 22). He mourns also then, not (like the later elegists) especially then.

2. "The Fifth Pastoral," *The Poetical Works of Dryden*, ed. George R. Noyes, 2d ed. (Cambridge, Mass., 1950), p. 429, line 26.

3. In Pope's lament the darkness confers primarily a sense of calm, and death seems subsumed by her benign sister, sleep:

> Thyrsis, *the Musick of that murm'ring Spring*
> *Is not so mournful as the Strains you sing,*
> *Nor Rivers winding thro' the Vales below,*
> *So sweetly warble, or so smoothly flow.*
> *Now sleeping Flocks on their soft Fleeces lye,*
> *The Moon, serene in Glory, mounts the Sky,*
> *While silent Birds forget their tuneful Lays,*
> *Oh sing of* Daphne's *Fate, and* Daphne's *Praise!*

Pastoral Poetry and an Essay on Criticism, ed. E. Audra and Aubrey Williams, in *The Twickenham Edition of the Poems of Alexander Pope*, 6 vols. (London and New Haven, 1961), 1:88–89, lines 1–8.

4. On eighteenth- and nineteenth-century funeral poetry, see John W. Draper, *The Funeral Elegy and the Rise of English Romanticism* (New York, 1929).

5. *Poems of Thomas Gray*, ed. Austin Lane Poole, in *The Poems of Gray and Collins*, 3d ed. (Oxford, 1937), p. 91.

6. Notice that Joseph Warton, commenting on the setting in which the singers converse in Vergil's fifth, sees it as a solemn place as well as a shadowy one: "The scene of it is not only beautiful in itself but adapted to the solemnity of the subject; the shepherds sit and sing in the awful gloom of a grotto, which is overhung by wild vines." *The Works of Virgil in Latin and English*, ed. Joseph Warton, 4 vols. (London, 1753), 1:97. For the eighteenth-century poet a setting which conforms to the solemnity of the subject itself is the only appropriate setting. The pastoralist's intermingling of the sweet and playful with the sad and serious is distasteful to him. There is no room in Warton's Virgil for play.

7. *The Complete Poetical Works of Percy Bysshe Shelley*, ed. Thomas Hutchinson (Oxford, 1905, 1956), p. 444, 55.486–95.

8. Philippe Ariès has an interesting discussion of the "attractive mystery" the Romantics make of death in *Western Attitudes toward Death: From the Middle Ages to the Present*, trans. Patricia M. Ranum (Baltimore and London, 1974); see esp. pp. 55–82. His analysis of earlier attitudes toward death (particularly on the earlier concern for the place of death in the larger rhythms of life) also has some bearing on the pastoral elegist's way of placing sorrow.

9. *The Poetical Works of Matthew Arnold*, ed. C. B. Tinker and H. F. Lowry, 3d ed. (Oxford, 1950), p. 267, line 145.

10. "Wash Far Away" was found among Berryman's papers after his death. According to his editor, Robert Giroux, the story existed in draft form in 1957 and may have been written earlier; see the notes on "Contributors" in *American Review* 22, ed. Theodore Solotaroff (Toronto, New York, and London, 1975), p. 273.

11. Text: *AR* 22, pp. 1–26.

12. The critical assumptions about "Lycidas" which lie behind the Professor's first reading of the poem and the "lesson" he draws from it go back to the 1930s.

One thinks particularly of E. M. W. Tillyard's essay on "Lycidas" (in *Milton*, [London, 1930], pp. 79–85, reprinted in *Milton's "Lycidas": The Tradition and the Poem*, ed. C. A. Patrides [New York, 1961], pp. 58–63), with its distinction between the poem's ostensible subject and its real one, and of John Crowe Ransom's "A Poem Nearly Anonymous" (*American Review* 1, pt. 4 [May 1933]: 179–203; 1, pt. 4 [Sept. 1933]: 444–467, reprinted in Patrides, pp. 64–81), which sets the anonymity of art against the personal emotions of the artist.

INDEX

chus," 27, in Vergil's tenth *Eclogue*, 48, in Petrarch, 60–61, in Boccaccio, 68, in Castiglione, 69, 73–75, in Scève, 117–18. *See also* Reversal

Convention, as way of seeing things, xi, xiii

Couteau, Nicolas, *OEvres de Virgille translatees de latin en françoys*, 107n

Custos, death of: in Vergil's fifth *Eclogue*, 36–37; in Petrarch's second *Eclogue*, 55, 57, 58; in Sannazaro's "Phyllis," 80; in French pastoral elegy, 107; in Milton's "Lycidas," 178–79

D

Daphnis, myth of, xxxii–xxxiii, 13

Death: in pastoral world, xv; denial of, in Theocritus, 15–16, in Sannazaro's *Arcadia*, 98, in Milton's "Epitaphium," 186; as sweet, in Trissino, 101, in Scève, 118

Del Virgilio, Giovanni, 54n

Diodorus, of Sicily, xxxii

Dolphin, and Arion: in Scève, 113; in William Browne's *Britannias Pastorals*, 148n; in Milton's "Lycidas," 176

Donne, John, "Twickenham Garden," 165

Drayton, Michael, *Idea The Shepheards Garland*: fourth *Eclogue* (1593), 145–46; sixth *Eclogue* (1606), 146

Drummond, William, "Tears on the Death of Moeliades," 147n

Dryden, John, "Fifth Pastoral," 187

Du Bellay, Joachim: as subject of Belleau's "Chant pastoral," 107n; *La Deffence et Illustration*, 107; *Antiquités*, 143n

E

Eden: contrasted to pastoral world, xv; and "other-pastoral" world, 66; in Milton's "Lycidas," 174; in *Paradise Lost*, 174n

Empson, William, xxii

Encomium, 95n

English pastoral poetry, characteristics of, 125–26

Epic poetry, and pastoral, xxiii

Epic themes, anticipated in pastoral: in Vergil, 39; in Spenser, 133–34, 136–37; in Milton, 161, 170, 174

Escapism: in pastoral poetry, xiv; in Vergil, 30

F

Falcone, Matteo, as subject of Castiglione's "Alcon," 69–70

Fletcher, Giles, "Upon the . . . departure of . . . Henry Prince of Wales," 147n

Fontana, Marco Publio, "Caprea," 85–88

Frame: in Theocritus' first *Idyll*, 3–8, 19–20; in other Theocritean idylls, 3n; in Vergil's fifth *Eclogue*, 31–35, 43–45; in Vergil's tenth *Eclogue*, 45–46, 48–49; in Renaissance pastoral elegy, 53–54; in Marot, 110; in Milton's "Epitaphium Damonis," 185; pentration of sorrow into, in Renaissance pastoral elegy, 51, 75, in Petrarch's second *Eclogue*, 55–58, 59, in Castiglione's "Alcon," 70, in Sannazaro's "Phyllis," 77–78, 81, in Tasso, 101–02, in Spenser, 127, 135–36; unique handling of in Milton's "Lycidas," 156–57, 179–82

Frazer, Sir James George, xxix

Freud, Sigmund, 98

Frye, Northrop, xxx, 25

G

Gathering of mourners: in Theocritus, 11–12, 17; in Vergil, 94; in Nemesian, 94–95; in Marot, 110–11

Giamatti, A. Bartlett, 67n

Golden age: and "other-pastoral" world, 67; in Ronsard, 121, 123; in Ben Jonson, 151–52

Grant, W. Leonard, 82

Gray, Thomas, "Elegy in a Country Church-yard," 188–89

Greek pastoral poetry: first collected edition of, 23n, Renaissance editions of, 85

H

Harrison, Jr., Thomas Perrin, xxx

Henry, Prince of Wales (1594–1612), as subject of English funeral laments, 146–47

Henry II, of France, as subject of Ronsard's second *Eclogue*, 121–22

"Hereness": xiv; in Theocritus, 5, 16; in Vergil's tenth *Eclogue*, 47; in Castiglione, 72; in Tasso, 106; in Marot, 108, 111–12; in Ben Jonson, 150–51; in Milton's "Lycidas," 171–72

zaro's *Arcadia*, 74n; in neo-Latin pas-
toral elegy, 84; in Spenser, 131–32; in
Sidney, 140–41; revision of, in Mil-
ton's "Lycidas," 176–77; in Milton's
"Epitaphium," 184–85
Nemesian, *Eclogues*: influence on San-
nazaro's *Arcadia*, 91, 94–95; influence
on Renaissance pastoral elegy, 95n
Night Setting: in Boccaccio, 62, 187n; in
post-Renaissance funeral lament,
187–92; in Gray's "Elegy," 188–89; in
Arnold's "Thyrsis," 191
Noon setting: in Theocritus, 6–7; in
Sannazaro's "Phyllis," 78; in Milton's
"Lycidas," 160–61; in pastoral elegy,
187; in Berryman's "Wash Far Away,"
193, 195–96
Nymphs, absence of: in Theocritus, 10;
in "Lycidas," 163

O

Orpheus: in "Moschus," 27; in Sanna-
zaro's *Arcadia*, 97; in "Lycidas,"
164–65
"Other-pastoral" world: threshold of,
in Vergil, 40–41; in Petrarch, 59–60; in
Boccaccio, 61, 64–67; in Renaissance
pastoral elegy, 67, 126; in Sannazaro's
"Phyllis," 80; in Fontana, 86–87; in
Sannazaro's *Arcadia*, 95–96; in Tasso,
103–04; in Marot, 111–12; in Ronsard,
122–23; in Spenser, 134–35; in Wil-
liam Drummond, 147n; in Milton's
"Lycidas," 177–78; in Milton's
Epitaphium Damonis, 185–86
Otium: in Vergil, 28–31, 49–50, fifth
Eclogue, 40–44; in Christian interpre-
tation of Vergil's fifth *Eclogue*, 52; in
Petrarch, 54–55; in Castiglione, 72; in
French pastoral poetry, 107–8; in
Marot, 108–9; in Scève, 116; in Ron-
sard, 121
oysiveté, in Marot, 109
ozio, in Tasso, 101, 103–04, 106

P

Panofsky, Erwin, xvn, 90n
Parry, Adam: xiv; on origins of pastoral
poetry, xxiii
Pastoral elegist, as lunatic, in Ben Jon-
son, 152–53
Pastoral elegy: and other forms of fu-
neral lament, xvii–xix; anachronistic
term, xix; other names for, xx; studies

of, xxin; in Middle Ages, 54; neo-
Latin, characteristics of, 81–88; popu-
larity of, in Renaissance, 81; bur-
lesqued, 85–88; and modern funeral
lament, 142–43; popularity of, in En-
gland, 143, decline of, in England,
144–53; detached from pastoral se-
quence, 147–48; and "metaphysical"
lament, 148–49, 153n; as misnomer
for "Adonais" and "Thyrsis," 187,
196. *See also* Subject(s) of lament, *Topoi*
Pastoral elegy, origins of convention: xii;
xxi–xxxiv, in folk poetry, xxiv; in
primitive attitudes toward death,
xxiv–xxvi; in vegetation rites, xxix–
xxxii; in Daphnis myths, xxxii–xxxiii;
in folk ritual, xxxiiin
Pastoral genre: origins of, xv, xxii–xxiv,
xxxii–xxxiii; Renaissance revival of, 54
Pastoral landscape as royal realm: in
Marot, 107–8, 110; in Giles Fletcher,
147n; in William Drummond, 147n; in
Milton's "Lycidas," 175. *See also*
Landscape
Pastoral poetry, Renaissance collections
of, 81
Pastoral theory, in Renaissance, xxn,
76n
Pathetic fallacy: xxvi–xxix; in *Old Testa-
ment*, xxvi; in pastoral elegy, xxvi; in
primitive lament, xxvi; in Theocritus'
seventh *Idyll*, xxvii–xxix; in Theoc-
ritus' first *Idyll*, xxviii–xxix, 11; in
neo-Latin lament, 82; in Spenser, 129;
in Milton's "Lycidas," 161–62. *See also*
Lament of nature
Pearl, and Boccaccio's "Olympia," 68n
Pericles, funeral oration of, xvii
Petrarch (Francesco Petrarca): *Bucolicum
Carmen*, 54–55, first *Eclogue*, and Ver-
gil's first, 55n, second *Eclogue*, 55–61,
83, 84; *De vita solitaria*, 54n; *Epist.
Fam.* 41 (ascent of Mt. Ventoux), 54n;
Epist. Met. 14, 54n
Poggioli, Renato, xixn
Pontano, Giovanni, "Meliseus": 76n,
82; influence on Sannazaro's *Arcadia*,
91n
Pope, Alexander, "Winter," xiii, 187
Priapus, in Theocritus, 12–14, 15, 16
Prince, F. T., 158–59
Private voice: in Renaissance pastoral
elegy, 51, 75, 83–84; in Scève, 114,
118; in Spenser, 132; in Milton's

"Lycidas," 154–55. *See also* Isolation of elegist, Self-absorption

R

Rajan, B., 155n

Refrain: in Theocritus, 9; in Milton's "Epitaphium," 182

Reversal: in Vergil, 39–40; in Spenser, 133–34; in Milton's "Lycidas," 175–76. *See also* Consolation

Robert of Naples, as subject of Petrarch's second *Eclogue*, 55–60

Ronsard, Pierre de: *Bergerie*, 120–24; first *Eclogue*, 121–24; Elégie (contre les bûcherons de la forêst de Gastine), 120; "Ode, aux cendres de Marguerite de Navarre, 119–20

Rosenmeyer, Thomas, xxvi, 5n

Ruskin, John, xxvi

S

Sannazaro, Jacopo: *Arcadia*, 89–98, popularity of, 89, 97–98, influence on Marot's lament for Louise, 110, influence on Scève's "Arion," 112, 118, fifth prose chapter, 94–95, fifth *Eclogue*, 95–96, eleventh *Eclogue*, 74n, 91–94, 97, influence on Sidney's "Dicus," 138, twelfth *Eclogue*, 91n; "Phyllis" (first *Piscatory Eclogue*), 76–81, 84, 89

Scaliger, Julius Caesar, *Poetices libri septem*, xxn

Scattering of leaves: in Vergil's fifth *Eclogue*, 38, 155; in "Lycidas," 155–56

Scève, Maurice, "Arion": 112–18, 148; and Sidney's "Dicus," 142

Sébillet, *L'Art poétique françoys*, xxn

Self-absorption: in Petrarch, 54; in Tasso, 103; in Scève, 118. *See also* Isolation of elegist, Private voice

Servius Marius Honoratus, xxn, 35n, 74n

Shadows: in Vergil, 29, tenth *Eclogue*, 49; in Boccaccio, 68; in Milton's "Lycidas," 181; in post-Renaissance funeral lament, 187–92

Shakespeare, William, *King Lear*, xviii, 17–18

Shelley, Percy Bysshe, "Adonais," xiii, 189–90

Shore: in Petrarch, 60; in Renaissance pastoral elegy, 60–61; in Boccaccio, 68; in Castilione, 69; in Sannazaro's

"Phyllis," 76–77; in Scève, 113, 114, 118; in Milton's "Lycidas," 175, 178–79; in Shelley, 190

Sidney, Sir Philip: as subject of English pastoral elegy, 143, 145–46; *Arcadia*, characteristics of, 137–38; "Dicus" (*Old Arcadia 75*), 138–43, 148

Spenser, Edmund: "Astrophel," 143n; "Daphnaida," 143n; "Epithalamion," 143n; *Faerie Queene* 1.10.63 ff., 136n, "Mutabilitie Cantos," 126, 136–37; "Lay of Clorinda," 143n; "Ruins of Time," 143n; *Shepheardes Calender*, characteristics of, 126–27, 134, "June" 65–74, influence on Milton's "Lycidas," 167, "November," xiii, 84, 127–36, influence on English pastoral elegy, 143, influence on Drayton's *Idea*, 145–46, influence on William Browne's *Eclogues*, 147, and Milton's "Lycidas," 178

Subject(s) of lament: varied, xii, 85; mythological, in Theocritus, xxxii–xxxiii, 3, 13–14; vegetation god, in Bion, 24; actual man, in "Moschus," 25; *custos*, in Vergil's fifth *Eclogue*, 35–37, in Petrarch, 55–60, in neo-Latin pastoral elegy, 85, in French pastoral elegy, 107, in Marot 107–09, in Scève, 113, in Ronsard, 119–24, in Sidney, 138, in William Drummond, 147n; friend and fellow poet, in "Moschus," 25–26, in Castiglione, 69–70, in Milton's "Lycidas," 160, 164, 194–95, in Milton's "Epitaphium Damonis," 182–85, in Arnold, 191–92, in Berryman, 192–93; filial, in Boccaccio, 61; female, in Sannazaro's "Phyllis," 76, in Pontano, 76n, in Marot, 108, in Spenser, 128; unidentified, in Sannazaro's "Phyllis," 76, in Sannazaro's eleventh Arcadian *Eclogue*, 93, in Spenser, 128, in Gray's "Elegy," 189; pet goat, in Fontana, 85–88

Sweetness: in Theocritus, 4–5, 20; in Vergil's fifth *Eclogue*, 40; in classical pastoral elegy, 51–52; in Fontana, 87; in Sannazaro's *Arcadia*, 94, 98; in Tasso, 102; in Milton's "Lycidas," 172

T

Tasso, Bernardo, "Alcippo," 143n

Tasso, Torquato: *Aminta*, 104n;